SCOTTISH VILLAINS & VICTIMS

Other books by John Kellie:

Ayrshire Echoes
Ayrshire Folk
Hanged Until Dead

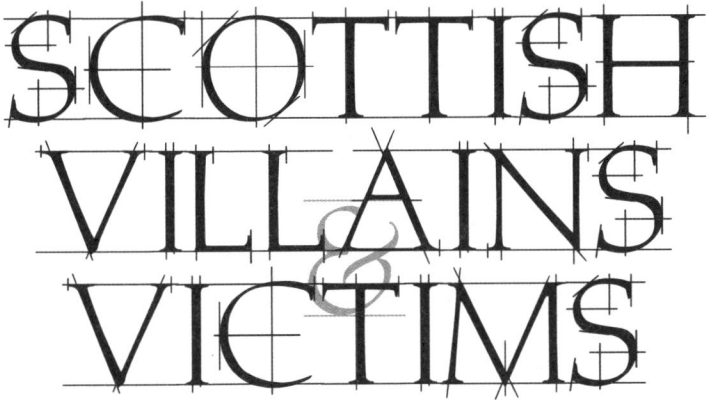

SCOTTISH VILLAINS & VICTIMS

True Tales 1799-1890

John Kellie

CARN PUBLISHING

© John Kellie, 2023.
First Published in Great Britain, 2023.

ISBN – 978 1 911043 15 7

Published by Carn Publishing,
Lochnoran House,
Auchinleck, Ayrshire, KA18 3JW.

www.carnpublishing.com

Printed by Bell & Bain Ltd,
Glasgow, G46 7UQ.

The right of the author to be identified as the author of this work has been asserted by him in accordance with the Copyright, Designs and Patents Act 1988.

All rights reserved. No part of this publication may be reproduced, stored, or transmitted in any form, or by any means, electronic, mechanical or photocopying, recording or otherwise, without the express written permission of the publisher.

JOHN KELLIE

John Kellie was born in Ayrshire and educated at Pinmore, Kilmarnock and Glasgow. An enthusiastic outdoorsman and freelance writer, over the years his work has found its way into a variety of magazines on both sides of the Atlantic, as well as broadsheet and tabloid newspapers. After teaching secondary school English for the best part of three decades, he seized the opportunity of an early exit and he is now researching and writing full-time.
Scottish Villains & Victims is his fourth book.

*To the memory of my paternal grandparents,
William Kellie (1883-1918) and Annie Boddan (1881-1954).*

Contents

	Introduction	9
1	Peter Gray & Colin McCallum, Luss, Dunbartonshire - December 1799	11
2.	Unidentified Murderer, Tweeddale Court, Edinburgh - November 1806	19
3.	Adam & John Lyall, Sheriffmuir, Stirlingshire - October 1810	29
4.	James Whiteford, Hopetoun, West Lothian - March 1819, & Peter Bowers, Coalston, East Lothian - April 1819	41
5.	John Forrest, Stirling - November 1822	49
6.	Alexander Martin, Kemnay, Aberdeenshire - April 1824	59
7.	David Landale, Kirkcaldy, Fife - August 1826	67
8.	John & Catherine Stuart, Firth of Clyde - December 1828	81
9.	Alexander Arthur & William Strang, Glasgow East End - April 1829	97
10.	John Adam, Millbuie, Ross & Cromarty - April 1835	103
11.	Malcolm Macleod, Bayble, Isle of Lewis - January 1838	125
12.	David Patterson, Dolphinton, Lanarkshire - May 1838	133
13.	Christina Gilmour, Inchinnan, Renfrewshire - December 1842	137
14.	Darby Furie & Theodore Dowd, New Cumnock, Ayrshire - March 1851	153
15.	Catherine Beaton, Claddach Kyles, North Uist - June 1856	167
16.	Thomas Ross, Kirkoswald, Ayrshire - January 1859	177
17.	Edwin Salt, Juniper Green, Midlothian - November 1859	185

18. Robert Watt & James Kerr, North Atlantic Ocean - April/May 1868 197
19. George Chalmers, Braco, Perthshire - December 1869 209
20. Thomas Scobbie, Monifieth, Angus - September 1872 227
21. Unidentified Assailant, Moscow, Ayrshire - March 1884 239
22. Hector Mackenzie, Ardersier, Inverness-shire - December 1888 245
23. Loreto Palombo, Possil, City of Glasgow - December 1890 255
    Afterword..267
    Index..269

INTRODUCTION

'... we should pass over all biographies of "the good and the great", while we search carefully the slight records of wretches who died in prison, in Bedlam, or upon the gallows.'
(Edgar Allan Poe)

We might as well face it. Like it or not, there's something in our make-up that draws us to the darker corners of human existence. If you doubt it, take a few seconds to scan the shelves in the fiction section of your local library or bookshop. Or alternatively scroll through the programmes showing on tonight's TV schedules, or take a look at what's trending on streaming platforms. I'm confident you'll find that crime fiction, police drama and true crime documentaries will be right up there.

It's not anything new. Continuing in an age-old tradition, throughout the eighteenth and early nineteenth centuries ballad singers were regularly to be seen setting up shop on street corners in our towns and cities where, in exchange for a few small coins, they regaled our forefathers with musical renditions of stories of infamous crimes, both local and from farther afield, to the accompaniment perhaps of a simple instrument such as a melodeon. In rural districts singers passed from place to place, performing their repertoire in village alehouses and at country fairs. As the nineteenth century progressed and literacy rates expanded, the trade of the ballad singers declined and 'broadsides' and 'broadsheets' came into their own - single-use documents printed on inexpensive paper. Regularly peddled by hawkers working the crowds at public executions, readers might expect to see a lurid account of the condemned person's crime, frequently with his or her confession attached - and sometimes a doggerel verse thrown in for good measure exhorting others not to copy the ill-fated individual's example. Often crudely illustrated with a portrait of the criminal, a depiction of the crime and a generic woodcut of a hanging, nineteenth-century broadsides sold in their thousands, typically at the modest cost of a penny or a halfpenny. The rapid spread of cheap newspapers took over where the broadsides left off, offering editors boundless column inches to satisfy the reading public's appetite to pore over the detail of crimes committed, those responsible identified and convicted, and justice dispensed.

Of course, not all crime stories had the necessary ingredients to fire the popular imagination. No different from today, the sad fact was that in earlier times a high percentage of crime was provoked by desperation, addiction or the damaging effect of destructive relationships, and reports of mindless alcohol-fuelled violence, petty dishonesty and squalid domestic abuse were standard daily fodder for the press, varying little between one case and another. In the pages that follow I have tried to avoid stories of this kind but have concentrated instead on those which are a little more eye-catching. Some I have chosen because of an interesting quirk, an unexpected turn of events perhaps or an unpredictable outcome. Others are set in an unusual location. They cover the country from Highlands to Lowlands, inner cities to outer isles, and they take place both on land and at sea. Possibly most crucially of all, many revolve around a character who succeeds in engaging our attention for either positive or - more often - unfavourable reasons.

I am aware that some of my villains and victims have been studied by earlier authors but in order to make them fit my own requirements I have done my best to start again from scratch, working from court papers, newspaper reports and other available materials. Other cases I have chosen to feature are, to the best of my knowledge, appearing in print for the first time. I should add that the names at the head of each chapter refer to the person, or persons charged or convicted. The date that follows relates to when their crime was committed.

During the course of writing I have received generous assistance from a variety of quarters but I would like to single out the following people for particular thanks: Dane Love of Carn Publishing for his continuing faith in my work; Fiona Campbell of Galston and Middlesex for patiently tracking several of my subjects through their continuing lives; and, as in my previous efforts, special mention goes to my longtime friend, Frances Smith of Cumnock, whose unflagging support has once again made all the difference.

Peter Gray & Colin McCallum
Luss, Dunbartonshire - December 1799

Clearly the late evening of Boxing Day 1799 had been earmarked for a relaxed, companionable supper. On behalf of his eldest brother and clan chief, Ludovic Colquhoun had spent most of the day at Arnburn, collecting rent money due from the Luss Estate's various tenants. The weather had been bitter with snow underfoot and what felt like the beginnings of a gale blowing up. With his day's work complete sometime between eight and nine o'clock, it seems certain he would have been relieved to come indoors, shake the snow off his boots and join his two guests by the fireside.

Ludovic's family had been a powerful force on Loch Lomondside for nigh on five hundred years, ever since his early ancestor, Sir Humphrey de Colquhoun, received a grant of lands around the village of Luss from King Robert the Bruce. (Five years on Sir Humphrey repaid the king's generosity in full, fighting shoulder to shoulder on the banks of the Bannock Burn.) Situated on a promontory projecting into the loch, the medieval tower house of Rossdhu became the Colquhoun family home and remained as such until the mid-eighteenth century when the current chief - Ludovic's brother - set about constructing a three-storey mansion in classical style, recycling masonry from its ancient predecessor in the process. It was said that his mother, Lady Helen, wept as her old home was dismantled stone by stone before her eyes.

In Rossdhu's new incarnation Ludovic found himself accommodated at Ross Lodge, a stone's throw from the great house itself. One of three brothers and six sisters, he had been born in July 1757 and, in common with many younger sons of the nobility, he had enlisted in the army where his aristocratic lineage appears to have done nothing to hinder his career. Serving initially in Fraser's Highlanders he was promoted to Lieutenant at age twenty and Captain two years later, rose to the rank of Major in 1783 and finally to Lieutenant Colonel. During his time in the military, he saw several years' service overseas during the American War of Independence, including a lengthy term of internment after the city of Boston was wrested from British control by American forces. On Boxing Day 1799 he was a 42-year-old bachelor.

His guests that evening were Rev. George Drummond, Minister of Rosneath - a small settlement on the shores of the Gare Loch, some miles west of Rossdhu - and a Dumbarton businessman, Alexander Connel. It is easy to conjure up a cosy picture as the wind whistled around the chimney-pots and a great fire crackled in the grate - a convivial atmosphere that unfortunately was soon to be shattered.

An hour or two earlier two strangers had stopped off at Archibald Bell's public house at Auchendennan, seven miles south of Ross Lodge, whose behaviour came across to the locals as a little odd. They paid for their drinks and left without waiting for their change, indicating as they went that they would return to collect it later. Without doubt, these were the same two men who slipped into Ross Lodge sometime later, entering the kitchen via a back door before launching a brutal attack on its occupants. The first of their victims was one of Ludovic's two female servants who, hearing an unfamiliar noise coming from a walk-in pantry, approached to investigate. Holding her candle aloft, she barely had time to peer inside before two figures, their faces blackened with coal dust, leapt out, one of whom struck her a blow to the head with a heavy wooden baton that knocked her unconscious to the floor. Witness to such savagery, the second housemaid let out a scream and fled into an adjoining passageway where she met Colquhoun's manservant, James MacFarlane, rushing towards her who, on hearing the commotion, had hurried from the front room where he had been attending to his employer and his guests. In the face of such ruthless violence MacFarlane was powerless. Seized by one of the intruders, he was clubbed by the man's accomplice and fell helpless to the floor.

With the house staff duly dealt with, the raiders then burst into the parlour where, claiming they had pistols secreted about their persons, they used their bludgeons to launch a violent assault on its three occupants, dealing Colquhoun a mighty blow to the arm as they did so. His guests were quickly incapacitated but he himself managed to lay hold of a fireside poker and lashed out, injuring one of his assailants before making his escape through a window and out into the winter night. Left to their own devices, the housebreakers were free to ransack the house, bursting open drawers and lockfast presses in what turned out to be a fruitless search for money. They turned to the manservant, James MacFarlane, and threatened him with instant death if he refused to disclose where the cash was held but bravely he held out and refused to cooperate. Then, for fear of the alarm being raised, the two men left as swiftly as they had come and slipped away into the darkness. In their haste to be gone, however, what they had failed to see tucked inside one of the cupboards was the rent money in its entirety - all £700 of it - a veritable fortune at the time.

The following morning Colquhoun and his two guests had recovered sufficiently to recall that their attackers had addressed one another in Gaelic (a language they denoted as 'Eirish', or Irish). A search of the lodge's environs turned up a number of abandoned items: a well-worn hat, a small tin box containing culm (a form of coal dust commonly used at the time for face-blackening) and a scrap of cloth used to apply it, and finally a plaid - this last of these to prove highly significant at a later date. Since Boxing Day signalled the customary date for rent collection on the estate it struck Ludovic as perhaps a little more than coincidental that the housebreakers had picked out that particular night for their raid and he speculated whether their original intention had been to intercept him somewhere between Arnburn and Rossdhu and relieve him of his cash. Following their stopover for a dram, however, they had arrived too late to follow their plan to the letter. Inquiries carried out locally turned up the fact that two hours or so after the break-in a pair of suspicious-looking characters had been spotted tramping southwards through the snow near Burnfoot of Auchendennan, and in the early hours of Friday morning what sounded very much like the same two, weary no doubt, had been spied walking from Dumbarton towards Glasgow. Asked by a passer-by for the time, they scarcely paused in their stride and their reply when it came was brusque. Conspicuously, one of the two was seen to have his head bandaged with a length of fabric.

When a notice offering a 100-guineas (£105) reward appeared in the national press, it didn't take long for one of the suspects to be named, identified and arrested. On Friday, 3 January 1800 - little more than a week after the incident - 45-year-old Peter Gray, a cotton-spinner to trade, was apprehended at his home in the mill-town of Johnstone, Renfrewshire, forty miles or so south from Rossdhu if travelling via Glasgow but a journey which could be considerably shortened by taking a ferry across the River Clyde. Confirming suspicions of inside information, it emerged that Gray had formerly been a small farmer on the Luss Estate though the reason why his tenancy was ended is unclear. He was charged in due course with the capital offence of hamesucken.

Also a mill worker, his suspected accomplice, Colin McCallum, had shown a clean pair of heels and his description was circulated widely in the press. According to the *Caledonian Mercury* of Thursday, 9 January, McCallum was around thirty years old, 'rather stout made' and 5' 10" in height, though, like many tallish men, he had a tendency to slouch when walking. He had a 'fair complexion ... pitted with smallpox', by no means uncommon at the time, and he wore his dark brown hair 'long [and] plaited'. He was in the habit of wearing a short blue coat to work but kept another more presentable bottle-green one exclusively for Sundays. Unhelpfully to his pursuers, from time to time he was also to be seen dressed in black. The *Mercury* added that McCallum was a Highlandman, a Gaelic-speaker, and 'there was reason to think that recent ... marks of violence, [would] be found upon his body'. No mention was made of the poker responsible.

Meanwhile Peter Gray was held at the tolbooth in Paisley until his case came up at the Circuit Court of Justiciary in Glasgow on Tuesday, 22 April 1800, before Lord Eskgrove and his fellow judge, Lord Methven. Eskgrove was a man whose eccentricities were legend. In the distinguished High Court judge, Lord Cockburn's *Memoirs*, published fifty years after Eskgrove's death, the author paints an amusing picture, highlighting amongst other things his insistence on conducting proceedings in good broad Scots as well as his notoriously longwinded delivery. 'Often,'

Cockburn wrote, 'have I gone back to the court at midnight and found him, whom I had left mumbling hours before, still going on, with the smoky, unsnuffed tallow candles in greasy tin-candle sticks, and the poor despairing jurymen.' 'His oddities,' he summed up, were such that they 'almost drove Napoleon himself out of the talk of the Edinburgh world.' A convincing impersonator of old 'Esky' and his distinctive manner was a young Edinburgh lawyer who would later become known for rather greater accomplishments. The young man's name was Walter Scott.

Nearly eighty at the time of Peter Gray's trial, Lord Eskgrove had shed nothing of his eccentricity. When Gray pled 'Not Guilty' his legal representative decided that the best option open to him was to quibble over the charge of hamesucken laid against him. Though a serious capital offence, hamesucken was a peculiar crime which could be a little tricky to pin down. Put in its simplest form, it could be defined as the assault upon an individual within his or her own home but, straightforward though that may sound, various potential complications often required to be ironed out. First, must there have been a prior intention to carry out a violent act for the crime to be classified as hamesucken? Opinions varied but, if indeed so, then incidental violence - carried out during a robbery for example - would not then be sufficient to qualify as hamesucken.

Secondly, an assault within a shop, office or other outbuilding could be ruled out since hamesucken was an offence which must categorically be perpetrated within the victim's customary dwelling-house. An attack on a visiting guest (such as Rev. Drummond or Merchant Connel) or on a temporary lodger would not constitute an act of hamesucken. And if all that wasn't curious enough, it was not a requirement that the attacker actually be inside the building when the assault took place. Examples of this might be where the victim was dragged out of his home prior to being assaulted or alternatively if a firearm were to be discharged into a building through a window, thus injuring the householder: both of these instances would be regarded as cases of hamesucken. With respect to such fine distinctions, we may be sure that Lord Eskgrove spared the men of the jury no smallest detail.

As Gray's trial got off the ground his counsel's first line of defence rested on the contention that the crime of hamesucken implied personal hatred towards a victim or a desire for revenge, neither of which could be shown. In addition, it was argued that the offence dated from 'ancient times when the people of Scotland were rude and revengeful, but that since their manners were happily reformed the crime of Hamesucken had become obsolete' and, as such, should not be treated as a capital crime. Countering for the prosecution, the Advocate Depute rejected this suggestion outright, declaring that to accept such a line of argument would be to effectively undermine the safety of an individual within his or her own home. As the trial proceeded, various witnesses were called upon to testify, among them Ludovic Colquhoun himself as well as his guests and house staff plus a number of Peter Gray's co-workers at Johnstone who could vouch for the fact that the plaid abandoned at Ross Lodge had been woven at the mill where he was employed. In the end the evidence proved too powerful and, following deliberations, the men of the jury found Gray guilty by a majority verdict. Hearing their decision, Lord Eskgrove addressed the convicted man, highlighting the depravity of his crime, and - in a moment of unintended dark humour - vented his particular outrage at the timing of his assault on Colquhoun and his friends: 'All this you did,' he barked, 'and God preserve us, joost when they were setten' doon to their denner!' Within seconds, however, grim reality reasserted itself as Eskgrove wound up proceedings by passing sentence of death. The date for his execution, the judge informed Gray, would be Wednesday, 28 May, and he concluded matters by stating that he was not in a position to offer him any hope of mercy.

But, against the odds, Gray's story was not yet at an end. On the very day appointed for his execution he was granted a fourteen-day reprieve in response to a growing groundswell of public sympathy and the remorse he was said to have shown since the time of his conviction. To his credit, Ludovic Colquhoun was one of those who threw his weight behind the case for clemency on the grounds that neither he nor any of the other victims of the Boxing Day raid had suffered any long-term harm as a result but ultimately his efforts were in vain. Gray's hopes were finally dashed when an order was received by the magistrates of Glasgow indicating that no mercy was to be shown and that the original ruling of the court must be carried out to the letter. So, on Wednesday, 11 June, Peter Gray paid for his sins with his life when he was launched into eternity before a crowd of eager onlookers at Glasgow Cross.

When push comes to shove, it goes without saying that of the two housebreakers Colin McCallum was undoubtedly the lucky one. After his flight from justice, there is no way of knowing what might have become of him. It seems at least possible that he chose to retreat into his native hills to the north of the Highland line or alternatively he might have embarked on a new life under a new identity who knows where? - a common enough ploy at the time. Whatever his plan, such was his haste to flee that he left his wife Jean behind, though whether an arrangement had been made between the two to meet up later we can only speculate. And, equally uncertain, a central question which contemporary papers failed to address was whether, in the ill-divided society that they inhabited, Gray and McCallum's crimes had been motivated purely by greed or by genuine, desperate need. So, at the end of the day - villains, then, the pair of them? Well, that may be. Or more the victims of a social structure whereby the poor were seen simply as props to uphold the privileged lifestyles of those who happened to be born rich? In the case of Gray and McCallum it is impossible to tell.

Unidentified Murderer
Tweeddale Court, Edinburgh - November 1806

The Edinburgh residence of the Marquesses of Tweeddale was a large, impressive mansion, just what you might expect of a family of such wealth, antiquity and influence. Coach access was from the Cowgate to the rear while the front of the house overlooked Tweeddale Court and was linked to the High Street through a narrow close, fifteen yards or so in length, which emerged almost directly opposite John Knox's house. However, by the early years of the nineteenth century the property had passed from the Tweeddale family into the hands of the British Linen Company whose banking operations in Edinburgh were now based there.

In late autumn of 1806 a grisly discovery was made in the cramped passageway connecting the bank buildings and the High Street. It was pretty well dark around 5 p.m. on Thursday, 13 November, when a wee girl from a neighbouring dwelling-house was sent by her mother to fill a kettle at a nearby well. Making her way out to the street, as the child passed through the gloomy close she tripped over something unseen on the ground. Presumably she cried out when she realised that the crumpled bundle she had trampled on was the body of a dying man. The alarm was raised but by then it was too late to do anything to save the life of William Begbie, a porter in the employ of the British Linen Company, who lay with the blade of a knife embedded deep in his chest and who sadly bled to death before he could gasp out any information about the assault. The murderer's motive was not hard to divine. When his attacker struck, Begbie had been returning to headquarters from the bank's Leith branch, carrying a yellow canvas bag which contained a sealed package of banknotes of various banks and denominations amounting to £4,392 precisely. By the time the small child found him dying in Tweeddale's Close, of either the murderer or the money there was not a trace.

The knife-blow that ended Begbie's life had been launched with great strength and precision to the extent that the blade had entered his body right up to the hilt, penetrating his heart. Investigations soon showed that the crime had been premeditated and well planned. The weapon used was a common bread knife complete with its customary long, thin blade but whose rounded front end had been ground with a whetstone to a sharp, vicious point and smoothed upon a hone afterwards. Immediately prior to the attack the knife's wooden handle - red in colour - had been muffled in soft paper so as to prevent any risk of the assailant's being sprayed with the blood of his victim, thereby rendering him conspicuous during his subsequent getaway. Looking back, it might surprise us that one man alone should have been charged with responsibility for crossing the city with such a vast sum in his care - according to the Bank of England's inflation calculator something akin to £400,000 today. Tragically, the price for the risk he took was paid not by William Begbie alone but also by the wife and four children whom he left behind to mourn his loss.

The British Linen Company lost no time in alerting the public to the shocking event in a blaze of publicity as broadsheets were distributed across the city and notifications published in a slew of newspapers both north and south of the border. These advertisements provided readers with details of Begbie's 'horrid murder', itemised the banknotes stolen, described the weapon which had dealt the fatal blow and requested any local cutler who might have sold such an item recently to make himself known. A reward of 500 guineas (£525) was offered to any person providing information that would lead to the conviction of the murderer and the notices added that if such an informant should happen to be an accomplice of the guilty party, then 'His Majesty's pardon [would] also be applied in his favour'. It was revealed too that William Begbie had been seen 'walking up Leith Walk between four and five o'clock in company with a man' and this unnamed individual was asked to step forward and provide whatever information he might have.

Later in the month it came to the company's notice that a knife matching the description previously given had been sold around 2 p.m. on the day of the murder and thereafter its newspaper advertisements invited any tradesman who had been asked to sharpen such an item to present himself at its head office at Tweeddale Court. Amongst all the talk of rewards, payments and pardons, whether Begbie's family received any form of compensation I do not know.

It emerged that children playing nearby had seen a man hurrying out of the close, crossing the crowded High Street and slipping down a lane known as Leith Wynd. A number of suspicious characters were taken in for questioning but all - with a single exception - were able to provide alibis or other evidence of their innocence and were quickly released. In Robert Chambers' *Traditions of Edinburgh* - published 1824 - the author identifies this solitary exception as 'a carrier between Perth and Edinburgh, a man of dissolute and irregular habits, of great bodily strength, and known to be a dangerous and desperate character' who had been seen in the Canongate, not far from Tweeddale Court shortly after the time of Begbie's murder. The individual in question was taken into custody and held for some considerable time but was eventually released, the author tells us, for lack of evidence. No wonder he kept his mouth shut: it turned out he had been engaged in committing a capital crime elsewhere. At no stage does Chambers name him. He also refers to another suspect: a certain Leith doctor (likewise unnamed) whom he describes as 'a dissolute man and a gambler', possibly with debts accumulating, who ended his own life not long after the murder, but Chambers admits to not knowing exactly what grounds there might have been for suspecting him.

Shockwaves caused by Begbie's brutal murder were felt throughout the Edinburgh area and a number of troubled citizens felt impelled to voice their concerns in print. In a letter to the *Caledonian Mercury*, 'Hamlet' outlines his fear that, if the murderer were not caught and punished, the message sent to others of a similar type would be that their best method of avoiding capture would be to permanently silence their victims. 'It may tend to hold out some hope to the highwayman, that if the murder is complete, he has every hope of escape', he warns, 'and it is only in the footpad doing the work of the assassin that he has any safety to expect.' Hamlet's proposed solution is that an additional fund should be set up 'by which £1,000 or £1,500 will be presently subscribed [by the general public] as further reward for the discovery of the ferocious villain'. Until that happens, he fears that 'the funds of every Banking and Commercial House are ... open to the hand of plunder, and the safety of the lonely traveller for ever undermined'.

Responding some days later, 'Horatio' disagrees, arguing that in the absence of new information no amount of money, no matter how great, would enable progress to be made. Instead he urges patience and expresses confidence that, given time, 'Providence' will disclose the murderer's identity, thereby allowing him to be suitably punished. Horatio finishes up with a literary flourish: 'We know,' he concludes, 'that, in the words of your correspondent's author, "Foul deeds will rise, Though all the earth o'erwhelm 'em, to men's eyes".' Well, it is certainly true that the evil-doer is revealed in Shakespeare's famous play but only time would tell whether the same would hold true in relation to the murderer of William Begbie.

Suspicion fell increasingly on one Robert Johnston, a burly former soldier in his thirties who had been condemned to death in the High Court four months earlier after being convicted of breaking into the shop premises of Edinburgh seedsmen, Dicksons, and stealing just over £35 in notes and coins. (His detection and arrest had relied in part on the classic Boy's Own technique of tracking his footprints through an expanse of dew-soaked grass.) Granted a pardon on condition that he submit to rejoining the armed forces and serving overseas, he deserted even before his regiment left the country. During December a series of advertisements appeared in the press offering a 50-guinea reward for information leading to his arrest. Apparently shortly after the murder he had been seen in the south of Scotland spending money hand over fist and he was spotted again, this time disguised in women's clothing in the city of Newcastle: 'a woman's dark great Coat, a Hat tied below the Chin, Petticoats [and] mixed coloured Worsted Stockings.' Small wonder, indeed, that this strapping, six-foot former army sergeant 'made a very awkward Appearance', according to a notice in *The Tyne Mercury*. As an added incentive to potential informants, if following his arrest Johnston were to go on to be convicted of William Begbie's murder, then whoever had notified the authorities would, of course, also be entitled to claim the British Linen Company's original 500-guinea reward, netting for himself a grand total of 550 guineas - not far short of £600. Despite the financial inducement, there appear to have been no further significant developments until late March when the suspect in question was tracked down and apprehended by an officer of the court, George Williamson, Edinburgh's Messenger-at-Arms, just south of Berwick on the English bank of the River Tweed, and escorted back to the city. He was questioned before the sheriff in relation to the murder of Begbie but ultimately nothing came of it. Presumably, he still had the charge of desertion to answer.

Nothing new emerged until four months later as three men - two masons and a gardener - were crossing an area of fields at Bellevue just outside the city when they happened to spot a package secreted in a hole in a wall and screened from view behind a hedge. When they opened it up they found that it was stuffed full of banknotes which from their perished condition had clearly been exposed to the elements for some time. They bundled the package together and handed it in to the sheriff's office where the notes - approximately £3,000 in large denominations - were identified as some of those stolen at Tweeddale Close nine months earlier. The assumption was that the robber had calculated the risks involved in changing notes of such large denominations too great and he had therefore chosen to abandon them while still holding on to well over £1,000 in smaller denominations. The three finders were rewarded for their honesty by the British Linen Company to the tune of £200 but the episode shed no further light on the identity of the robber and murderer.

For a long time after Begbie's murder rumours continued to circulate and various theories were proposed. In 1813 a story surfaced to the effect that a person recently deceased in London had left behind a written confession, while two years later it was reported that an army deserter, currently imprisoned on the Isle of Wight, had admitted to being the murderer. He preferred to face execution in Edinburgh, he was alleged to have stated, than continue as at present behind bars. Others stepped forward to confess who demonstrably had nothing to do with the crime - something not unusual, it seems, in similar cases. But probably the most popular theory - picked up and pondered many times over - involved an interesting character by the name of James Mackoull (or Maccoul).

Born around 1760, most accounts of Mackoull's life present him as a London ruffian but at least one suggests that in fact he was born in Berwickshire before his family moved south to the capital where his father established himself as a respectable tradesman. His mother, by contrast, was a woman cast from a different mould and was well known as a persistent shoplifter and low-grade thief. He received a rudimentary education and acquired basic competency in reading and writing but, in common with his two brothers and three sisters, followed his mother's moral lead and lapsed into a life of dishonesty and crime, progressing from initial petty pilfering from his fellow school pupils to involving himself with criminal gangs that operated outside theatres and other places of entertainment in the city. After carrying out a brazen daylight robbery in St James's Park, he escaped justice by enlisting as a volunteer in His Majesty's Navy and went on to spend the following nine years serving - apparently honourably - in the West Indies and along the North American coast. In 1785 he returned to London but soon fell in with bad company and resumed his old habits, attending bull-baiting, cock-fighting and boxing events where he gambled away the savings he had accumulated over his years abroad. As a means of starting afresh, he reinvented himself as Captain James Moffat, the former master of a West Indian trading vessel, and a certain gentlemanly polish he had acquired during his time in the Navy served him well in relieving a succession of well-heeled victims of their money and other valuables. On one notable occasion he was said to have picked the pocket of a clergyman on his way from the pulpit.

It was written of Mackoull that 'a thief throws out with a shovel what he brings in with a spoon' and, consistently overspent, he was constantly on the lookout for potential new sources of income. In his late twenties he married the madam of a house of ill repute whose business he diversified by taking in stolen goods which he cached in a concealed alcove behind a window bricked up to avoid payment of window tax. When the authorities picked up on his activities he was forced to flee once again, this time to Hamburg where, becoming proficient in the language, he lived by his usual methods of gambling, swindling and pickpocketing, moving from place to place around the country as soon as the shadow of suspicion fell upon him. He left Germany in 1805 and, after a brief stopover in London, he stepped ashore at Leith harbour on Tuesday, 10

September. He stayed for a short time at the Ship Tavern before, posing as a Hamburg merchant, he took lodgings in New Street, just off the Canongate - a relatively short walk, as it happened, from Tweeddale's Close.

Not until after Mackoull's death did his name come to be associated with the Begbie affair. Researched and written by James Denovan, a court officer and former Bow Street Runner (London policeman), an account of his life and criminal activities was published in 1822 which included a statement by a Leith schoolteacher who in November 1806 had been a fourteen-year-old sailor lad, currently home on leave after returning from a voyage to Lisbon. Newly disembarked at Leith, the boy had been making his way into the city with a small gift for his mother and sister when he became aware of two men on the street ahead of him, the foremost of whom was carrying under his arm a yellow-coloured parcel. It seemed he was being shadowed by the second man who was careful not to lose contact but at the same time maintain his distance, crossing and re-crossing the street in what looked like an effort to avoid being noticed. Conscious that no duty had been paid on his own small present, very probably the young sailor overreacted when he jumped to the conclusion that he was witnessing a smuggler in possession of contraband goods being pursued by a zealous officer of the customs and excise.

At the head of Leith Street 'the smuggler' - in reality, the bank courier William Begbie - turned to cross the North Bridge and, after a brief pause, 'the customs officer' followed. Coming along behind, when the young sailor reached the southern end of the bridge he found that the two men had disappeared from sight. Relieved, he put them from his mind and within a few moments arrived outside his mother's house in the Netherbow, directly opposite Tweeddale's Close. But if he thought he had seen the last of the supposed customs officer, then it turned out he was mistaken because just at that moment the self-same man rushed out of the close with an unseen bundle tucked underneath his coat and vanished among the crowd. Still feeling uneasy, the young lad quickly handed in his gift at his mother's door and returned as soon as he could to his ship. Although news of Begbie's murder reached him before his vessel set sail a few days later, he dismissed the idea of reporting what he had witnessed to the authorities for fear of his own small misdemeanour coming to light and, as it turned out, it was some considerable time before he returned to his native land. It was the time of the Napoleonic Wars and the young lad's ship was captured by an enemy privateer. He found himself imprisoned in a French jail and did not regain his freedom until peace was negotiated.

But what was there to link his supposed customs officer with the notorious criminal James Mackoull? Despite the intervening years, the schoolteacher was still able to paint a clear picture of the man's appearance for James Denovan. He had been fairly tall, he recalled, and solidly built. Well turned out in a black coat, he had about him an air of gentility. Taken alongside verified descriptions of Mackoull, it certainly seemed a reasonable match but realistically the fact cannot be ignored that, apart from a quick glimpse of his face as he emerged from Tweeddale's Close, the only views the sailor boy had of Begbie's killer were from some distance away and from the rear as they made their way up Leith Walk from the harbour.

After William Begbie's murder Mackoull didn't hang around but packed up and left Edinburgh in short order. It was said that back in England he lay low for a time but, a dyed-in-the-wool criminal, he was not one to settle down and turn over a new leaf. Many years later, after being convicted of robbing the Glasgow branch of the Paisley Union Bank, he was questioned shortly before his death in prison by James Denovan who broached in an oblique manner the subject of Begbie's murder. Mackoull seemed rattled in response but, even so, he gave nothing away. Lord Cockburn - Denovan's former classmate at the Royal High School, as it happened - referred briefly to the case in his *Memoirs* but made it clear that the evidence was not strong enough to convince him of Mackoull's guilt, and at the end of the day no-one ever faced charges relating to the murder of the unfortunate William Begbie.

Indeed, it was probably the very fact that the case remained unsolved that kept it alive in the public consciousness for so long. Twenty years after the event, in February 1827 Sir Walter Scott was invited to preside at a dinner for several hundred guests hosted by the Edinburgh Theatrical Fund. Although it was widely rumoured, Scott had never yet publicly acknowledged his authorship of the Waverley novels - the first of which, *Waverley*, had been published more than a decade earlier - but, prompted by a fellow guest, at long last Scott came clean to prolonged and enthusiastic applause from around the hall. As he resumed his seat he was said to have slipped a pencilled note to a friend who was due to speak later in the evening. It read: 'Confess something too - why not the murder of Begbie?'

Adam & John Lyall
Sherrifmuir, Stirlingshire - October 1810

Livestock-dealer Matthew Boyd's trip to Dunning Fair in October 1810 had proved a great success, so as he travelled home to West Lothian, alone and on horseback, he was carrying with him a significant sum of money. But, as things turned out, his good fortune was set not to last. Twenty-odd miles into his journey, he was crossing the high country of Sheriffmuir when he was waylaid around midday by two young men on foot - in fact, little more than boys - one of whom laid hold of his bridle and demanded that he deliver up his money. Initially Boyd was not remotely alarmed, never thinking for a moment that he could be held up in broad daylight, and he automatically assumed that he was the object of a prank played by one of his friends. But when the two men presented pistols, his view of the situation changed. For a time, he tried stalling, claiming that business at the market had left him penniless, but the robbers were not so easily fooled. 'Blow his brains out,' said one to the other, 'if he does not give up what is in his vest.' Realising that resistance was futile, Boyd reached into his waistcoat and produced from an inside pocket a leather wallet whose contents of £29 and 9 shillings he duly handed over. In doing so, however, he did his best to conceal the wallet's inner compartment where he had hidden the bulk of his money, but to no avail. Before he could return it to his pocket one of the robbers ordered him to surrender the entire wallet containing four £20 notes issued by the Falkirk Union Bank plus a further four £5 notes by the Stirling Bank

- £100 in all. Once the two highwaymen had finished totalling up their haul, they must surely have marvelled at their luck. In today's terms they had relieved their victim of something to the tune of £10,000.

Instructed to ride on, only after a hundred yards or so had Boyd sufficiently regained his composure for it to occur to him that taking note of what direction the robbers took as they fled might come in useful later. Aiming for a higher vantage point, he dismounted and scrambled over a nearby stone dyke where by sheer chance he landed beside two large bags which had apparently been stashed out of sight. Thinking that the contents of the mysterious bundles might provide a clue to his attackers' identity, he approached to take a closer look but before he had time to investigate, he became aware that one of the robbers was hurrying in his direction, pistol in hand. With no time wasted, he snatched up the bags, quickly remounted and galloped off in the direction of Stirling, the nearest large town. After a mile or so he arrived at Roy's farmhouse where he breathlessly gasped out his account of recent events, finishing off with a request for assistance in apprehending his attackers. The response he received was somewhat lame and it looked very much as though the farmer was chary of becoming involved in another man's troubles. So urgent was the job of bringing in the harvest, he told Boyd, that he could not spare any of his workers. Realising he had been given short shrift, Boyd was left with no option other than to continue alone so, leaving the two bundles at the farm, he dropped out of the hills, passed through the village of Blairlogie and travelled on to Stirling where he successfully applied to obtain a warrant. Now accompanied by Stirlingshire's Messenger-at-Arms - a sheriff court official named Thomas Miller - he rode straight back to Roy's farm where the two men set about opening up the bags that Boyd had left behind. Inside they found articles of clothing such as shawls and pelisses (lightweight women's gowns much in vogue at the time) but, most significant of all, they unearthed a man's jacket which Roy recognised as one worn by a former employee of his brother's. The individual in question went by the name of John Lyall.

Leaving the farm, Boyd and Miller resumed their journey, tracing the highwaymen's suspected route to the village of Menstrie where they halted for refreshments at a local inn. When they made enquiries about whether anyone matching the highwaymen's description had been seen in the vicinity, they were told that, yes, two such men had spent the previous night there. Encouraged by what looked like a reliable sighting, Boyd and Miller proceeded to itemise the various articles of clothing found in the robbers' bags and, as soon the landlord's daughter heard the garments described, she grew suspicious. She went to check on a number of wardrobes which she found had indeed been rifled of their contents. Following a positive lead, Boyd and Miller left Menstrie in the direction of Alloa, four miles south-east, where they met the proprietor of a second public house, John Stewart, who could tell them that the men they were chasing had set off for North Queensferry by carriage during the late afternoon. Riding alongside the River Forth where it broadened out into the firth, Boyd and Miller had twenty more gruelling miles to cover in pitch black before they reached the ferry's northern terminus at 3 a.m. and learned, to their intense frustration, that the men they sought had preceded them by some five hours. Boyd presumed that, after making the two-mile crossing, it would be the robbers' intention to travel into Edinburgh.

Scarcely pausing for breath, Boyd and Miller set about hiring a boatman of their own to guide them across the Firth. Stepping ashore at South Queensferry, they made inquiries at the Newhalls Inn and were directed towards Robert Henderson, the very chaise-driver, it transpired, who had earlier conveyed the fleeing fugitives into the city. Offering him the sum of five guineas as an incentive, they asked Henderson to drop them off at the exact spot where he had set down his previous passengers. At the end of a dark ten-mile journey, the coachman brought his horses to a halt at the door of Shaw's Hotel on Princes Street. The hour of their arrival was 7 a.m.

If Miller and Boyd's expectations had been high, then they must have been dashed pretty quickly when they learned that they had been pipped once again. Hotel staff confirmed that two men answering the robbers' descriptions had indeed stayed as overnight guests but they had settled their bill and checked out during the early hours. Hoping against hope that he was not already too late, Boyd immediately went about organising a search party, half of which would be led by Archibald Campbell, Edinburgh's Messenger-at-Arms, who promptly led his group down into the Grassmarket area of the Old Town. Meanwhile Miller and Boyd's men began to comb the New Town area. Wandering the streets without success, it was looking increasingly like a wild goose chase and when

Matthew Boyd came over faint around 9 a.m. - no surprise after an exhausting full day on the go - he returned to Shaw's Hotel where he bought a bottle of porter as a pick-me-up. All out of options, he was seriously contemplating throwing in the towel when, lo and behold, a pair of natty-looking gents came swaggering past the hotel whom he instantly recognised as the two men who had robbed him. It was obvious that they had wasted no time before kitting themselves out in style. Earlier in the day they had visited the premises of John Brown, shoemaker, where they paid for expensive, top-quality boots, complete with spurs, using a Falkirk Bank £20 note. At Shaw's Merchant Tailors they had treated themselves to a new wardrobe, paid for once again with Falkirk banknotes, and acquired in addition fashionable whips which they brandished with evident pride. Had they but known it, they would not have long to enjoy their extravagant purchases.

Conscious of being recognised, the robbers attempted to flee but in a classic case of poetic justice Matthew Boyd laid hold of one man in person and his accomplice was seized soon after. In a desperate last-ditch effort to evade the law, one of the prisoners proposed that all concerned should adjourn to a nearby hostelry to negotiate acceptable restorative measures over a glass or two of spirits. 'Take us to a public house,' he suggested, 'and we will give up the money and pay all expenses.' It was a suggestion that fell on deaf ears and the men were huckled off to jail without further ado. When searched, each was found to be carrying a pistol complete with lead bullets which were confiscated on the spot. Also in the men's possession were banknotes and coins, both gold and silver, that amounted to the greater part by far of Boyd's stolen money. As for the cattle-trader himself, we might imagine that he felt highly gratified at the day's satisfactory outcome as he headed home to West Lothian to catch up on lost sleep.

Just as the farmer at Sheriffmuir had suspected, one of the two captives did indeed turn out to be John Lyall, and the other his brother, Adam Lyall. At the opening of their trial in the High Court in January 1811 Adam pleaded not guilty but the only defence his lawyer, John Reid, could muster was to highlight what he claimed was an error on the original charge sheet that had placed the crime scene in Perthshire rather than Stirlingshire. The sheriff officer at Stirling, John Kerr, was no help, not entirely clear himself about the positioning of the boundary for the county he was responsible for. At the end of the day the lawyer's gallant (if forlorn) efforts cut no ice with the jury who dismissed his argument as a mere technicality and were not long in unanimously finding the prisoner guilty as charged of highway robbery. In atonement for his sins, Adam Lyall went to the gallows in Edinburgh three months later. He met his death, it was reported, in a calm and dignified manner.

Disposing of John Lyall's case proved a bit trickier. Standing alongside his brother in the dock, when asked how he pleaded he remained sullen and silent. One person unlikely to have been surprised was Captain Sibbald, the Edinburgh jailer. When Lyall was first locked up he had found him surly and uncooperative, refusing to respond to any questions put to him. After a few days his behaviour grew ever more eccentric when he started to insist that his brother had been murdered and that his ghost had appeared in his cell during the night. He fell into a fever and raved randomly about unnamed castles. A doctor was consulted who recommended a week's total rest before he was subjected to further questioning. During the days that followed, Lyall ate nothing until his temperature eventually returned to normal, his appetite returned and, as if to make up for lost time, he began to devour any foodstuffs placed before him. Suspecting that he was play-acting and his whole performance was simply a ruse, Sibbald removed his outdoor shoes one day and tip-toed upstairs where he peeped through a spy-hole on the door of Lyall's cell. What he saw was the prisoner, sitting motionless while gazing blankly at the wall, but it was the manic glint in his eyes that unnerved Sibbald most and convinced him that Lyall was not of sound mind. In the days and weeks that followed his prodigious appetite showed no sign of abating and he continued to gobble down his meals 'like a dog'. He put on weight until the buttons on his clothing could no longer be fastened.

With Lyall's outright refusal to enter a plea, his lawyer, Robert Rollo, was forced to step forward on his behalf to request a postponement on the grounds that his client was incapable of speaking in his own defence. Backing up Rollo's claim, Captain Sibbald recounted various instances of Lyall's peculiar behaviour during the time he spent behind bars pending trial. Dr Farquharson was next to take the stand and testified that, while treating Lyall in prison, he had formed the impression that - in the blunt language of the time - he was 'in a perfect state of idiotry [sic]' and 'totally incapable of knowing the right hand from the left'. Their evidence was strong enough to convince the Lord Justice Clerk that Lyall was unfit to stand trial and accordingly he issued instructions that he be remanded back to prison and passed in due course into the safekeeping of his sister and brother-in-law, Catherine and Robert Lyon of Glasgow, to be cared for by them indefinitely. But, as later events might suggest, maybe John wasn't so daft. It didn't take long before he absconded and went on the run, vanishing completely for a time. Only by a curious combination of circumstances was he eventually brought to book.

Then as now, Edinburgh's New Year was invariably accompanied by celebrations and all manner of merry-making, but on Hogmanay of 1811 things got seriously out of hand. An hour or so before midnight the festivities turned sour when, at the pre-arranged peep of a whistle, a gang of keelies - young city thugs - emerged out of stairwells and closes and proceeded to rampage through the streets. To shroud their dark deeds from view they destroyed street lamps and assaulted anyone in their path with clubs and bludgeons, robbing them of money, jewellery and any other valuables that came to hand. The night's most serious casualty was a policeman, Dugald Campbell, who was kicked and brutally beaten about the head. Three days later he died of his injuries in the Royal Infirmary. Following a major overnight operation a number of those responsible were arrested on New Year's Day, some with stolen items still in their possession, and, in an effort to identify and apprehend any of the hooligans still at large, a reward of one hundred guineas was put up by Lord Provost William Creech and the city magistrates. At the end of the day, if the episode generated any tangible silver lining, it acted as a wake-up call to inadequacies in the policing of the capital.

In mid-January one of the principal suspects, Hugh McIntosh, was tracked down to Glasgow where he was arrested and placed behind bars. Here he found himself sharing a cell with a teenager, John Dunkison (or Duncanson), who was being held for his alleged involvement in a recent highway robbery during which an Ayrshire haulier, Hugh Dunn of Maybole, had been relieved of a substantial sum of money. Before McIntosh was transferred back to Edinburgh to face trial, Duncanson and he put their heads together and hatched a plot to retrieve various items stolen during the New Year riots from where they had been cached in a house in the High Street of Glasgow. The valuables, it was understood, were to be split two ways and McIntosh's share would be forwarded - by whatever underground means - to his place of confinement in the capital. The first part of the arrangement went without hitch as regular consignments of stolen goods - wallets, banknotes, articles of jewellery - were smuggled in to Duncanson's cell courtesy of a lady of the night named Anne Gemmel [sic], one of his most regular visitors, and her sister, Janet. When it came to sidestepping the rules, Anne was no slouch, and on one notable occasion she sneaked in a number of pocket-watches concealed in a basket beneath an upper layer of potatoes. By then, however, Duncanson was starting to have second thoughts. If such a thing exists as loyalty among thieves, then no-one had informed him. He decided to renege on his deal with McIntosh and keep the stolen items entirely to himself. Furious at being duped, McIntosh reported his former co-conspirator's treachery to the authorities - but the taste of his revenge was brief. Three months later - on Wednesday, 22 April - Hugh McIntosh and two other convicted rioters were hanged for the part they had played in the New Year affray. The crowd, it was estimated, was one of the largest ever seen in the capital.

Back in January, of course, McIntosh was still on remand in Edinburgh, smarting at being betrayed by his former cellmate. In order to investigate his allegations concerning Duncanson's handling of stolen goods, Archibald Campbell (the same Messenger-at-Arms who had supported Matthew Boyd three months earlier) travelled to Glasgow, and when he entered the prison and came face to face with Duncanson it must have made for a memorable occasion. The two men's surprise was surely impossible to hide when they realised that this was not the first time they had met. Campbell instantly recognised Duncanson as the slippery runaway, John Lyall, who had been charged with highway robbery precisely a year before and dismissed from the dock as mentally incapable. Cornered at last, it seemed certain that it would be only a matter of time before he followed his brother Adam's example and gasped out his final breaths in front of a baying Edinburgh crowd. Well, maybe or maybe not, one thing was for sure: given his previous record, he wasn't about to give up his life without a struggle. He'd been lucky so far and there was always a chance, no matter how slight, that he might yet pull something out of the hat.

Transferred to jail in Edinburgh, Lyall made a bid for freedom which was nipped in the bud when Captain Sibbald unearthed a plot whereby he had colluded with two fellow inmates, Alexander Thomson and John Armour, to make good their escape by disarming their guards, overpowering the prison turnkey and liberating themselves using his keys. Their scheme was rumbled just in time, and from that point on Lyall was kept shackled in irons. In spite of his best efforts, this time round there was no question that he was fit to be tried and on Monday, 15 June, he pleaded not guilty to the charge of highway robbery. What followed bore a strong resemblance to his brother's trial the previous year: Matthew Boyd repeated his testimony virtually verbatim, and Thomas Miller and Archibald Campbell, court officials for Stirlingshire and Edinburgh respectively, recounted once again the part they had played. Just as in Adam's trial, the jury were unequivocal in reaching a guilty verdict.

But there all similarities ended. Whereas Adam Lyall was condemned to pay the ultimate price, the final twist in John's tale emerged when the prosecuting Solicitor General, David Moneypenny, addressed the judges in rather unexpected terms. The ends of justice, Moneypenny argued, had already been served in large measure when Adam Lyall was executed the previous April for the same crime that his brother, John, stood convicted of now. Moneypenny went on to highlight the length of time that had passed since the robbery took place - more than a year and a half - and suggested that this too should be taken into consideration. Enigmatically, he alluded to certain circumstances which, for reasons unstated, he chose not to divulge to the court. Before resuming his seat, he closed by exhorting the judges to treat the prisoner as leniently as lay within their powers. Despite being somewhat unorthodox, Moneypenny's remarks were well received by the bench and the Lord Justice Clerk, David Boyle, went so far as to compliment him for the humanity he had shown. Boyle then turned to direct his concluding remarks toward the man in the dock, underscoring the responsibility invested in him as an instrument of the law to safeguard members of the public. In accordance with these principles, the judges brought the court proceedings to an end by sentencing John Lyall to be transported overseas for the remaining duration of his natural life - a weighty punishment, for sure, but one which could easily have been so much worse.

So - a satisfactory outcome all round? Well, as far as the plucky cattle-dealer, Matthew Boyd, was concerned, undeniably he had been put through the mill but at the end of the day he had successfully recovered most of his stolen money. Not only that but he had in addition been granted an award of twenty guineas by 'the Gentlemen of Stirlingshire' at their annual meeting - 'as a testimony of their approbation of the great activity and exertion, successfully used by him, in pursuing, apprehending, and bringing to justice, two men, who had robbed him in the Sheriffmuir, of a large sum of money'. Likewise, a fund had been set up to ensure that the Maybole deliveryman, Hugh Dunn - another of Lyall's victims - was not left out of pocket after his own ordeal: 'in consideration of his excellent character for attention and honesty, and of the determined resolution which he displayed in defending his property'. But what of John Lyall himself? What awaited him thousands of miles away at the bottom end of the globe?

The way things turned out, Lyall spent the best part of a year, sleeping on straw and quite possibly shackled in irons, on the *Retribution* - one of the squalid prison ships known as hulks that were anchored at the mouth of the River Thames. Not till May 1813 was he permitted to board the *Earl Spencer* at Portsmouth, bound for Australia. Of his two hundred fellow passengers (all male), fourteen were convicted Scots, four of whom - including Lyall himself - were exiled for life. After a brief stopover at Madeira, the vessel sailed directly to Port Jackson, Sydney, where she arrived on Saturday, 9 October 1813, at the end of a four-month voyage. Once ashore, Lyall was assigned to work with a carpenters' gang, but old habits die hard and it was not long before before he was up to his old tricks. A public notice placed in April 1814 in the *Sydney Gazette & New South Wales Advertiser* enumerates various convicts 'who have absented themselves from their respective employments'. Alongside stonemasons, a bullock driver, bricklayers and labourers, there features the name of a certain John Lyall, carpenter. 'All constables and others,' the advertisement declares, 'are strictly required to use their utmost exertions in apprehending, and lodging them in safe custody'. As time would tell, Lyall proved tricky to pin down and similar notices seeking his whereabouts appeared in the press periodically until the early months of 1818.

Within such a tight European community - a mere 12,000 souls - how, one might ask, could an individual simply go missing, unseen and undetected? Contemporary records are patchy but it seems that the method Lyall settled upon was one with a time-honoured history. When he spied the transport ship, *Windham*, preparing to leave King's Wharf, Sydney, to ferry soldiers of the 73rd Regiment to the island of Sri Lanka, he grasped his opportunity, and in the company of a band of like-minded convicts, seventeen in all, he slipped aboard on Saturday, 2 April 1814. Once at sea it was only a matter of time before the stowaways were obliged to reveal their presence and, faced with a battalion of seasoned army men, they were in no position to dictate terms. By then, however, there was no possibility of returning them to Port Jackson, so they duly accompanied the 73rd to Sri Lanka from where they were transferred in due course to Calcutta, a popular end-point for successful escapees. In the circumstances Lyall and his companions were less fortunate, held behind bars until finally escorted back from India aboard the convict ship, *Greyhound*, following an absence from Australia of four whole years.

Despite his failed escape bid, Lyall was still not ready to toe the line. He was sent to Newcastle, a tough coastal settlement one hundred miles north of Sydney, where records show that in January 1822 he was subjected to fifty strokes of the lash for disobeying orders and being absent from quarters after hours. He was similarly punished three years later for an infringement that sounds a good deal more serious. In the early hours of Sunday, 2 January 1825, Lyall was the only Scot among a group of seven convicts who, with the connivance of the duty sentry, Private William Yams, took possession of a government-owned 'gig' - a boat guided by oars - in the hope of seizing control of a larger vessel, *Mars*, which was currently standing out to sea. Thwarted in their attempt by a squally north-easterly, nevertheless they made good their escape by allowing the gig to run freely before the wind. Their absence was not picked up on till the following morning when the local commandant, Lieutenant Thomas Owen, manned a whaleboat with five of the fugitives' fellow convicts, supervised by two soldiers of his company, and set off in pursuit. That evening the searchers landed at Reid's Mistake, a projecting headland twenty miles south of Newcastle, where they found five oars of the stolen gig lying abandoned on the beach. Assisted by two Aboriginal trackers, they spent the night combing the surrounding countryside and by shortly after daybreak all of the absconders had been successfully recaptured. The men were duly returned to Newcastle where they were kept in jail pending trial in three months' time. Despite their claim that they knew nothing of the stolen gig but were simply 'kangarooing' in the bush, they were found guilty of 'piratically seizing, carrying away and destroying a boat, the property of the Crown'. Lyall was sentenced to fifty lashes.

By the time he reached the age of forty it seems fairly likely that Lyall would have acquired a wife, perhaps amassed a family around him, and settled down to a steadier existence. Certainly by April 1834 he had mended his ways enough to be granted his ticket-of-leave - a document that permitted him certain freedoms while still limiting his movements and placing him on a form of parole. Undoubtedly this easing of restrictions would imply a degree of confidence on the part of the authorities that he had turned his life around - though leopards, as we know, are not known for changing their spots and maybe it shouldn't come as too much of a surprise to learn that the old Lyall resurfaced three years later when he was sentenced to six hours in the stocks for misconduct. A newspaper account of his court appearance provides readers with a glimpse of his appearance: the prisoner's nose, the report states, was 'of such dimensions that even we shall decline any attempt to describe it'. Looks aside, his infringement of the law was not viewed as sufficiently serious as to prevent him from receiving a Conditional Pardon in April 1841, granted - it was made crystal clear - through 'Her Majesty's gracious approbation and allowance'. Whilst not revoking his original life sentence, the pardon entitled him to unrestricted freedom of movement so long as he did not leave Australia. Now approaching fifty, it was clear that in spite of his chequered past he was a lucky man. For his brother, Adam, on the other hand, half a world away and thirty years dead, a life such as John's - adversity, hardship and all - would have been preferable by far to his own grim end.

VILLAINS AND VICTIMS

James Whiteford, Hopetoun, West Lothian - March 1819
Peter Bowers, Coalston, East Lothian - April 1819

During the summer of 1819 two men shared the condemned cell in Edinburgh. For the more fortunate of the two, imprisonment would prove short-lived and a reprieve would allow him to escape the rope and embark instead on a ten-thousand-mile voyage down under where he would live out the rest of his days in relative peace. But his companion on death row would be less fortunate and for him there was to be no such second chance. On Wednesday, 18 August, he had no option but to climb the steps to the gallows and pay for his crimes with his life.

Initially Peter Bowers had been the one who seemed in much deeper trouble. It had started off innocently enough on Wednesday, 15 April 1819, when the 21-year-old millwright left Gifford, East Lothian, to walk the four or five miles to his home in Haddington in the company of his employer's son. For the previous week the two men had been working on a job at Gifford and, before leaving their temporary lodgings, they had drunk a half-mutchkin of spirits between them - no more than half a pint - courtesy of James Trail, for whom they had been working. But along the way they continued to drink, stopping off at various public houses to top up with whisky before finally calling it a day and heading for home. That they had overdone things would have been obvious to anyone.

That same evening a quarryman, Alexander Napier, was making his way home after work when he found a sporting contest in progress near the Coalston House tollbar. Two young farm labourers - Henry Phillips and Alexander Watt - were competing at long jump while their more mature colleague, John Sandilands, spectated from the sidelines. A few moments later Bowers and his companion happened along, the latter carrying his workman's tools and the former swinging an axe. Fuelled by alcoholic bravado, Bowers offered to take on either of the two jumpers, adding for good measure that he would be willing to bet tuppence that he would emerge as the winner. Watt was quick to take up the challenge, but when the contest got underway it quickly became clear that Bowers had bitten off more than he could chew. Comprehensively trounced, he grew surly, reneged on the deal and refused point blank to pay up.

Understandably, his actions gave rise to friction. As Watt pressed his claim Bowers grew belligerent, raising his axe in a threatening manner. In the scuffle that ensued Watt managed to disarm him and threw the axe to the ground where Alexander Napier quickly laid hold of it and passed it for safekeeping to the onlooking tollkeeper. For another quarter of an hour or so Bowers continued to bicker until, appearing to calm down, he said that he would leave peaceably as soon as his axe was returned to him. Once it was handed over, he turned to go, but his temper was still smouldering. A second exchange of words took place with John Sandilands during which Bowers challenged him to fight, 'old as he was', and he raised the axe and plunged the blunt end down on to the left side of Sandilands' head. As Sandilands crumpled to the ground, Bowers turned his attention to Alexander Watt, landing a blow on the farm worker's forearm before the two men watching - Napier and Phillips - succeeded in wrestling him to the ground and removing the axe from his grip. Throughout this entire time John Sandilands lay silent and motionless where he had fallen.

When spoken to he failed to respond, and he was carried into the tollhouse where he was placed on a chair. Although his head-wound did not produce a great deal of blood, his friends suspected that his injury was a serious one and never at any point did he show any sign of regaining consciousness. Meanwhile, Peter Bowers was still spoiling for a fight and he muscled his way inside the tollhouse but his boss's son finally managed to calm him down and cajole him into leaving. Soon after the two men's departure, Sandilands' colleagues set out to carry him home but before they were able to do so his life ebbed away. The man responsible for his death was in no fit state to be questioned that evening, and when Peter Bowers was interviewed the following morning, he claimed to have no more than the haziest recollection of his actions the previous day.

Bowers' prospects looked bleak indeed when he appeared two months later at the High Court in Edinburgh to answer a charge of murder. The evidence of the witnesses was to prove pivotal, their testimony consistent and unequivocal. Bowers' behaviour, however, was apparently out of character. His employer, Richard Catleugh, spoke in his defence, stating that during the year that he had worked for him he had 'always behaved well [and] was regular and peaceable', an observation echoed by a further two of his former employers. One of them saw fit to add that, during the eight or nine months that Bowers had lodged with him, he had been in the habit of devoting his free time to the harmless pastime of sketching. His landlady at Gifford stated that, during the week he had stayed with her, he had neither drunk alcohol nor at any point come across as in any way quarrelsome. But at the end of the day, it was not enough. A barmaid at Hogg's public house, Elizabeth Boag, told of how she had formed the impression that Bowers and Catleugh were drunk even before they entered Hogg's premises. They drank three gills of spirits, she continued, and before leaving one of the two men was so clumsy and uncoordinated that he dropped and broke a glass.

When all the evidence had been laid out, it was down to the Lord Justice Clerk to sum up for the Crown. Addressing members of the jury, he reminded them that in the eyes of the law drunkenness was no excuse for criminal behaviour. Naturally Peter Bowers' own lawyer opted for a different tack, focusing instead on the difference between a habitual drunkard and a young man 'altogether unused to liquor ... at a time when his stomach was empty' which might go some way, he suggested, to explaining his client's outrageous behaviour. But even he could see what way the wind was blowing when he concluded by imploring the jury to recommend that, in the event of a guilty verdict, Bowers should be granted a reprieve. His fears, as it turned out, were justified though his plea for mercy did not go unheeded. Following an absence of an hour and a half, the members of the jury returned to the courtroom where their spokesman announced that, by a majority verdict, they found the prisoner guilty as charged though they were unanimous in recommending him to mercy. Passing sentence, the judge, Lord

Hermand, warned Bowers that it would be a mistake to place too much faith in the jury's plea for clemency, and he concluded matters by stating that one month hence, on Wednesday, 21 July, he would be executed between eight and ten o'clock in the morning, and that his body would then be given over for medical dissection. Hearing his gloomy fate spelt out, Bowers appeared stunned and had to be supported as he stepped down from the dock. It was later revealed that, in a compassionate gesture, the members of the jury had donated their entire combined allowance of seven pounds, seventeen shillings and sixpence for the welfare of his wife and family.

Turning to Bowers' cellmate, the crime that James Whiteford was alleged to have committed had taken place in West Lothian. At around three o'clock in the morning of Saturday, 27 March, the tollkeeper at Hopetoun Wood, Henry Duncan, had been startled by a loud knock at the door. Before risking opening up, he called out to ask who was there and the voice that replied was an unfamiliar one which bluntly demanded a bottle of porter - a form of dark sweet ale. Telling his late-night visitor that he possessed no such item, Duncan had no intention of opening his door owing to the lateness of the hour and, not least, the fact that the man was a total stranger. His unknown caller, however, was persistent and went on to ask for a gill of spirits - a ruse, quite clearly, to gain entry but, more wary than ever, the tollkeeper continued to refuse and told him to leave immediately. This was the point when things turned nasty. There was an almighty crash as the wooden shutters on one of Duncan's cottage windows burst open - it would later be said as the result of a single mighty blow - but, strangely, the tollkeeper's sister, Mary, chose this as the moment to throw open the front door. Perhaps she thought fleetingly that she recognised the man's voice or that her action might defuse his anger but, either way, she soon had cause to regret the rashness of her action. Quick as lightning, the stranger struck her a blow to the head that caused her to stagger backwards into the cottage, dazed and bleeding. Though her attacker now had free access to the tollhouse, he took care to remain in the shadows, grimly warning the occupants not to look him directly in the face. He produced a pistol from his coat pocket, cocked it and levelled it at Duncan, warning the tollkeeper that he would 'blow his brains out' if he refused to hand over his money. Duncan pleaded for mercy, begging, 'Spare ma life and I'll gie ye a' I hae', and with no option other than to cooperate, he removed £10 in banknotes from his cash box which he duly handed over.

Not yet content, the robber wanted more. With nothing else to give, Duncan invited him to check for himself that the cash box was empty but the stranger still held back, careful to keep his face hidden. One of the banknotes had fluttered to the floor during the two men's exchange, and he ordered Duncan to pick it up and hand it over, then, confident of having secured all of the paper money, he demanded what cash there was in silver. Duncan opened up the press and lifted out a small brass box which he handed over, complete with its contents of silver coins. At this point matters took rather an odd turn. From somewhere about his person, the robber produced a whistle which he proceeded to blow on, muttering darkly about companions close by who might easily be summoned. Fairly confident this was a bluff designed to intimidate, even so Duncan was not prepared to take the risk and he scrabbled together 'a handful of penny pieces' which he thrust at the intruder who continued to blow his whistle, repeatedly warning the tollkeeper that his accomplices would soon be here to 'do for them all'.

Probably it was sheer desperation that forced Duncan's hand. As the robber backed out of the cottage, still blowing his whistle, the tollkeeper laid hold of an iron poker and struck out and, though the weapon missed its mark, his action took the stranger by surprise and provided the tollkeeper with the opportunity to slam the door shut. Before leaving the scene, the robber fired off his pistol, possibly to quash any thought of pursuit. Later when it grew light and Duncan risked opening his front door, the marks made by lead pellets were clearly visible on the outside. His brass box, minus its contents, had been abandoned in a nearby field.

The villain who put Duncan and his family through their ordeal was James Whiteford, a shoemaker in his early twenties from Balerno. A few hours after leaving Hopetoun Wood, he was seen at Keir's Hill tollhouse, just west of Edinburgh, where he put it about that he was a master shoemaker from Lanark. His tired appearance he explained by claiming he had been out on the road all night. A fellow traveller, James Fordyce, saw him draw a bottle of whisky from one of his pockets and could not help noticing that he was carrying a pistol in the other. At that Whiteford's story began to unravel and when his true identity came to light he departed post-haste and hurried west from Keir's Hill in an effort to evade capture. He succeeded in travelling nearly sixty miles across the mossy slopes of the southern uplands before eventually the forces of the law caught up with him at Muirkirk in Ayrshire. A few weeks later his case was heard at the High Court in Edinburgh where he faced charges of robbery and hamesucken. In his sworn declaration to the court Whiteford had already admitted the charges against him, and his legal counsel saw no point in rising to address the jury. To all intents and purposes the case against his client appeared cut and dried, and it was notable that members of the jury felt no need to withdraw from the courtroom before finding him guilty as libelled of both hamesucken and robbery. Although no-one had lost his life as a result of Whiteford's actions, nonetheless the Lord Justice Clerk wound up proceedings by sentencing him to death. He would be executed four weeks thence, on Wednesday, 18 August, between the hours of eight and ten o'clock in the morning.

During their weeks in prison James Whiteford and Peter Bowers were thrown into one another's company twenty-four hours a day. Cooperative and apparently contrite, Whiteford made no effort to play down the seriousness of his crime and he was willing to accept the justice of his sentence. As far as Bowers was concerned, the date assigned for his execution - Wednesday, 21 July - slipped by while he waited pending the outcome of an appeal for mercy made on his behalf, and he was still waiting on the morning of Wednesday, 18 August, when Whiteford was escorted from the condemned cell on his final journey in this life. It was reported at the time that Bowers' positive influence had been instrumental in reconciling Whiteford to his fate, and the two men's leave-taking, we might imagine, must surely have made for a poignant occasion.

Respectably dressed and dignified in his manner, Whiteford was accompanied by two clergymen and two town bailies dressed in their municipal robes to the spot at the head of Libberton's Wynd where the scaffold had been erected. In front of an assembled group of onlookers, prayers were said and a hymn sung before he took his place on the drop. A few minutes before nine o'clock the bolt was drawn and when he stepped into space Whiteford paid a hefty price for his crimes. His struggles, it was said, were mercifully brief and half an hour later his body was cut down. By shortly after ten o'clock the crowd of spectators had dispersed and the entire apparatus of the scaffold had been dismantled and removed. Tragically, he left behind a widow and two small children.

Less than a week after Whiteford's execution the good news reached his former cellmate Peter Bowers that his death sentence had been commuted to transportation for life, and at the end of September he was one of twenty-four Scots to embark at Leith, bound for the hulks on the south coast of England to await his departure. There he remained for six months until, at the end of March 1820, he and nearly two hundred fellow prisoners set sail aboard the *Mangles*, arriving in Australia four months later. Life went on for Peter Bowers in his new homeland and it seems he put his past firmly behind him and settled in to life down under, finding work as a carpenter and taking a second wife - fairly routine for transported men - in 1829. Sarah Wantling was a mere fourteen years old at the time of their marriage and the couple went on to have two daughters: Mary Ann, born later that same year, and Isabella two years later. Sadly, Sarah did not live long enough to see her girls grow to maturity for she passed away in 1846 while both were still in their teens. A widower for more than three decades, Bowers lived on in Armidale, New South Wales, until he too reached the end of the line when he died - an octogenarian - in March 1879. However hard to believe, he had outlived his old cellmate, James Whiteford, by a remarkable sixty years.

VILLAINS AND VICTIMS

John Forrest
Stirling - November 1822

The tell-tale signs were there for all to see. The ground immediately above the grave had been disturbed and was several inches lower than the level of the surrounding turf. Investigations revealed a length of rope leading down to where the lid of the coffin had been burst open and its occupant hauled to the surface. The looted corpse was that of a stonemason's widow, 55-year-old Mary Witherspoon, who had died of dropsy - or oedema - three days earlier and been laid to rest in the burial ground of the Church of the Holy Rude, a short distance from her home in Cowane Street, Stirling, in November 1822. All that had been left behind was a pile of her discarded clothing. Based on the reports of nightwatchmen it was concluded that the desecration had been an inside job with the man responsible none other than James McNab - the very gravedigger who had been responsible for burying Mary - assisted by an accomplice, Daniel Mitchell, a street sweeper. A third man, James Shiels, an employee at a local public house, was also said to have been involved in some way but, for whatever reason, was never summonsed to appear in court. Their crime, it transpired, had been carried out to order and, after being liberally plied with whisky, they had been paid four guineas in exchange for Mary's body by an eighteen-year-old Edinburgh University medical student, John Forrest, who required a fresh corpse for the purpose of dissection.

Around that time university medical schools had a growing problem on their hands. The only legal channel by which they were able to obtain corpses for anatomical study was through the law courts which, in passing the death sentence on a convicted criminal, might order his or her body to be handed over for medical research. In earlier times when relatively large numbers of men and women had been put to death each year this system had operated satisfactorily but with the passage of time the number of executions carried out had steadily decreased, resulting in a growing shortage of corpses made available and this was the situation that led to an upsurge in grave-robbing at the latter end of the eighteenth century. Technically speaking, the unauthorised taking of a dead body did not represent an illegal act - the law did not view a corpse as any individual's personal property - but items such as clothing were often deliberately left behind by the 'resurrection men' (as in Mary Witherspoon's case) as removing these along with the body would constitute theft. Therefore, when cases came to court, the accused was more likely to face a charge of violating a grave or suchlike rather than specifically bodysnatching. This illogical situation would not be remedied until 1832 when the passing of the Anatomy Act injected some sanity into the system by, among its other provisions, permitting anyone with rightful possession of a dead body to donate it to medical science, subject to certain conditions.

Around that time the desecration of Mary Witherspoon's grave was not a unique event in the Stirlingshire area and, given the prevailing circumstances, there would always be men who viewed bodysnatching as an easy way of making money and were willing to risk being caught. One dark evening a worker at Gilston farm, midway between Falkirk and Linlithgow, was puzzled when he spotted an unknown man digging in the midden at his place of work. As he continued to watch unobserved, he saw the stranger unearth a large sack that appeared to have been secreted there and drag it a short distance from the dunghill before returning and repeating the process two more times. The man then trailed each of the three bundles roughly fifty yards away to where a horse and gig were standing by and, after loading them on board, he hopped up alongside the driver who promptly geed up the horse and took off. Strongly suspecting he had witnessed body traders at work, the farm worker reported what he had seen to his employer, Adam Scott, who immediately saddled up his mare and set off in pursuit, riding hard in the direction of Linlithgow. Scott first caught sight of the gig a quarter of a mile short of the built-up area where he saw a passenger being dropped off, and by the time he caught up with it in the town centre only the driver, a young man wearing a tartan cloak and 'glazed' (waterproofed) hat, was still aboard. Scott reached across and seized hold of the reins, thereby forcing the vehicle to a standstill. As a crowd of curious onlookers gathered, he voiced his suspicions of wrongdoing and loudly demanded to be shown what goods the gig was carrying. In response the young man in tartan refused to cooperate, insisting that he was under no obligation to disclose the nature of his load but, as Scott hurried off in the hope of securing an official search warrant, the crowd grew increasingly restive and finally its members took matters into their own hands.

First to lose patience was James Douglas who stepped forward and drew down the apron of the gig. The shock was palpable as what looked unmistakably like body bags, two large and one small, were revealed for all to see. Realising the game was up, the young driver leaped from his seat and tried to make a break for it but he was intercepted by another member of the crowd, David Brown, who grabbed him by the front of his cloak and held on tight until officers of the law could be summoned to make an arrest. However, before the constables had time to arrive, certain members of the mob launched an attack on the young man, inflicting grievous wounds on his head and face, and left him bleeding, battered and bruised. After freeing the horse, they hauled his cart to the market cross where they set it ablaze to an accompaniment of whoops and cheers.

Meanwhile the body bags were carried into the town-house where they were opened up and found to contain the corpses of a man, woman and child, each bound by a rope around the neck and ankles. Best preserved of the three was the body of the woman, subsequently identified by her father and brother as nineteen-year-old Janet Moir who had died two months earlier in mid-January and been buried in Larbert churchyard, twelve or so miles north-west of Linlithgow, in a grave between eight and nine feet deep. It was suggested that the remarkably fresh state of her body was accounted for by recent unseasonably cold weather. Janet's alleged bodysnatcher, tartan-clad Thomas Stevenson, alias Thomas Hodge, gave his address as Jack's Close in the Canongate district of

Edinburgh and stated that, after undergoing training as a weaver, he had gone on to spend six years at sea before taking up employment in his current role as a porter. Appearing at the Edinburgh High Court charged with 'violating the sepulchres of the dead', he pled Not Guilty and offered the following explanation in his defence. He had been walking east towards Linlithgow, he claimed, when he had accepted a lift from 'a gentleman driving a gig'. A short time later he had been asked to step down briefly while the gentleman turned aside from the main road in order to conduct some private business. When he was uplifted again a little later, he admitted he was aware that goods had been taken on board but insisted he had given no thought to what these might consist of. Approaching the western edge of Linlithgow, the gentleman had got down from the gig and asked him to drive through the town alone and pick him up again on the eastern outskirts. No explanation for this odd request had been offered and that, of course, was the last he had seen of this shadowy figure whose identity never subsequently came to light. In the event, the jury found Stevenson's story unconvincing and returned a guilty verdict. It emerged that he had a previous conviction for plundering graves at Lanark for which he had already served a six-month prison term, but for this second offence the Law Lords took a stricter line and sentenced him to seven years' transportation overseas.

So, this was the backcloth against which the trial of trainee doctor John Forrest and his accomplices James McNab and Daniel Mitchell was due to take place on 19 April 1823 following the breaching of the grave of Mary Witherspoon. Locked up pending trial, McNab and Mitchell took their places at the bar, but when called upon to do likewise Forrest - the son, it so happened, of Dr John Forrest of Stirling and brother-in-law of another medical man, Dr Alexander Johnston of Edinburgh - failed to make an appearance. It turned out that not having been held in custody had given him ample opportunity to flee to Europe and avoid facing up to the consequences of his actions. Acting as prosecutor, the Advocate-Depute responded to this state of affairs by naming Forrest as the principal offender and stating that the evidence against his two co-accused appeared to him conflicting and incomplete, therefore his decision was to drop the case against them 'pro loco et tempore'. Theoretically at least this meant that they could be called back to answer charges at a future date - but, in practice, quite possibly never. The

Advocate-Depute concluded by pronouncing a sentence of fugitation against Forrest and declaring his goods 'escheat to the king', meaning that from that point on he was officially viewed as a fugitive from justice, liable to arrest any time he set foot in Scotland, and that his possessions were confiscated by the Crown. Objections raised by his lawyer were swiftly overruled. Once proceedings relating to the absent Forrest had been attended to, his flunkeys, McNab and Mitchell, were released from the bar and the matter appeared to be concluded.

Not so. Throughout the town of Stirling ill-feeling had never faded regarding the violation of the widow Witherspoon's grave, and when word got out that those believed responsible had been freed from jail and were once again at large in the community the townsfolk's resentment boiled over. Crowds assembled demanding justice for the dead and appropriate punishment for the two offenders who had meantime retreated quietly to their respective homes. Never having anticipated that the court proceedings might be wrapped up so soon, Provost Thomson was caught on the hop and, fearing an outbreak of serious violence, he quickly began the process of procuring a warrant to allow McNab and Mitchell to be rearrested for their own safety but by then it was too late. Fronted by a band of enraged women, a mob had marched on McNab's home and attempted to gain entry by breaking down the door. This proved unsuccessful but a heavy stone lobbed through one of the windows struck the unfortunate man on the head as he sat by his own fireside and knocked him unconscious, raising cheers of delight from the crowd. Constables arrived on the scene and carried him from the house under a hail of stones and whatever other missiles lay within reach.

A similar situation played out at the house of Daniel Mitchell in St John Street, conveniently close to the town jail. Through the efforts of a solitary policeman, the mob's intended victim was enabled to sneak out of a back door whereupon the officer himself became a substitute target for enraged rioters who flung him to the ground, kicked and beat him and tore the clothes from his body. In desperation, he struggled to his feet, stumbled to a neighbouring property and barred the door against his attackers. Meantime, Mitchell himself had sought refuge in an adjacent building where he climbed to the top floor and concealed himself in the darkness of the attic. It did not take long, however, for his pursuers to sniff out his hiding place and his skin was only saved through the intervention of Provost Thomson and other town officials who reasoned with those at the forefront of the mob and persuaded them to clear a path and allow police officers access to arrest Mitchell and escort him back to jail. But not everyone, it turned out, was willing to go along with the plan and a certain number of the rioters, both men and women, remained intransigent. 'We're no' wanting him to prison,' the *Stirling Journal* quoted one of their number - 'Only gie him up till us, and we'll tak the b-----'s heart out of him and tear him to pieces.' In spite of Provost Thomson and Sheriff McDonald's warnings and entreaties, a stubborn portion of the crowd refused to disperse so soldiers of the 77th Regiment of Foot were called in from their barracks at Stirling Castle to clear the streets, some armed with muskets with fixed bayonets attached and others bearing halberds - tall, ferocious spears with axe-heads near the top. In the event, it turned out to be a bad move with their presence only adding fuel to the flames.

As soon as the troops arrived, Daniel Mitchell was retrieved from his sanctuary beneath the roof tiles and when he appeared downstairs at the mouth of the close the crowd went wild, hurling insults and volleys of abuse. The chaos that ensued seems to have resulted from an initial accident when one of a number of soldiers who were incapably drunk at the time staggered and fell among the legs of the crowd. He was assisted back to his feet, reinstated among the ranks of his more sober comrades and his rifle passed into the care of an officer but the confusion this small distraction had created allowed the rioters to press forward more closely on the soldiers, one of whom was unwise enough to raise the butt of his musket and strike out at several members of the crowd. His violent actions provoked an angry response and two of the rioters reached out and attempted to seize hold of his weapon, prompting him to pull the trigger and fire. Several more shots rang out and a number of the soldiers attempted to charge the rioters, though the majority held back in accordance with their orders and did their best to bring their wayward comrades back into line. A hail of stones poured down, striking many of the soldiers including their commanding officer who continued nonetheless in his attempts to reimpose order.

When the man at the centre of the entire furore, Daniel Mitchell, was taken to within a short distance of the prison door Provost Thomson and Sheriff McDonald took charge and escorted him to the cells. As they were doing so, they heard more shots being fired outside. Once their prisoner was safely under lock and key, the two men returned to the street where they were successful at last in pacifying the mob and bringing the violence to an end. The troops of the 77th Regiment were ordered to retire to their barracks at the castle and normality gradually reasserted itself. All things considered, the outcome of this chaotic day could have been a great deal worse: although their rifles had been loaded with live ammunition, the soldiers had fired high and no-one had been on the receiving end of a musket ball. Several members of the crowd had incurred bayonet wounds and one young townsman had been more seriously injured by the glancing blow of a halberd but, even so, fortunately there had been no loss of life. For their part, the soldiers had suffered nothing worse than grazes, bumps and bruises. In an interesting postscript, disciplinary action was taken against those five of their number who had discharged their weapons without receiving the order to fire. With consummate irony, their actions in the midst of a riot were classed as a breach of the peace.

So - what became of the grave-robbers McNab and Mitchell when they eventually got out of jail and in the months and years that followed? Stirling's day of disorder had made it crystal clear that picking up where they left off and resuming their old lives as gravedigger and street sweeper was simply not an option. Well, it seems that as soon as they were released the notorious pair slipped into obscurity and what their future held, I have not been able to discover. As for their slippery accomplice, the medical student, John Forrest, it turns out he did rather well for himself. Having been outlawed by the courts six months earlier didn't prevent him from being one of three students who presented themselves before the 'examinators' of the Royal College of Surgeons of Edinburgh in November 1823 and 'being severally examined on their skill in anatomy surgery and Pharmacy [all three] were found duly qualified to practise these arts and received Diplomas'. Why he went on to be granted a royal pardon in July of the following year is unknown (might strings have been pulled?) but, whatever the explanation, King George IV's action allowed him to continue his studies at Edinburgh University and he received his doctorate in 1825. Composed in the contemporary language of scholarship, Latin, his dissertation consisted of an investigation into the topic of gangrene and, given the path his life would take, the knowledge he gained during his research would be put to good use in the years that followed.

After graduating, Dr John Forrest joined the British army medical staff, a decision that would define the next thirty-six years of his life. His first posting was to Kolhapur in the hill country of the Western Ghats in India where he was quickly promoted from Hospital Assistant to the position of Assistant Surgeon. He returned home to Stirling in 1832 and settled down to work in St Ninian's Hospital for a number of years. During this time he met and married Ann McLachlan and a mere month after their wedding the couple took the major step of migrating to Cape Town, South Africa, where their two children were born soon after: a daughter Mary in 1840, with her brother John following on a year later. Tragically, Ann died in August 1842, eighteen months after the birth of her second child. During the years that followed, Forrest was present during such conflicts as the 1845 Boer uprising at the Orange River and the Xhosa War of 1846 - viewed perhaps as morally dubious today, less so in the age of empire and assumed white supremacy - and in recognition of his efforts he was awarded the South African Medal. In 1850 he was promoted to Surgeon of the First Class and returned to Britain where he was employed in hospitals in Glasgow and at Chatham in Kent.

As Deputy-Inspector of Army Hospitals, he left Britain a few years later to take part in the Crimean War and was present at many of its most significant engagements such as the capture of Balaklava, the battles of Alma and Inkerman and the siege of Sebastopol. He was named in Lord Raglan's despatch after the Battle of Inkerman - 'for his able exertions, as deserving to be most honourably mentioned'. In his capacity as Principal Medical Officer at Scutari Hospital, Istanbul, where thousands of Crimean casualties were taken to be cared for, he became acquainted with the legendary 'Lady with the Lamp', the heroine Florence Nightingale. Suffering from kidney disease, he was forced to return to Britain in January 1855 and four months later he received the Crimea Medal from Queen Victoria at Horse Guards Parade in London. He was decorated also by Sultan Abdülmecid I who awarded him the Turkish Crimean War Medal. Once sufficiently recovered, he travelled to Malta as Principal Medical Officer where his efforts to adapt the existing infirmary in St Julian's into an army hospital were recognised when it was renamed Forrest Hospital in his honour, a name it retained until its closure in 1922.

Remarried in 1858 to Emma Jenkin, he was promoted that same year to the position of Inspector-General of Army Hospitals and in 1859 he was given the title of Honorary Physician to Queen Victoria. On his retiral he and his second wife settled in the south of England where he died at his home in Queen's Parade, Bath, in September 1865 at the age of 61. His widow survived him by nearly 35 years and was buried by his side in Locksbrook Cemetery in 1899. Well into her eighties at the time of her death, she would surely have been among the last of her time to retain memories of the days of the bodysnatchers.

No-one could deny that Dr John Forrest's life was an eventful one and his career anything other than illustrious. But, now that the sound and the fury have died down and the dust has settled, what are we to make of him? A craven young medical student perhaps who scuttled off at the age of eighteen, dodged his responsibilities and left two humble accomplices in the lurch, a gravedigger and a street sweeper, to face whatever punishment the law might choose to mete out? A young man from a privileged background who made use of influence, we might suspect, to secure a royal pardon for the part he played in a grave-robbing plot - a similar offence, let's not forget, to the one for which Thomas Stevenson of Jack's Close in the Canongate found himself convicted and heading to a penal settlement down under on a seven-year term?

Or might we portray him instead as a young man with a vocation to follow in his family tradition of healing the sick, operating in a system that effectively ensured a scarcity of corpses for medical research and where it might be argued that the end justified the means? Or in later life as a medical man whose courage was beyond question, whose work eased the suffering of many and whose studies contributed to the cure for disease and the preservation of life?

Which one of the two? I leave it to you to decide.

Alexander Martin
Kemnay, Aberdeenshire - April 1824

In April 1816 eight men were indicted to stand trial at Aberdeen for a variety of offences ranging from crimes of dishonesty at one end of the scale to murder at the other. One of them was a Kincardineshire man in his mid-twenties, Alexander Martin, the circumstances of whose case were particularly repellent. The crime in question was that of rape, the victim of which had been a young deaf and dumb woman. In the event, Martin failed to turn up for his trial and was duly outlawed by the court. It was a whole seven years before the law finally caught up with him and on Saturday, 12 April 1823, he made his much-belated appearance in the dock at Aberdeen. It was to be a brief affair. Since the circumstances of his case were believed to be the first of their kind in Scotland, the decision was taken to postpone proceedings until he could be tried in the High Court in Edinburgh. A warrant was issued accordingly which authorised his transfer to the capital, and on Monday, 30 June, Martin found himself at the bar for a second time faced with a charge of raping, or assaulting with intent to rape, the deaf and dumb woman, Christian Moir, on Thursday, 12 October 1815. As was normal in similar cases, the trial was conducted behind closed doors. Asked for his plea, Martin replied firmly, 'Not Guilty,' but before matters could go any further the defence raised an objection, questioning Christian Moir's ability to act as principal witness and postulating a link - unthinkable today - between her condition and possible learning difficulties. In line with the standards of the time, the intervention was accepted by the court and proceedings deferred until it could be established whether she was fit to testify or not. This was the point where a representative of the Deaf and Dumb Institution in Aberdeen, a teacher by the name of Taylor, stepped in.

Although Great Britain's first school for the deaf had been established in Edinburgh more than sixty years earlier, a belief persisted that deaf or dumb people were incapable of being educated. Addressing the court, Taylor countered this misconception by demonstrating the methods currently in use for teaching pupils new vocabulary and abstract ideas. In relation to Christian Moir specifically, he had no doubt concerning her ability to distinguish truth from fiction. She had conveyed to him, he told the court, her firm belief in God - well-nigh universal in 1820s Scotland - and in the existence likewise of heaven and hell. When he stepped down from the witness box, Taylor's testimony was corroborated by various others to whom Christian was known, and the evidence they provided proved sufficient for her to be accepted as a credible witness.

Taking the stand, she started out by communicating her clear understanding of the oath she was called upon to swear and, with Taylor interpreting, proceeded to give an account of her ordeal seven years earlier when she had been approached and assaulted by an unknown man in an area of woodland close to her home. Her attacker, she recalled, had been wearing a 'sailor's jacket', and, asked what colour, without hesitation she pointed at a court official dressed in blue. So far so good, but it took only a matter of seconds for the prosecution's case to stall. Faced with the most crucial question of all, Christian admitted to being unsure whether the man in the dock was her attacker and, despite being pressed further, she declined even to venture an opinion. Left with nowhere to go, the prosecution case crumbled and the jury had no option but to find the prisoner not guilty. Before matters concluded, however, both prosecution and defence made a point of complimenting Taylor on the knowledge and intelligence he had shown throughout his testimony. In marked contrast, Christian Moir's courage in facing up to the daunting machinery of the law - most likely for the first time - and in confronting her possible rapist eye to eye went entirely unrecognised. For his part, Alexander Martin was dismissed from the bar and left the court a free man though, as future events unfolded it wouldn't be too long before he was back.

At around nine o'clock in the morning of Thursday, 15 April 1824, a stranger calling himself Alexander Milne knocked at the door of Agnes Allan to ask for directions to Kemnay, a small settlement in the Garioch district of rural Aberdeenshire. She pointed west and the last she saw before closing the door he was walking towards Picktillum where an elderly man, Alexander Hervie, occupied a small cottage along with his daughter, by coincidence also named Christian. As it happened, both were absent from home that morning but when they returned a few hours later she noticed immediately that a number of items were missing from the house, most notably a blue silk napkin and a quantity of silver coins had been removed from where they had been kept in a chest. Worse was yet to come. During the late evening just as she and Alexander were preparing for bed, she was startled to see an unfamiliar face staring in at her through the cottage window. After recovering from the initial shock, she had sufficient presence of mind to screen the fire and darken the room, while her feisty father - already in his eighties - threw open the door and stepped out into the night. Peering through the darkness, however, he saw no-one and came back inside, assuming that the stranger had fled. It turned out he was wrong.

A few moments later Christian became aware of sounds overhead and she went outside to investigate. Looking up, she made out the form of a man, silhouetted against the night sky, as he made his way crab-like along the ridge of the cottage roof. Aiming in the direction of the chimney, he was presumably intent on covering the vent and smoking out those inhabitants below. Instinctively Christian cried out and, alerted to her presence, the sturdily-built stranger jumped down and launched an immediate attack, grabbing her by the throat in what seemed a determined effort to strangle her. She struggled, screamed, and in desperation raked her nails over his face. Hearing the altercation, Alexander rushed out and seized hold of his daughter's attacker by the arm and, although he did his best to restrain him the younger man's superior strength proved telling and he overcame the old man with relative ease. Next, he bundled both Christian and her father back inside, then, following on behind, ominously turned and locked the door behind him. Disposing of the old man first, he struck a savage blow that knocked him to the floor, then kicked him viciously and effectively ensured he could play no further part in the conflict. Next, he turned his attention to Christian, gripping her fiercely by the arms and throwing her repeatedly against the table and chairs until she begged him for mercy and to take whatever of her possessions he wanted if only he would spare her own and her father's lives. Forcing the old man back on to his feet, he ordered him to light a 'fir-caunle' - a sliver of resinous firwood, the poor man's lighting - and place it upon a saucer in order to illuminate his search of the cottage. Opening a drawer, he drew out a knife and brandished it in the two Hervies' faces while uttering a grim warning: 'If you make the least resistance, this if for you.' With no option but to comply, Christian handed over two silk handkerchiefs, one of them jet black, a circumstance which would later prove significant. He also seized silver coins to the value of fifty shillings - a sizeable sum - which he counted out before tossing back a shilling and a sixpence which he judged to be counterfeit. Now apparently satisfied, he pointed the knife directly at Christian and ordered her to raise her right hand and solemnly swear an oath to the effect that never at any point in future would she either describe his appearance or give an account of his actions to the authorities. So, after one hour and three quarters the violent intruder left the Hervies behind him, shocked and injured, ensuring as he did so that they were securely locked inside the cottage and unable to raise the alarm. Not till around 6 a.m. when a local farm worker, James Mitchell, had begun his day's work of harrowing in the fields were Christian's cries overheard. When he reached the cottage, Mitchell spoke to her through the window and listened to her distressing account of the night's events. After scouting around for a few minutes, he found the house key not far away and when he unlocked the door she was first to emerge. He was shocked to see that articles of her clothing were saturated with blood.

It would emerge in due course that the villain who put the frail octogenarian and his daughter through the mill that night was the same Alexander Martin who had been acquitted of rape less than a year before. After leaving Picktillum, he travelled south-east and in the early hours of the following morning stopped off at a public-house where he bragged to a fellow-drinker, George Reid, that he was carrying about his person the considerable sum of fifty shillings. At around four o'clock in the afternoon he met a twelve-year-old boy, Alexander Smith, who was herding livestock at the farm of Drumnaheath and offered to sell him a silk handkerchief. The boy showed no interest so Martin continued on his way, anxious to keep on the move. Where he spent Friday and Saturday nights is uncertain, but by Sunday morning he had crossed to the south bank of the River Dee and reached his home country of Durris.

Being back on home turf did nothing to curb his criminal tendencies. As he was passing Mains of Durris farm, he encountered an acquaintance, John Walker, to whom he was known under his alias of Alexander Milne. At the time the two men's paths crossed, Martin was conspicuously dressed in a pair of white corduroy trousers, a light-coloured 'fustian' coat (a hardwearing cotton-based fabric much in use at the time) and, most eye-catching of all, a red waistcoat with contrasting black spots. Walker noticed too, a stylish black silk handkerchief he had tied around his neck. A boy of ten, Charles Pearson, saw him standing in a wood around 11 a.m. and he too was struck by the colourful way he was dressed. A little later he arrived at the small village of Kirkton of Durris where much of the devout population was at church. The schoolmaster, Alexander Duncan, and his unmarried sister were no exception, a circumstance which provided Martin with an opportunity. The two Duncans shared a house a short walk from the village centre and that Sunday the schoolmaster's sister left a little later than her brother, securing the door firmly behind her. Duncan was still at church when she returned after the service and, shocked to find that the house had been broken into, she asked a neighbour, George Watt, to deliver the bad news to her brother. The schoolmaster hurried home immediately, and when his sister and he went over their house they found that the drawers of a writing desk had been burst open and a considerable quantity of old silver coins were missing from a locked press. Other valuables, possibly too bulky to remove, were untouched. There was no sign that the front door had been forced and they quickly deduced that the intruder had gained entry through a window close to ground level that had not been properly closed.

A connection was not hard to make between the schoolhouse burglary and the brightly-dressed Martin's arrival that same morning - not to mention his abrupt departure - and the obvious next step was to link it with the robbery at Picktillum two days earlier. He had put the best part of fifty miles behind him by the time he was picked up on the Brechin road near Forfar, still dressed as he had been at Durris, even down to his black handkerchief. Once removed to the county courtroom, a search of his clothing turned up a significant quantity of silver coins secreted in an inner pocket of his waistcoat, as well as a 'steel purse' - a pocket-sized metal box used for carrying coins. His face, it was noted, was badly scratched. After a night in jail, he was escorted by John Fyfe, the court's Messenger-at-Arms, to Aberdeen where he proved unforthcoming and gave away nothing when questioned. By this stage in proceedings his black silk handkerchief was not to be seen, though it was possibly significant that a fire had been kept burning in his cell all night.

Given the weight of evidence stacked up against him, convincing a jury of his innocence was never likely to be easy. Looking across from the witness box, both Christian and Alexander Hervie identified Martin without hesitation as the merciless intruder who had assaulted them and plundered their home. (Old Alexander was deaf to the extent that he required the services of an interpreter but it did nothing to hinder him from delivering his evidence 'with great animation in the broad dialect of Aberdeenshire'.) The herdboy, Alexander Smith, followed on, recalling how Martin had offered to sell him a black silk handkerchief, then ten-year-old Charles Pearson described how he'd seen the man he knew as 'Sandy' Martin lurking in the woods near Kirkton. To finish up, his captor near Forfar recounted how he had caught up with Martin and found him sporting a black silk handkerchief and with a large sum of money in his possession. Once all of the witnesses had been heard, it took the members of the jury only a few moments to intimate that they felt no need to withdraw from the courtroom before delivering their verdict. In relation to the crimes both of theft and of stouthrief - theft accompanied by violence - they unanimously found the prisoner guilty as charged.

The first of two presiding judges, Lord Succoth, turned then to Martin and addressed him directly, stating that it did not matter whether a crime had been committed in 'the cottage of a peasant or the palace of a peer'. Both, the judge told him, were of equal status in the eyes of the law. Since the punishment appropriate to his crimes, he continued, was one set by statute he had no option but to sentence him to death. In six weeks' time, he pronounced, Martin would be executed at Aberdeen. All that remained now was for the second judge, Lord Meadowbank, to express his agreement with his colleague's remarks, but before resuming his seat he made an additional comment which hinted perhaps at an unspoken suspicion. This was not the first time, he recalled, that the prisoner had been accused of serious wrongdoing but on the previous occasion he had been tried and acquitted in unusual circumstances. Throughout his trial Martin had appeared subdued and downbeat, but hearing his fate spelt out unambiguously he was unable to hide his distress.

By the day of his execution - Friday, 14 July - Martin had managed to recover a degree of composure. Shortly before 3 p.m. he entered the Court House, dressed all in black and flanked by three ministers. Here he gave a short speech (for which he had almost certainly been coached) offering thanks for his kind treatment to a number of persons including the Lord Provost and magistrates of Aberdeen, various local clergymen, even the jailor and his turnkey. A short time later he left the building and appeared before a smallish crowd of assembled spectators, supervised by a large body of constables. Some verses of the 23rd psalm were sung - *The Lord is my Shepherd* - and a prayer was offered up by Rev. Thom. When the clergyman fell silent, Martin turned to address the crowd and, speaking clearly and with no sign of faltering, attributed his downfall to his failure to observe the sabbath and by resorting to bad company, particularly during the formative years of his youth. Immediately afterwards he ascended the drop where for several minutes he knelt in prayer before giving the final signal to the hangman (his identity unknown) who drew back the lever and plunged him into thin air. Death did not come instantly and in a harrowing scene, mercifully brief, his body was racked by convulsions before finally all signs of life departed. A short time later the corpse was cut down and passed into the care of friends who removed it in a horse-drawn hearse for burial. The spectators, it was noted, dispersed quietly and without fuss.

It would later be claimed that while awaiting execution Martin had confessed to a number of other crimes which up till then had gone unsolved. The rape of Christian Moir, it seems, was not one of them.

VILLAINS AND VICTIMS

David Landale
Kirkcaldy, Fife - August 1826

In the early morning of Wednesday, 23 August 1826, two men faced one another with pistols at the ready in a field north-west of Kirkcaldy. One was in his mid-forties, an ex-military man who had seen active service overseas, while his adversary by contrast was a local merchant some five years younger who was totally unschooled in the handling of firearms and who had travelled to Edinburgh the previous day to purchase his very first pair of pistols. A short distance off, the two men's representatives - known as 'seconds' - were conferring in a last-ditch attempt to fend off disaster but when the army man barked out 'No apology!' he quickly put paid to their efforts. Faced with a total impasse, the two combatants took up their final positions twelve paces apart and, in line with standard practice, were asked the question - 'Gentlemen, are you ready?' - but before matters could go any further a halt had to be called when the former soldier was seen raising his pistol prematurely, an action known as jumping the gun. The procedure was then repeated, this time according to form, and at the command - 'Present - fire!' - a deafening report rang out. For a brief, excruciating moment time seemed to stand still until finally one of the two men gave an audible groan and lurched forward as his legs crumpled helplessly beneath him. He was dead before hitting the ground.

The years leading up to the duel had witnessed a major downturn in an industry crucial to the town of Kirkcaldy's prosperity, and Landale & Co was one of the many businesses that took a hit. A leading producer of linen, David Landale had done good business during the Napoleonic Wars when demand for woven fabric was steady - and high prices assured - to kit out the large number of British servicemen overseas. But the peace accord of 1815 turned the situation on its head when hordes of those same demobbed men arrived back in Britain with families to feed and small prospect of employment, a situation that - understandably - provoked social unrest and plunged the economy into crisis. Hopes of an upturn proved premature when the banking sector took a serious dip in 1825, undermining investment, causing businesses to fail and trade of all kinds to stall. A widower since his early thirties, David Landale had appeared to be weathering the slump better than some, but by the early months of 1826 he too was feeling the pinch. His business was suffering from cash flow problems and the linen merchant's debts amounted to several thousand pounds. The natural thing for him to do was to approach his bank to seek a solution.

Landale & Co's accounts were held by the Kirkcaldy branch of the Bank of Scotland which was operated by its two local agents, brothers David and George Morgan. As a substitute for cash the linen merchant suggested to the Morgans that he clear £600 of his debts using 'bills of exchange' - the equivalent of a post-dated cheque today - which he had received from business clients and were routinely accepted at the time as a form of currency. In such cases the bank would serve its own interests by charging a fee, known as 'discount', in payment for handling these documents. In this particular instance, however, its agents refused outright to accept Landale's bills of exchange, implying on their part a lack of confidence in his business prospects and thus placing him in the humiliating position of having to go back to his creditors to ask them to exchange their bonds for hard cash. As it turned out, this loss of face was only just the start. A succession of obstructive measures followed until the last straw came on Tuesday, 25 April, when the Morgan brothers reneged on a verbal agreement - reached a matter of hours earlier - under whose terms the linen merchant was to be provided with a short-term overdraft of £1,000 to allow him to settle an important bill. Finally at snapping-point, Landale immediately transferred his business to the local branch of the National Bank whose agent, the town provost George

Millar, was prepared to agree to the overdraft. Thus, Landale & Co closed all of its Bank of Scotland accounts and ended a financial relationship lasting more than forty years. There was no question that David Landale had emphatically made his point but, with the benefit of hindsight, he would have done well to leave it at that and let the matter drop.

No doubt there was antagonism on both sides. The younger of the Morgan brothers, George, had come to banking late and it was not perhaps a business he was naturally cut out for. Fourteen years earlier he had enlisted as an officer of the 45th Regiment of Foot and had travelled abroad where he spent the next two years fighting his way through some of the toughest campaigns of the Napoleonic Wars. His military service ended in 1817 when he returned to civilian life, now aged 36, and embarked on a new career, working alongside his brother as joint agent for the local branch of the Bank of Scotland. He quickly became known in the locality as an irascible man, easily roused to anger and quick to take offence - as a local tobacconist, Robert Kirk, found out to his cost. The two men happened to be travelling on the same Edinburgh ferry one morning when Morgan knocked the tobacconist's walking-stick out from under him, causing him to stumble and trip. 'Why didn't you keep your stick out of the way?' snapped Morgan. On another occasion he sparked a major row with a Kirkcaldy draper, George Graham, over the trivial matter of borrowing a library book. For a man of such legendary ill-temper, he could hardly have failed to react when he found himself and his brother's business snubbed by David Landale.

Morgan set about getting his revenge by circulating rumours that Landale & Co was in financial trouble and that its proprietor had been forced to remortgage part of his property to allow him to service his debts. Though totally unfounded, such gossip spread quickly throughout the town's business community. Times were hard, the economy remained depressed, and Landale's business associates - even many of his oldest and most trusted friends - felt the need to protect themselves and their companies, so they played safe by cutting their credit to him and calling in their debts. Beleaguered and under pressure, Landale managed to identify Morgan as the source of the rumours but when he confronted his former banker he was met with a blunt denial of any responsibility. Incensed and unconvinced, Landale was not prepared to let matters rest. On Friday, 23 June, he penned a strongly-worded letter of complaint to the Bank of Scotland's head office in Edinburgh, explaining his reasons for transferring his company's business elsewhere and reporting George Morgan's 'baseness and ill nature' in his attempts to discredit him. Ultimately, at the end of a six-week investigation, the bank's top officials closed ranks and presented their conclusions to the effect that the Morgans had been justified in protecting the bank's interests, though they added rather limply that 'generally agents of the Bank ought to abstain as much as possible from speaking of the Bank's concerns - or those of parties concerned with the Bank - unless on the proper occasions'. Such criticism notwithstanding, there appears to have been no question that the two brothers should be dismissed from their posts or disciplined in any other way.

Ostensibly absolved of wrongdoing, George Morgan now felt free to write to Landale to demand a written apology for what, by his way of it, were the disrespectful allegations he had made behind his back. As a former soldier, almost certainly Morgan felt his honour had been called into question and, given his military background, considered that the matter would best be settled if Landale could be goaded into throwing down the proverbial gauntlet. If that was indeed his intention, then he must surely have been disappointed when no challenge followed as a result. Instead the linen merchant wrote back, stating in a calm and reasoned manner that he had no idea what he was expected to apologise for since he could substantiate every one of the accusations he had made to head office in Edinburgh. A tense exchange of letters then ensued, none of which contained any trace of an apology from Landale. A long drawn-out correspondence was the last thing Morgan wanted so why, we might ask, did he not simply hurry matters along and issue a challenge of his own? His reticence may be explained at least in part by a reluctance to attract the notice of his superiors in Edinburgh so soon after they had dealt with Landale's recent complaint. On top of that, he seems also to have been labouring under the misapprehension that the issuer of a challenge risked putting himself on the wrong side of the law and, if convicted, would be liable to transportation overseas. Whatever his thinking, Morgan came to realise that if he were to succeed in provoking a challenge then more decisive measures were called for.

Of course, he was no stranger to aggressive, irrational behaviour. A year or so after his confrontation aboard the Edinburgh ferry, Morgan collided with the same man, Robert Kirk, in a Kirkcaldy street - apparently deliberately - and almost knocked him to the ground. 'You are a damned scoundrel,' muttered Morgan as he turned and left the scene. Some days later he escalated matters when he challenged the tobacconist to settle the two men's differences down a dark close nearby. Reaching the end of his tether, Kirk was willing to comply but before a punch could be thrown or a blow landed, Morgan inexplicably fled the scene and left the men's dispute unresolved. A few weeks afterwards he approached the tobacconist yet again and this time went so far as to raise his walking-cane and strike him across the face. With what can only be viewed as commendable restraint, Kirk laid hold of the stick and thrust it back at Morgan, saying, 'Go about your business, sir.' With the benefit of hindsight, all these skirmishes might be seen as forerunners of yet worse to come.

Morgan made no secret of his plans, in fact it looked very much as though he went out of his way to advertise them openly. In the afternoon of Monday, 14 August, he boasted to a friend, James Fleming, that he intended to horsewhip Landale in a public place - 'to lay a cane across his shoulders for the purpose,' so he explained, 'of forcing him to challenge me'. He made similar remarks to Landale's friend, wood merchant Alexander Barker, whom he encountered a little later near the harbour. A delay of several days followed while Landale attended his godson's christening in the neighbouring county of Angus, and Morgan meanwhile commissioned the manufacture of 'two or three dozen' new pistol bullets from a local blacksmith. A day or two later gunshots were heard in the vicinity of his home, in preparation, one might assume, for what most likely lay ahead. The back wall of the house would later be found to be riddled with bullet holes. By Saturday, 19 August, word had reached Landale regarding Morgan's violent intentions and he realised that if his plan to publicly assault him were to be put into effect then he would have no option but to respond by issuing a challenge. He approached his friend, William Millie, a merchant at nearby Pathhead, and asked him to act as his second if required.

The crunch wasn't long in coming. The morning of Tuesday, 22 August, was one of heavy rain and when George Morgan went to pick up his morning paper at around ten o'clock he was carrying an umbrella instead of his more usual walking-stick. Just as he was turning to leave the newsagent's shop, he spotted David Landale passing outside. He immediately rushed out on to the street and, raising his umbrella, struck Landale across the shoulders from behind - the equivalent, to all intents and purposes, of the medieval slap of a glove. The ensuing conversation, as recorded, comes across as a little stiff and formal, as though lifted perhaps from a Boy's Own magazine. 'Take that, sir!' Morgan is supposed to have cried, before adding: 'By God, sir, you shall have more of it.' Landale's response was one of outrage. 'I have never had such treatment in my life,' he exclaimed. 'You are a poor, silly creature. You are a coward, sir, a poor, silly coward.' And with that, he turned his back and walked away. Just as Morgan had intended, his actions had backed Landale into a corner, and if the merchant were to uphold his standing within the community and recover his dignity, then he was left with one single option. Early that afternoon he put together a brief, written challenge to Morgan. Belying any sense of heightened emotion, the letter's tone was one of studied formality. 'In consequence of the ungentlemanlike insult you gave me this morning,' he wrote, 'I must request that you meet me tomorrow morning at seven o'clock precisely... with pistols.' He went on to demand 'the satisfaction which as a gentleman' he felt entitled to. Concluding with consummate politeness, he signed off with the words: 'I am, Sir, Your most obedient servant, D. Landale.'

Before the letter could be delivered there was a second essential task to be completed. Writing to William Millie, Landale gave a brief account of the recent assault and, in line with established practice, he asked his second to hand over the challenge to Morgan on his behalf. He added in a postscript that he was about to leave by the two o'clock coach for Edinburgh where he intended 'to purchase a pair of detonating pistols', and he asked Millie to meet him at a quarter-past six the following morning. Arriving in the city Landale found himself somewhat at sea as he browsed randomly in the premises of a Princes Street gunsmith with little idea of what he was looking for. Pointing at a particular pair of pistols, he inquired of an assistant whether they could be relied upon to carry out the job in hand. 'You may depend on thae pistols,' replied the boy at the counter. 'Thae's the pistols that shot the man on the ferry.' Purely by chance, as it happened, Landale had stumbled across weapons put to the test two years earlier when a certain Mr Westall had duelled with his former friend, Captain Gourlay, at North Queensferry following a dispute over money. In the event, Westall had come out on top. Satisfied with what he heard, Landale handed over his cash and took possession of the pistols in exchange.

Meanwhile back in Kirkcaldy William Millie had experienced some difficulty in tracking down George Morgan. He called first at the banker's residence where he learned from a maid that he no longer lived there. Following her directions, he arrived at Morgan's new house in Kirk Wynd only to be told that the master of the house was not at home. Out of options, Millie set out for Morgan's workplace at the bank but, as he did so, he happened to meet him on the street. Millie swithered. The etiquette relating to 'une affaire d'honneur' stipulated that a challenge ought not to be delivered in a public place, but after a short hesitation Millie made up his mind to go ahead and intercept Morgan and inform him that he had a letter to deliver from David Landale. Morgan was fairly certain about what to expect. He took Millie to his home and when he sliced open the envelope and read the letter within, his response to Landale's challenge was brief and unequivocal. 'Certainly, by all means,' he replied. Despite the firmness of his words, Millie judged - perhaps in error - that Morgan 'appeared flurried a little', but within a few hours the banker had evidently recovered his composure sufficiently to invite a friend, Captain Henry Brown Wood, to join him for dinner the following evening, twelve or so hours after the duel.

What might strike us as a little odd is that by this late stage Morgan had not already nominated a second. Granted, he was not a sociable man and he appears to have had some difficulty in co-opting the services of a friend at such short notice. Eventually, however, he found a Royal Navy veteran, Lieutenant William Milne of Burntisland, who agreed to accept the role. Milne immediately set about trying to broker a compromise between the two men at loggerheads and he met William Millie that evening at McGlashan's Inn to talk things over but, despite his best attempts, no solution was to be found. Duelling protocol stipulated that each of the combatants should be attended by a doctor and now that a duel was inevitable Landale and Morgan each arranged for his own routine practitioner, Drs Alexander Smith and James Johnston respectively, to be present.

For his part, David Landale spent a quiet evening at home ensuring that his financial and business affairs were all in order. He wrote to his land agent, John Anderson, outlining what action he was to take 'in the event that I fall', but despite his inexperience he did not dismiss out of hand the possibility of a more cheerful outcome. If on the other hand he were to survive the duel, his plan was to flee from Fife to Glasgow so he asked Anderson to send a suitcase containing items of his clothing to an address in the city and to manage his affairs until his younger brother, Alexander, could return from Calcutta, India, to take over. At one point during the evening Robert Stocks, Landale's friend for 25 years, dropped in on him. Stocks apparently knew nothing of his host's assignation the following morning and, remarkably, as the two men chatted over a glass of wine, Landale failed even to mention it.

Predictably there had been a spell of wrangling before agreement could be reached on a mutually acceptable location for Morgan and Landale's upcoming confrontation. The venue eventually chosen was an open area near Kirkcaldy known as the East Park, close to Cardenbarns farmhouse, and it was here that the duellists and their seconds arrived by carriage early the next morning. Conspicuously absent was Morgan's doctor, James Johnston, who turned up at the last moment in his bedroom slippers, so it was said, after his wife had hidden his outdoor shoes in an effort to prevent him leaving home. Be that as it may, what is beyond doubt is that last-gasp attempts to negotiate a peaceful solution were unsuccessful and, once the various preliminaries had been attended to, there was nothing left for the duellists but to follow prescribed protocol. When they had taken up their respective positions, Lieutenant Milne gave the signal without further ado and the early-morning tranquillity was shattered by the blast of gunshots. The fatal outcome was recorded in an old, rough-hewn rhyme, its author now forgotten:

> *Between Torbrain and Cardenden*
> *A bloody duel was fought.*
> *Morgan fell and Landale fled*
> *From off the bloody spot.*

Yes, against all expectations the man who lay slumped on the ground, pierced through the heart and lungs, was the wartime veteran, George Morgan, while his opponent left standing was David Landale, the linen merchant who had never before fired a gun. Had he but known it, Landale had newly survived what would turn out to be the last duel on record ever fought on Scottish soil.

With Morgan's death his honour might have been upheld, but David Landale and his second were still in hot water since, technically speaking, both men were guilty of having committed a capital offence. 'We had better be off,' he told Millie bluntly. Perhaps surprisingly, at no stage did he display any sign of contrition, voicing instead his firm conviction that the outcome of the duel was an expression of God's will which 'providence had decreed'. Maybe it was that same providence that placed an obstacle in Landale's own path when his coachman, John Mason, refused to drive him to Stirling, forty miles away, on the grounds that his horses were already exhausted. This had the effect of scuppering Landale's plan to slip quietly across the country and melt into the anonymity of Glasgow where he was little known. Instead, he and Millie had no option but to catch a local ferry across the Firth of Forth to Edinburgh where they boarded a westbound coach. Meanwhile Drs Smith and Johnson were left at Cardenbarns to deal with the bloodstained aftermath of the tragic encounter. Johnson was the man allotted the unenviable task of informing David Morgan of his brother's death. The banker's first response was telling. Straightaway he wanted to know whether everything had been conducted above board, and later in the day he paid a call to a local mason, John Leslie, who was known throughout Kirkcaldy as the man who made coffins.

Within hours of George Morgan's death, arrest warrants were issued for Landale, William Millie and Lieutenant Milne. From his lodgings in Glasgow, Landale maintained communications with his land agent, John Anderson, asking him to let it be known that he was perfectly willing to return to Fife to face justice. For William Millie, at least, the pressure eased when it was acknowledged that he and Lieutenant Milne had done all in their power to prevent loss of life and they could therefore expect to be treated relatively leniently. In an effort to apprehend Landale, the net was spread ever wider until on Thursday, 24 August, he was forced to decamp once again. On the same day that George Morgan's body was laid to rest in an unmarked grave in Kirkcaldy, Landale crossed the border into England where, still accompanied by the faithful William Millie, he paused at Carlisle before travelling thirty miles farther south to Keswick, deep in the heart of the Cumbrian mountains. He continued to communicate with John Anderson during this time whose evident anxiety was given short shrift. 'Your feelings about the late affair,' Landale wrote to him, 'appear to have agitated you by far too much and caused you to be alarmed at your shadow.' He advised Anderson to 'dismiss the matter from [his] mind' as he had already done himself. Strangely, Landale's letters from the Lake District communicated less the sense of a flight from justice and more the flavour of a pleasure trip through countryside recently popularised by such Lake Poets as Wordsworth and Coleridge: 'Mr Millie has just arrived from a tour among the mountains, lakes etc.,' he wrote on Tuesday, 29 August, 'and [we are] making the most of our time.' Almost as an aside, he mentioned that he had 'now fixed upon remaining in Britain'. Poor John Anderson - it looks very much as though the task of worrying had been devolved to him alone.

On Saturday, 2 September, William Millie returned from exile and, by prior arrangement, both he and Lieutenant Milne handed themselves in to the authorities and were immediately placed in custody. In did not take long, however, for both men to be freed: Millie on bail of £100; and Milne, a more modest £60. In his absence Landale was charged that same day with having 'wickedly and maliciously' challenged George Morgan to a duel during the course of which the latter 'was ... murdered by the said David Landale.' 'Being conscious of his guilt,' the charge added, the accused 'did abscond and flee from justice.' He was required, it continued, to report to the relevant authorities within fifteen days of a specific, stated time and, in the event of his failure to do so, he would be 'put to the horn' - that is, declared an outlaw - and his property in its entirety confiscated by the state. In preparation for what he knew was inevitable, Landale left Cumbria and returned to Edinburgh in secret. From a safe house in the city, he wrote a letter to John Anderson which expressed his total confidence of being acquitted. 'I have no fear,' he insisted - 'I am convinced [that] a respectable jury will at once clear me of all crime.' That said, he added a small request, namely that Anderson provide him with 'stomach powders' as his recent experiences, he admitted, had left him feeling a little 'out of sorts'.

David Landale stood trial at Perth Sheriff Court on Friday, 22 September, one month to the day after the fateful encounter at Cardenbarns. The judge presiding was the Honourable Lord Gillies, and the courtroom was packed to capacity with members of the public, all eager to view what promised to be a fascinating spectacle. When the charge of murder was read out and Lord Gillies asked how Landale pleaded, his reply was firm and unhesitating - 'Not guilty, my Lord.' His defence was to be conducted by one of the foremost Scots lawyers of the day - the same Henry Cockburn whose acquaintance we made previously - much of whose energy throughout the trial was focused on highlighting his client's probity, both personal and financial, and the esteem in which he was held by his local community. Impossible to ignore, Cockburn contended, was the high degree of provocation to which he had been subjected. He referred specifically to George Morgan's well-known quarrelsome nature and to the banker's indiscretion in openly discussing Landale's affairs. His client had no option, Cockburn stated, than to transfer his accounts elsewhere, and his subsequent letter of complaint to Bank of Scotland head office the lawyer described as polite, professional and entirely justified. At every stage of the dispute, he went on, even a verbal apology on George Morgan's part would have been enough to satisfy his client and bring the affair to a satisfactory conclusion - but none was forthcoming. (For strategic reasons he avoided mentioning the fact that this same argument held true for both duellers.) In the aftermath of Morgan's death Landale had fled south of the border not, he asserted, in an attempt to evade justice but simply as a means of avoiding the disgrace of temporary imprisonment. When Henry Cockburn finally wrapped up his argument and resumed his seat, the judge, Lord Gillies, let slip his own view of the case when he complimented Landale's lawyer on his clarity of speech and fluent delivery.

The case for the prosecution was led by the Advocate Depute, Alexander Wood, who from the outset made no bones about the scale of the task that confronted him. He had no intention of questioning Landale's integrity, he said, but when push came to shove there could be no doubt that in the eye of the law, he had committed a capital offence. When Wood concluded his argument and sat down, a hush descended on the courtroom. It was now up to the fifteen jurymen, and them alone, to decide Landale's fate. A brief, huddled conference took place before their foreman, George Campbell, stood up and intimated that the jury members would have no need to withdraw from the courtroom to deliberate since they had already come to a unanimous conclusion. When their verdict of Not Guilty was read out, a loud whooping and cheering erupted from the public benches, prompting the court reporter to comment - with some restraint - that 'the decision seemed to give high satisfaction to an extremely crowded court'. As far as Landale was concerned, after an excruciating five hours on trial his month-long ordeal was finally over and he was dismissed from the dock - in Lord Gillies's words, 'with [his] character unsullied'.

And, true enough, the duel and its consequences did nothing to hamper his prospects or inhibit his future career. Despite prompting discussion of duelling generally, no criticism appears to have been levelled at Landale in particular and within months of the fatal conflict he became chairman of the local Chamber of Commerce, a position he held for the following four years. As Landale & Co expanded its operations into shipping, he became politically active and was an enthusiastic supporter of the 1832 Reform Act, a significant step towards establishing genuine democracy in Great Britain. In 1835 his star rose yet higher when he was elected Provost of Kirkcaldy and, just as his business dealings prospered, likewise his personal life. In March 1828, less than two years after the duel, he married his second wife, Mary Russell, the 23-year-old daughter of a family friend, and in the years that followed the couple produced no fewer than four sons and seven daughters. But in spite of his comfort and prosperity, things took a catastrophic downturn for David Landale when he suffered a stroke at the age of 60 which left him paralysed until his death ten years later in 1861. Latterly he was incapable even of speaking.

The years and decades that followed Landale and Morgan's fateful confrontation saw time, the great healer, step in. In September 1851 Alexander - nephew of the late George Morgan - took his wedding vows in the Free Church of Scotland in Kirkcaldy. His new bride was Ellen, David Landale's nineteen-year-old daughter. Any lingering suspicion of rancour must surely have been laid to rest once and for all when the couple named the youngest of their subsequent nine children George. During the 1880s three of the couple's other sons - Alexander, David and Robert - travelled together to the farthest reaches of the British Empire where they teamed up with David Landale's youngest son, Alexander, to set up a joint trading company, Landale & Morgan, in Calcutta. One of the firm's main trade goods was jute, a fibrous material made from tree bark, which they sent home to Kirkcaldy to be used in the manufacture of linoleum.

Before finally drawing down the curtain on Morgan and Landale's story, I wonder if it might pay to pause briefly and take a glance at events of 1826 from a slightly different viewpoint. It is perhaps a little too easy to go along with the accepted view that depicts David Landale entirely as the victim and injured party, and George Morgan as the unalloyed villain of the piece. Unarguably this is in large measure justified, but maybe also oversimplified. In Landale's letter of complaint to Edinburgh, might one detect perhaps a touch of malice too - a suggestion his counsel, Henry Cockburn, felt the need to deny in court? Despite claims - unsubstantiated - that Landale suffered bouts of remorse in later life, what comes across very much like an unfeeling self-righteousness, both at the time of Morgan's death and afterwards, might incline us toward a different view. And crucially, on top of that, a potentially important piece of the jigsaw that appears to have gone wholly unnoticed, then as now, is the possibility that Morgan had been scarred by his experience overseas, and that his quarrelsome nature and haughty pride had their roots in the bloody trauma of the Napoleonic Wars.

VILLAINS AND VICTIMS

John & Catherine Stuart
Firth of Clyde - December 1828

On Christmas Day of 1828 one of the most notorious figures in nineteenth-century Scotland, William Burke, was convicted at the High Court in Edinburgh of the murder of sixteen men, women and children after his partner in crime, William Hare, saved his own neck by turning King's evidence. Famously, the two ne'er-dae-weils had sold on the corpses of their victims for the purposes of medical research. But only a few short months after Burke's execution, another case came before the High Court which generated a similar torrent of public interest due in part to the curious circumstances surrounding the alleged crime but also because of its unusual setting.

Only through a chance combination of circumstances did Robert Lamont, a merchant on the tiny Hebridean island of Ulva, find himself aboard the steamship *Toward Castle* in the company of John and Catherine Stuart, a couple previously unknown to him, as she made her way from Lochgilphead in Argyll towards her destination at the Glasgow Broomielaw on Monday, 15 December 1828. Accompanied by his second cousin, John Lamont, a farmer on the same small island, Robert was travelling to the city on an annual business trip while the Stuarts were heading home to John's native Ireland by a somewhat circuitous route.

Up till now the couple's journey had been anything but straightforward. A blacksmith to trade, until fairly recently 32-year-old

John had been earning a living in the Newcastle area but work had dried up there and with no future prospects on the horizon he and his wife, ten years younger than himself, had made the decision to gather up their belongings and travel to Glasgow where they embarked upon the vessel *Eclipse* bound for Belfast. For a time the crossing went well enough until, caught in rough seas between Arran and Kintyre, the ship was forced to make a run for the port of Campbeltown in order to sit out the storm. Given to understand that she would resume her journey at six o'clock the following morning, the Stuarts left the quay to find accommodation in the town but when they returned at 5 a.m. they discovered to their dismay that the *Eclipse* had sailed at midnight without them and, what made matters worse, their luggage was still on board, leaving them with neither change of clothing nor the means to support themselves. As events would later show, this was a pivotal moment - a misunderstanding that set in motion the fateful series of events that led to their making the acquaintance of Robert Lamont and the grievous consequences that followed as a result.

With no option but to return to Glasgow and start out for Belfast all over again, it must surely have been with heavy hearts that the pair left Campbeltown to travel the thirty-odd miles to Tarbert where their plan was to intercept the *Toward Castle* as she stopped off on her journey south from Lochgilphead. Whether they were able to arrange transport or were forced to trudge north on foot I cannot say but it is on record that in order to keep body and soul together John was obliged to sell his pocket watch - he was desperate enough to accept £1, a paltry quarter of what he believed its true value to be. Surely only the stoniest of hearts could have avoided feeling for the couple in their miserable plight.

After reaching Tarbert the Stuarts joined a group of people drinking in a public house while awaiting the arrival of the steamboat at 5 a.m. on Monday, 15 December. One of those waiting was a whisky smuggler from Glasgow, Catherine (or Katie) McPhail, currently returning home to the Gorbals with her young daughter, Margaret, after what had been a successful outing to the West Highlands; successful, that is, up till then when she was collared by a vigilant excise officer who confiscated the proceeds of her trip - two gallons of illicit spirits. Despite her loss, she was by no means left penniless and consoled herself with a cup of coffee in the public house kitchen. Unable to read without assistance, she was forced to inquire whether she was presenting a one-pound or a one-guinea note in order to settle up for what she owed. Waiting by the fireside nearby, it seems likely that the Stuarts sat up and paid close attention as they watched her secrete the rest of her money - close to £17 in coins and paper money - within her layers of outdoor winter clothing. Some conversation seems to have taken place since, before turning to leave, she footed the bill for Catherine Stuart's coffee. It was a gesture likely to be appreciated since, boarding the *Toward Castle* at around eight o'clock, she and her husband claimed to be unable to pay the six-shilling fare from Tarbert to Glasgow but, put under pressure by the ship's master, Captain William Stewart, they finally stumped up.

During the subsequent crossing it can be tricky to pin down what exactly happened and when. Recollections did not always tally, alcohol inevitably took its toll on the various participants' memories and the following is basically a distillation of several different accounts. Possibly the witness who came across as most dependable was John Lamont who recounted how, once the vessel had passed through the Kyles of Bute, he and his cousin Robert descended from the deck to the downstairs saloon where they settled down to a gill of whisky at a table in a candlelit alcove. Between ten and eleven o'clock John and Catherine Stuart arrived below deck and, with seating to spare, Robert invited them to join himself and his cousin. It could be that he was influenced by Catherine's looks. She was a slim, dark-haired woman with a fetching manner that, some have suggested, was inclined to draw men's attention. After sitting awhile John Lamont excused himself and returned to the upper deck. For a time afterwards he could tell from the sounds of laughter drifting up from below that Robert and his new companions were enjoying making each other's acquaintance, and after a while his cousin appeared on deck to persuade him to rejoin them: 'I've fallen in with fine company,' he told John, 'You had better come down and take a share.' Overcoming a degree of reluctance, John assented and followed him downstairs. If not yet *roarin' fou*, they had clearly grown merry in one another's company and he observed John Stuart make his cousin the gift of a knife.

Also aboard since Tarbert were the whisky smuggler, Katie McPhail, and her daughter. Mindful of the cash in her possession, Catherine Stuart approached McPhail under the pretext of expressing sympathy for the loss of her spirits to the keen-eyed exciseman. She went on to offer to buy her a drink - a token of appreciation, she insisted, for her earlier gift of coffee. Initially McPhail declined but Stuart was persistent and eventually she gave in. After joining the Stuarts and Lamonts for a quick nip of whisky, McPhail rose from the table and returned with her daughter to the upper deck but Catherine Stuart was not done with her yet. One of the puzzling aspects of the story is what powers of persuasion she brought to bear to coax her back to the saloon later on in the trip - McPhail would later state that Stuart made no fewer than three attempts to encourage her to rejoin the company before she agreed to fall in with her wishes. Why, we might ask, didn't McPhail smell a rat? Who knows? But one thing we can be sure of: now that all the principal actors were united, smoking around the candlelit table - McPhail and her daughter; the two Hebridean gentlemen; and John and Catherine Stuart - the scene was set for the day's tragic events to unfold.

With strong ale at 9d a bottle (nine old pence - about 4p today) the canny Robert Lamont mumped about the price but when his turn came round to pay he forked out nonetheless and the drink flowed freely. Each newly purchased bottle was handed by the steward first to Catherine Stuart who poured its contents into a tumbler which was then passed from person to person around the dimly lit table. As one such glass did the rounds, when Katie McPhail took her first mouthful she instantly screwed up her face and spat it out, wiping her mouth on her apron to remove what she described as 'a bad, bad bitter taste'. Unperturbed, Catherine Stuart handed the glass back to her. 'Drink this, Katie,' she told her, 'and damn my soul you'll drink every drop.' Seeking an explanation for the taste, McPhail dismissed the idea that the ale might have been tainted by birch bark she had been chewing earlier (for its perceived health-giving benefits) and, bracing herself, she forced down another mouthful or two before - unthinkably! - passing the glass along to her small daughter. Anyway, her unpleasant experience was soon glossed over, treated as a minor blip, before the drinking continued as before. When it came John Lamont's turn, he drank sparingly but for Robert the glass was topped up to the brim. 'This is your drink,' Catherine Stuart told him. 'Drink some of it.' Robert did better than that, draining the glass to the bottom without a second's hesitation and, not only that, but he capped it off with a stiff shot of whisky for good measure.

Filling up the glass, Catherine Stuart passed it round once again but just as it was her husband's turn to drink, she suddenly reached out and snatched the ale from his hand, announcing that he had already had enough and spilling the entire contents of the glass down his front as she did so. He swore viciously as he turned on her and, fearing things might take a violent turn, Katie McPhail intervened, crying - 'Don't strike her!' The couple's drunken spat subsided just as quickly as it had blown up but, recalling the event later, both she and John Lamont indicated having sensed a whiff of the bogus about what took place. In the fullness of time it would emerge that their instincts were well founded for what they had witnessed was in reality an elaborate and well-practised hoax.

With calm apparently restored, things looked likely to continue as before had not Robert Lamont drawn attention to Margaret McPhail who seemed to have turned ill. The girl appeared groggy with her head lolling forward over her chest, so her mother helped her up from the table and escorted her to the upper deck in the hope that fresh sea air might act as a tonic and perk her up. Although well accustomed to drinking ale, McPhail became conscious of feeling confused and disorientated herself at this point and she found herself leaning over the rail and vomiting. By then the *Toward Castle* was somewhere between Dunoon and Gourock, edging closer to the Clyde mouth, but before the vessel would reach her destination there was more drama still to come.

Most likely the Ulva men (tipsy to varying degrees) automatically put young Margaret's illness down either to seasickness or possibly unaccustomed alcohol. Not long after her hurried departure, John Lamont too left the table, feeling off-colour himself. Living far from the world of crowds and cities, he was unfamiliar with malt liquor and not in a position to pass judgment on the ale whose taste had so nauseated Katie McPhail. Not until the *Toward Castle* was nearing the Renfrew Ferry did he return to the saloon where he found that the Stuarts had disappeared from the candlelit alcove, leaving Robert alone, slumped on a bench with his head hanging between his knees. When spoken to, he was unresponsive and he seemed to have lost control over his limbs. John noticed that his coat had been unbuttoned which led him to suspect that he had been the victim of a robbery. He was familiar with Robert's habit of carrying money in his left 'oxter pootch' - inside pocket - in a wallet outwardly visible by the bulge it created in the material of his clothing. He knew too that the previous day this wallet had contained notes to the value of roughly £20. Reaching into Robert's pocket, he confirmed that, just as he had suspected, the wallet was gone. An onlooking female passenger spoke out, saying, 'You should not be trying that man's pocket,' but John explained that the drunk man was in fact his relation and that he had been robbed. That Robert Lamont had become easy prey for thieves was hardly surprising: of the three gills of whisky, three bottles of porter and eleven bottles of ale sold aboard the *Toward Castle* during the crossing, all but one bottle of ale had gone to the candlelit alcove in the saloon. But the puzzle was - why was the Hebridean merchant the only one of the drinkers to become totally incapacitated?

John Lamont hurried back on to the deck where he found Captain Stewart at the gangway, awaiting the arrival of a small boat off shore, and he reported to him the news that his cousin had been robbed. As soon as he was free to come away, Stewart accompanied John down to the saloon where by now Robert had slipped from the bench on to his knees. The captain lifted the candle from the table and peered underneath and by the faint light it provided the two men spied Robert's wallet, rifled of its contents and discarded on the floor with various letters (equivalent to modern-day cheques) lying alongside. Of banknotes there were none. Captain Stewart's next move was to round up Robert's fellow drinkers and, once assembled in his cabin, he set about the task of interrogating them. Queasy and befuddled, Katie McPhail had not recovered sufficiently to provide much help, so he turned his attention next to the Stuarts. Had they spent time in Robert Lamont's company? 'Yes,' John Stuart replied, 'and very good company he was till he got drunk.' The captain continued, asking if Stuart had any money in his possession. 'I have, Captain, plenty - nearly £20,' he replied, laying a wallet on the table and a black silk purse by its side. Removing their contents, the captain counted out £19 and seven shillings in both notes and silver coins. Thinking back to Tarbert and the couple's apparent difficulty in covering the cost of their passage, his suspicion of theft grew strong enough to place restrictions on their movements during the rest of the voyage. During questioning, John Stuart had struck Captain Stewart as much the worse for drink but he couldn't help noticing that when matters started to become serious, he appeared to sober up pretty rapidly. As soon as the *Toward Castle* docked at the Broomielaw quay, Stewart referred the matter to the harbour master, James Russell, who in turn contacted the River Clyde police at their office in Robertson Street with the result that the Stuarts were arrested on suspicion of theft and escorted from the boat. It had become clear by then that there was something more seriously wrong with Robert Lamont than routine drunkenness so the captain requested that a doctor be sent for as a matter of urgency.

Immediately after arriving on board, Dr Joseph Fleming of Main Street, Anderston, conducted an examination of Robert Lamont, assisted by Angus Cameron, police watchman, and harbour master, James Russell, who supported the patient in an upright position. The doctor's initial findings suggested a severe case of alcoholic poisoning: his extremities were cold to the touch, his pulse barely perceptible and his lips were swollen and bluish in colour. Throughout the procedure the patient remained unconscious. In order to flush the alcohol from his system, Fleming applied a stomach pump and replaced the fluid thus removed by injecting a similar quantity of water. As a precaution, a sample of Lamont's stomach contents was retained, placed in a jar and transferred to Robertson Street for possible later analysis.

After treating his patient Dr Fleming went directly to Robertson Street police station where the two suspected thieves, John and Catherine Stuart, were currently detained. A dramatic development had taken place. While he was being searched, two green bottles had been found in John Stuart's coat pockets and when the larger of the two was uncorked it had - to no-one's surprise - emitted a powerful aroma of whisky. But when police officer James Young investigated the second bottle, he found something of greater interest. Inside were a few drops of a whitish liquid that gave off an unpleasantly bitter odour that he recognised straightaway as the smell of laudanum. The aspirin of its day, laudanum was an opium-based solution in common use at the time for treating a wide variety of ailments but, among the many hazards attached to its use, administering the correct dosage was critical. Though widely used in Glasgow and Edinburgh as a recreational drug, if taken without due care it could lead to loss of consciousness, poisoning - even death. When Dr Fleming arrived at the police office, he was able to confirm that the smell from the green bottle was indeed that of laudanum, and potential links with the plight of Robert Lamont were evident to all.

Sadly for the sick man, the doctor's efforts proved unavailing and the unfortunate islander, still in his fifties, died aboard the *Toward Castle* at around five o'clock the following morning without ever surfacing from his unconscious state. Later that same day - Tuesday, 16 December - a post-mortem examination was carried out by Dr Fleming in collaboration with Dr James Corkindale of St Vincent Place which found no sign of external violence nor any evidence of disease. More detailed investigation did, however, uncover indications of laudanum poisoning. Not only that, but when the sample of fluid taken from Robert Lamont's stomach was subjected to analysis two days later by Dr Corkindale and his colleague Dr Andrew Ure (he whose experimental work in Glasgow was said by some to have sparked the idea behind Mary Shelley's classic novel, *Frankenstein*) the two physicians were able to confirm the presence of laudanum both by its highly distinctive smell but also by rigorous chemical testing. Although they were candid in acknowledging that their conclusions were not definitive, they nevertheless expressed confidence that Robert Lamont had very likely died of a laudanum overdose.

So, things didn't look good for the Stuarts and their prospects only got worse as investigations proceeded. Questioned about events aboard the *Toward Castle*, John Lamont recalled that as glasses of ale were passed around the table Catherine Stuart initially took her share like the others but at a certain point she seemed to bow out and, aside from doing the pouring, took a back seat from then on. Katie McPhail remembered seeing John Stuart knock back plenty of whisky but not so much in the way of ale. Through the dimness of the saloon her daughter, Margaret, had several times noticed Catherine Stuart screening the tumbler from view behind her tartan shawl before slipping it out again to be passed round the table. She had not known the reason. After arriving at Glasgow, John Lamont recounted how he was sick throughout that night and remained unwell for several days afterwards. There was no question of seasickness - he was well used to sailing - and at the time he put his illness down to the shock of his cousin's death. But increasingly it was looking as though there was more to it than that.

Despite being circumstantial in nature, the evidence was sufficient for charges of murder and robbery to be brought against John and Catherine Stuart - but that, of course, didn't guarantee that they could be made to stick. When their case was heard at the High Court in Edinburgh on Tuesday, 14 July 1829, they both pleaded not guilty which left the prosecution facing two major hurdles. First, to persuade the jury that a *high probability* - not absolute certainty - that Lamont's death was caused by laudanum poisoning was strong enough evidence upon which to base a conviction; and, secondly, to prove beyond reasonable doubt that a link existed between drops of laudanum found in a bottle in John Stuart's pocket (which he claimed was to treat complaints suffered by himself and his wife) and traces of the drug detected in the late Robert Lamont's stomach fluids. As the trial got underway, witnesses were called one after another to take their turn at the stand, both eyewitnesses aboard the *Toward Castle* - John Lamont, the McPhails, Captain Stewart and others - plus those who became involved in their various capacities later - policemen, doctors, pharmacists. After replicating her late husband's journey from the Hebrides, Robert Lamont's widow, Euphemia, spoke through a Gaelic translator. She was followed in the witness box by her daughter, Catherine, who identified her father's silk purse from stitching she personally had carried out. She told the court she had never known him to leave home without it.

Things took an unpredictable turn when two prisoners John Stuart had shared a cell with while awaiting trial stepped up to the witness box. Stuart, it transpired, had been surprisingly forthcoming in connection with his own and his wife's involvement in the death of Robert Lamont but, not only that, he had also admitted to being in the habit of carrying a small bottle of laudanum for 'giving the doctor' to anyone whose path he crossed whom he judged a suitable target for theft - i.e. by administering a dose of the drug sufficient to incapacitate them, thus enabling them to be robbed of their money and valuables. According to the first prisoner, Malcolm Logan, Stuart had also divulged the interesting titbit that, on realising he was suspected of having poisoned Robert Lamont, he had slipped into the *Toward Castle's* water-closet and urinated into the laudanum bottle in what turned out to be an unsuccessful attempt to disguise the drug's distinctive smell. A second prison inmate, Archibald Anderson, testified that Stuart had disclosed that it had been his wife, Catherine, who had been responsible for adulterating the ale. When challenged by the defence, Logan and Anderson declared that there had been no understanding given that Stuart was speaking to them in confidence.

Whilst not perhaps one hundred per cent conclusive, the evidence presented by the prosecution had all tended in one same direction. The testimony of those aboard the *Toward Castle*, damning enough on its own, was backed up in large measure by the medical men's findings and, if that still wasn't enough to convince a jury, Stuart's unguarded remarks to his fellow prisoners in the tolbooth had done nothing to help his own and his wife's case. With all this in mind, after withdrawing to consider their decision it took the jury members a mere two or three minutes to pass a unanimous verdict of guilty on both of the accused on charges of murder and robbery. The hour was late and the judge, Lord Pitmilly, kept his concluding remarks brief before assuming the black cap and closing the day's proceedings by proclaiming that John and Catherine Stuart would pay for their crimes with their lives at the city's customary place of execution in five weeks' time on Wednesday, 19 August 1829. Their bodies would then be forwarded to Dr Alexander Monro, Professor of Anatomy at the University of Edinburgh, to be dissected for medical research. Hearing their fate spelt out in such starkest of terms, both prisoners remained conspicuously impassive and neither showed any emotion. Their courtroom ordeal had lasted close to twelve hours.

Falling on the back of the Burke and Hare atrocities, when the circumstances surrounding Robert Lamont's death became known they created a national sensation and stirred up an appetite for more information. In response, several newspaper titles published purported accounts of the life of John Stuart. Readers were informed that the killer was born under the surname 'Broadfoot', not in Ireland but of Irish parents in the parish of Stoneykirk, near Stranraer, where they had managed to put together enough money to secure the lease of a small farm. For whatever reason, either the result of some unknown setback or (as *The Scotsman's* columnist seemed to favour) through 'mismanagement', they had run into financial difficulties and been obliged to vacate the property, at which point their son had gone into service with a neighbouring gentleman whose identity the press disguised somewhat thinly as 'Mr McM____n, a good-hearted man in the parish of Glenluce'. In what capacity John was engaged readers were not told but throughout his time at Glenluce he apparently conducted himself in an exemplary manner and was held in high regard by his employer.

Aged around twenty, Stuart became married to an unnamed young woman whose background was more affluent than his own and consequently he found himself the victim of social snobbery on the part of his new parents-in-law. Why their attitude had failed to become apparent during his courtship of their daughter is not made clear. 'Being of an independent, haughty, and rather imperious disposition' - *The Scotsman* again - Stuart found their manner intolerable and, perhaps acting in haste, he enlisted in the Royal Marines and was posted to Chatham in Kent. Estrangement from her parents coupled with the downturn in her fortunes took their toll on his young wife's health, and she fell ill and died in 1825 within months of arriving in England. Stuart sought and was granted a pass to return her body to her parents in Galloway but, after so doing, for reasons unstated he made the decision to abscond from his regiment. As a known deserter, he was shunned by former friends and, constantly haunted by fear of arrest, he began to associate with undesirable company and fell into a life of dissolution, dishonesty and crime. For nearly four years before the death of Robert Lamont, *The Scotsman* informed its readers, he had been 'prowling up and down the country, like the arch-enemy of mankind, seeking whom he might devour' - lurid prose indeed and a startling transition from the decent young man employed by Mr McM____n of Glenluce to no lesser a figure than His Satanic Majesty, Auld Nick himself.

Perhaps *The Scotsman* journalist realised he had over-egged the pudding somewhat when, taking a deep breath and a new paragraph, he went on to correct the record, conceding that never, even at his times of greatest need, had Stuart resorted to such brazen acts as housebreaking or highway robbery. Rather he made a living by more underhand means - as a light-fingered pickpocket, a gambler, a trickster at country fairs - and more than once he apparently signed up with the armed forces but decamped at the first opportunity with the king's shilling firmly secured in his pocket. The boldest of his criminal enterprises involved sheep-stealing for which he was convicted under the name of McGrady but he managed to evade the full weight of the law by performing a successful jail-break at Stranraer. His activities cranked up a gear when he fell in with a gang of forgers in the border country from whom he learned their methods and techniques before setting up on his own account in the town of Dumfries where he manufactured a set of casts and dies for his own exclusive use as a 'shanner', or counterfeiter of coins. In order to deflect his neighbours' suspicions, he took on various jobs in addition to his illicit activity and it was during this time that he first met Catherine Wright, the Glasgow-born woman now resident in Dumfries who would become his second wife.

Equipping themselves with a sizeable sum in fake coins, the two set off on a tour of the district with the object of passing off Stuart's forgeries in the various hamlets, villages and other small settlements they passed through. At Gretna they stopped off to be married before devoting the rest of their trip to the pleasures of eating, drinking and carousing with companions of a similar mould to themselves. Mere petty criminals, there was no suggestion of robbery or violence at this time, let alone any hint of murder to come in the future, and things might have continued along similar lines but for a chance wayside encounter. While travelling one evening between Edinburgh and Biggar, John Stuart happened to encounter a former comrade-in-crime, a man reputedly by the name of Henderson, whom he met lurking by the roadside waiting to carry out a burglary once darkness had fallen and the family in a nearby house had retired to bed for the night. This was to be his last ever housebreaking, Henderson told Stuart, since he had recently discovered a more profitable and less hazardous way of topping up his coffers. By administering a certain soporific drug, he explained, an unsuspecting victim's defences might be overcome, rendering him an easy target for an enterprising thief. Stuart's interest was piqued and, after hearing the details, he resolved to put his old acquaintance's method to the test. In order to do so, Catherine and he travelled to Glasgow where the drug in question - yes, laudanum - could be purchased cheaply from any local chemist. In the city they found it a surprisingly simple matter to befriend strangers in public houses, spike their drinks and, once their new companions became drowsy, relieve them of their cash. Catherine, reported *The Scotsman*, was always the one with responsibility for administering the drug and though murder was never their objective, the death of Robert Lamont was the third fatality for which the Stuarts were responsible. The first, in which an unnamed 'quiet, kind, good man' lost his life, had taken place at an unspecified location somewhere in the south of Scotland; the second in the west. (The *Caledonian Mercury* does a little better and identifies this second victim as a ferryman, still anonymous, at Kirkcudbright.) And there the curtain falls on Stuart's alleged biography: all very vague, with no sources cited and its mishmash of information at odds in places with High Court evidence. With readership numbers its main priority, it wouldn't do to trust its every detail.

Additional revelations appeared in a broadsheet published by Messrs Carmichael & Graham, printers, of the Trongate, Glasgow, and hawked around the city streets for a few coppers. According to the broadsheet's author, prior to Stuart's trial he had confessed to persons close to him to having murdered no fewer than seven persons before the death of Robert Lamont and since his conviction had admitted to three more, all by laudanum poisoning, thus making him responsible for eleven murders in total. At the end of the day, however, we might be wise to hold back a generous pinch of salt in reserve: with a keen eye to their market, broadsheet publishers leaned toward sensationalism. The truth of the matter was that the exact number of unfortunate strangers who fell prey to the couple's poisonous wiles, and either did, or did not, emerge with their lives intact was something impossible to know.

Other publications featured stories focusing on the Stuarts and how they conducted themselves in jail in the weeks between conviction and the date set for their executions, some perhaps more plausible than others. It was reported that John had twice read the New Testament cover to cover - that in spite of the fact that four months earlier he had declared himself illiterate and had his Declaration to the Court signed on his behalf. Also illiterate, Catherine was said to have shown herself capable of repeating a large part of the Shorter Catechism from memory. Her mother, it was reported in the press, had made the journey from Dumfries in order to visit her daughter in jail. John Stuart reportedly insisted under questioning that there had never been any intention to murder Robert Lamont: in line with their established practice, Catherine had added laudanum to his drink but, unaware that she had done so or believing it had not taken effect, he had followed this up with a second dose. 'We would have been mad to have committed murder knowingly in a steamboat,' he was said to have remarked. During the course of another conversation, he allegedly expressed the hope that their sad fate would act as a warning to law-abiding members of the public against sitting down to drink with persons previously unknown. The practice of laudanum poisoning was, he cautioned, a good deal more widespread than was generally realised. Viewed from an objective standpoint, one might be forgiven for suspecting that Stuart's reported warnings were perhaps a little too public-spirited to be authentic and - what with the newspaper disclosures, broadsheet revelations and anecdotes leaking from the condemned cell - it looks very much as though fact and mythology had started to merge on the printed page.

Rain was descending in torrents on the morning of Wednesday, 19 August, as crowds gathered at the head of Libberton Wynd in anticipation of the awful spectacle to come. By eight o'clock thousands filled the streets and every window space and rooftop vantage point had been claimed and occupied. Spying a commercial opportunity, hawkers worked the crowds with various items on offer to mark the occasion. Clearly turning a penny or two mattered more than the literary merit of the broadsheet ballads on sale:

> *A certain man upon a plan he put us both one day,*
> *How we could raise money with ease and no lives take away,*
> *By giving laudanum to them and putting them to sleep,*
> *So by an oath he bound us both the secret for to keep.*
> *In the Bridgegate of Glasgow once this horrid scheme we tried,*
> *The dose being strong, it was not long before the poor man died.*
> *Of the same death in the Trongate another died also;*
> *To shun disgrace we left the place, to Ireland we did go.*
> *We never thought we would be brought to trial for this crime.*

Up until the previous day the couple at the centre of it all had been jailed apart but for their final night Catherine and John Stuart had been granted leave to share a cell and a bed. Neither, it was reported, had shown any inclination to sleep but instead they had passed the long hours engaged in whispered conversation. Stuart was weighted down by leg irons, his reward for a thwarted escape attempt. A petition appealing for clemency, submitted on Catherine's behalf, had failed and it was said that she spent much of the night in tears, fearful of death to come in the morning. Earlier news reports of ill-treatment she had received at her husband's hands were belied by his tender attempts to relieve her distress as he reassured her that they were 'now in the hands of the Almighty'. He left their cell at half-past six and descended to the downstairs hall where, despite the greatcoat he was wearing, he complained of the cold - most likely the effect of nerves at work unseen. Tea was brought to him and he asked permission to smoke a final pipe of tobacco. Catherine joined him a quarter of an hour later and she too was given tea to drink. She asked to borrow a pipe which she lit and settled down to smoke on a chair close to the fire. Both were neatly dressed in black clothing provided for their use by the prison governor - in John's case the self-same garments, it was said, as had been worn by the mass-murderer Burke on the scaffold seven months earlier. Noticing that her husband's hair was untidy, Catherine Stuart took up a comb, saying, 'John, comb your hair that you may appear decent.'

Before leaving for the place of execution the couple were provided with spiritual support by two clergymen, Dr Gordon, and Rev. Porteous, Chaplain of the Calton Jail, who led them in prayer and in singing the 30th Paraphrase and 33rd Psalm. At 8.15 a.m. the ministers and Edinburgh Bailies Crighton and Small accompanied them to the head of Libberton Wynd where the city hangman, Thomas Williams, was making his last checks and adjustments. After climbing the steps of the scaffold, they spent their last few moments in quiet conversation as their arms were pinioned and nooses placed around their necks. Once Williams was satisfied that all was in order, the couple turned to face one another and, being denied permission to embrace, they simply shook hands and exchanged their final farewells. As ten thousand spectators looked on in near silence, John dropped the handkerchief to signal their readiness to die, the hangman drew back the bolt and Catherine and he dropped simultaneously from the platform. Some accounts recorded that John struggled hard for a moment at the end of the rope while Catherine's life slipped away instantaneously and without apparent pain. Inexplicably, others reported the manner of their deaths as precisely the other way around while still others suggested that neither one had suffered. Whatever the truth, there was general agreement that during their final ordeal the couple's demeanour had remained calm and dignified throughout.

What then are we to make of the poisoners, John and Catherine Stuart, with their story now at an end? It is not easy to settle on a consistent, credible picture as nineteenth-century accounts swing between extremes in seeking to manipulate their readers and their emotions. Murderers many times over? An 'arch-enemy of mankind' accompanied by a 'Fury in female form'? Or merely a fond couple, quietly shaking hands as they stand side by side on the brink of eternity? What we do know for sure is that the Stuarts were poor people, unemployed and of no settled abode, who were forced to sell John's watch simply to get back from Campbeltown to Glasgow - people who did a great wrong, no doubt, but who, by John's way of it, never had any intention to take anyone's life. That is all very well, but theirs is not the only story: others too were affected by their actions whose feelings must not be allowed to be forgotten. Travelling back from Edinburgh to their Hebridean home, Euphemia and Catherine Lamont - one without a husband, the second missing her father - would hardly have felt overburdened with sympathy. For them, life on their small, tide-washed island would never, ever be the same.

Alexander Arthur & William Strang
Glasgow East End - April 1829

The entire plot had been choreographed from start to finish with each player's part spelt out in advance. The target was the hardware business which Andrew Scott operated from within his home at Falconer's Land, Kirk Street, in the Calton district of the East End of Glasgow. First to set the wheels in motion was William Strang, a nineteen-year-old medical student, who entered Scott's premises purportedly to pass on a message from James Robertson, a large-scale ironmongery dealer in St Andrew's Square, requesting to see Scott on an urgent business matter. Loitering outside, Strang's twenty-one-year-old accomplice, Alexander Arthur, a blacksmith to trade, made sure Scott was well clear of the premises before he entered the shop and asked the young assistant, David Wilson, to speak to his boss. When told that he had just gone out, Arthur replied that he was happy to wait and he settled down in the adjoining kitchen, lighting up his pipe for a smoke.

Cue the third member of the gang, William Comb, to step forward, posing as a customer in the market for wrought iron which the gang must have known that Andrew Scott kept stored in a dark closet in his back shop. As well as engaging the attention of the shop assistant, Comb created as great a din as possible while rummaging through the bundles of iron, thus providing Alexander Arthur with the cover he needed to slip from his seat in the kitchen and force open a lockfast chest - using a scalpel belonging to Strang, it was said - and withdraw its contents of eight £1 notes and a number of bank drafts. Once Comb was satisfied that he had given Arthur enough time to carry out the theft, he left the shop after giving the assistant an undertaking that he would return later in the day to uplift a certain quantity of iron which Wilson agreed to reserve in his name and set to one side. Shortly after Comb's departure, Arthur emerged from the kitchen and told Wilson that he had waited long enough and had decided he would take a walk instead and come back a bit later when the boss was likely to have returned. For some reason, however, the assistant sensed something amiss. Hurrying back into the kitchen, he found the money chest had been forced open and immediately raised the alarm, crying - 'Stop the thief!' But by then it was too late. All three of the men - Strang, Arthur and Comb - had fled the scene. It transpired later that two more ne'er-dae-weils - John Brown and Robert Campbell - had also been involved in the ploy but what minor part they had played is unclear.

The five lay low overnight but they met up early the following morning when they hired a coach to carry them to the West Craigs Inn, a few miles from Bathgate, a venue well known for boxing matches that attracted large crowds of spectators sometimes numbering in the thousands. Here they enjoyed watching a prize-fight, eating and drinking before eventually they decided to call it a day and make tracks for home. Possibly by then funds were running low because they stopped off at the King's Arms Inn at Airdrie where William Strang manufactured a set-piece distraction, thus enabling Alexander Arthur to extricate three £1 notes, two guinea-notes and a quantity of silver coins from a locked drawer in the landlord's desk. They'd had an enjoyable day out but, sadly for them, the good times were set not to last. Within a few days the long arm of the law had reached out and collared them and they found themselves under lock and key in the Glasgow tolbooth.

When they appeared at the High Court in Edinburgh on Monday, 18 May, the charge they faced related to the robbery of Andrew Scott's hardware store. Of the five accused, only three appeared in the dock. Whatever John Brown's involvement in the affair might have been, he had managed to abscond in the interim, while William Comb had chosen to make life easier for himself - and the prosecution's job a little more straightforward - by turning his back on his friends and agreeing to turn King's evidence. During cross-examination, Strang's lawyer attempted to discredit Comb in the eyes of the jury by probing into his private life and activities, asking him to enumerate how many times he had ever been imprisoned. Initially hesitant, Comb eventually admitted to having spent time in Glasgow, Greenock, Paisley and Perth jails but he maintained that, despite these spells in prison, he had never been convicted of any crime. What was hard for the defence to dispute was the testimony of an impartial witness, a cobbler by the name of Neil Log, who had happened to be in Scott's shop at the time of the robbery and was able to identify Strang and Arthur as the men involved - despite the latter's having since shaved off his whiskers. It did not help Strang's case that he had admitted his part in the affair to a fellow prisoner in Glasgow Police Office, and his character was cast in an even more unfavourable light when it emerged that during his arrest he had been caught in the act of jettisoning two skeleton keys.

The verdict of the jury was unanimous: Alexander Arthur and William Strang were found guilty as charged while Robert Campbell, whose role in the business had always been pretty vague, was deemed to be not guilty. In an attempt to mitigate his sentence, Strang's lawyer spoke out, stressing that his client had been well educated and was of a respectable background but that he had fallen into bad habits after developing the habit of attending boxing matches. It sounds suspiciously like using social class to influence the justice system - and just maybe it worked when Lord Gillies, one of three presiding judges, announced that Alexander Arthur would be transported overseas on a fourteen-year term and William Strang for only seven. Addressing both prisoners, the Lord Justice-Clerk emphasised the seriousness of their crimes but it was noticeable how he focused on Strang in particular, warning him about his future choice of companions. What company was kept by the blacksmith, Alexander Arthur, was apparently of less importance.

As the two convicted men were led from the dock the matter might have looked to be done and dusted but, no, William Strang had other ideas and in the days that followed he wrote from his cell in Edinburgh to petition King George IV to intercede on his behalf. His words expressed shame at the 'disgraceful ... solitary instance' when he had '[carried] off a small sum of money' and he attempted to excuse his action by insisting that he had not been the instigator of the crime. (The incident at the King's Arms Inn had been conveniently expunged from his memory.) His enthusiasm for prize-fighting had led him into making the acquaintance of those who were, he explained sniffily, 'far below his proper sphere in life'. He followed this up by outlining his personal credentials. He had received a 'Liberal Education', he wrote, and been successful in gaining his Surgeon's Diploma. He was anxious to pursue his studies further, he continued, and wished to be granted permission to treat his fellow inmates in the Edinburgh tolbooth. Those of a more cynical disposition may experience a twinge of suspicion that only once he was confined behind bars did his interest in the welfare of others suddenly blossom and his interest in prize-fighting similarly wane...

Strang had no shortage of backers willing to champion his cause. Three staff members of the University of Glasgow - including the Principal, Rev. Dr Duncan Macfarlane, sent a letter to the Home Secretary, Robert Peel, which confirmed that Strang had completed four years' study of medicine and had shown particular aptitude in the areas of anatomy and surgery. The governor of Glasgow jail, Dugald McColl, and John Fisher, the prison chaplain, also wrote to Peel, commending Strang's good behaviour during his time behind bars on remand. A number of petitions likewise landed on the Home Secretary's desk, including one signed by neighbours of Strang's father, a publican in Glasgow's Jamaica Street. The Procurators Fiscal of Glasgow and Lanarkshire wrote to confirm that prior to this misdemeanour the person of William Strang had been unknown to their offices, and Peel received no fewer than three letters supporting Strang from the Earl of Glasgow. For a time, it looked as though this barrage of support from the great and the good of the West of Scotland might tilt things in the prisoner's favour. In response to one of the Earl of Glasgow's communications, the Home Secretary indicated that, as an alternative to transporting Strang overseas, he was minded to allow him to serve out his sentence in the General Penitentiary at Millbank, London, 'just as any other convict'. When this change of plan was relayed back to Strang's father, he started making arrangements for his son to be supplied with such items as he might require during his prison term. A pair of new shoes in particular was mentioned.

But it soon became clear that this entire array of luminaries had seriously misjudged William Strang's character. Everything changed abruptly in late July when he was named among a dozen inmates found to be implicated in a foiled escape attempt from Edinburgh prison. Interviewed one-to-one, he 'very readily and candidly disclosed the whole proceedings' to the governor but, even so, the Home Secretary felt he must annul his reprieve with the result that Strang was sent south to the prison hulk *Justitia* at Woolwich to await transportation. Notwithstanding this major setback, Strang senior refused to concede defeat but continued to petition Peel, requesting that his son be kept in England at a location apart from hardened criminals. William, however, did nothing to make his father's task any easier. While working ashore during daytime, he was found to have cached clothing and money for what was assumed to be a planned future escape bid. Not only that but papers were confiscated from him aboard the *Justitia* which set out instructions relating to the counterfeiting of coins. Not surprisingly, the Home Secretary's patience ran out. 'Transport him,' Peel wrote abruptly in October, and on Wednesday, 2 December 1829, Strang left England aboard the *Mermaid* bound for New South Wales. His old partner in crime, Alexander Arthur, fared no better. Petitions appealing for clemency had been filed by his elderly mother, Ann Reid of College Street, Glasgow, on the grounds that her health was precarious and she relied on her son for support. Among those countersigning her petition was Andrew Scott, her son's victim, and in an interesting change of perspective Ann Reid depicted him as an innocent led astray by the twin influences of William Comb - 'an old offender and expert lock picker' - and his highly educated, mischief-making associate, William Strang. But, for all her efforts, there was to be no change of heart at official level and Alexander Arthur too was among those two hundred convicts who departed aboard the *Mermaid* to embark upon a new life in Australia.

Five months later on Friday, 7 May 1830, the vessel reached New South Wales where she discharged her complement of passengers at Sydney Cove and this was the point where the lives of William Strang and Alexander Arthur took wildly divergent paths. Set to work as a medical attendant, Strang appears to have put his nose to the grindstone and endured his sentence with stoicism until he was granted his Certificate of Freedom in early 1836 which completely restored his rights as a free citizen and allowed him to relaunch his life while he was still in his mid-twenties. In stark contrast, after he stepped ashore from the *Mermaid* Alexander Arthur was put to work as a blacksmith but it was only a matter of weeks before he absconded and stowed away to Liverpool aboard the brig *Pacific* alongside 'a cargo of colonial produce'. At the end of the five-month voyage, he succeeded in making his way back to Scotland where he settled down in Dalkeith under the alias of Thomas Winter, but by autumn of the following year the authorities had tracked him down and he found himself arrested and charged with unlawfully returning from transportation. At the High Court he had little option but to plead guilty and this time round he was sentenced to transportation for life. After spending several months on the hulk *Ganymede* on the River Thames in East London, he was among the 222 transportees who set sail on the *Katherine Stewart Forbes* bound for Van Diemen's Land - present-day Tasmania - in February 1832. Although he survived a cholera outbreak that claimed the lives of thirteen of his fellow passengers, he only lived for three years afterwards himself and died in January 1835 in an infirmary and asylum for sick convicts at New Norfolk in south-east Tasmania. Listed in the burial register as an invalid, he was still in his twenties at the time of his death.

John Adam
Millbuie, Ross & Cromarty - April 1835

When word of the whole tragic affair got out, there were of course questions to be answered. Who was he, this John Adam - traced, arrested and locked behind bars? And what kind of a man might he be? No-one could deny that he came with a chequered past and for what we know of his early years we are largely indebted to Rev. Francis Cannan, minister of his home parish of Lintrathen, Angus. By the clergyman's recollection, John was an 'obliging' child, 'free from malice', but who was also known for 'concealing the truth and fabricating lies to escape the lash of the teacher' - not so very different, you might think, from the majority of his fellow schoolboys. Following his father's untimely death, during his mid-teens, he became responsible for working the small farm of Craigieloch, supporting through his efforts his widowed mother and younger siblings. A few years later, however, Rev. Cannan detected a change. According to the minister, 'a passion for women' bubbled to the surface when John developed an 'uncommon faculty of flattering the female sex', embarked on a variety of love affairs throughout the district and formed the habit of rising late in the mornings. Responsibility for running the farm fell increasingly to his more sober younger brother, James, and in 1825 John left Craigieloch under a cloud to take up employment as a ploughman at Newbarns farm, a few miles from Forfar.

But actions invariably lead to consequences. In June of the following year (1826) his 21-year-old cousin, Margaret Ogilvy, gave birth to an illegitimate daughter and when questioned before the kirk session she cited John Adam as the child's father. Deaf and unable to speak, Margaret gave her answers by signing which was then interpreted by her parents. Confronted with her allegation, Adam flatly denied any involvement but when another Lintrathen girl, sixteen-year-old Betsy Eason, produced a baby son the following month this time he chose not to dispute the boy's paternity. Both of these children, it was said, bore a striking resemblance to their father. In line with established custom, Adam was automatically deemed liable for the upkeep of both mothers and children but, in order to shirk his responsibilities, he chose instead to fly the coop overnight. And if the Rev. Cannan is to be believed, these two instances were only the tip of the iceberg. By the minister's way of it, John Adam conducted a good number of liaisons and yet, for all that, he remained 'a favourite with the young women of the district'. Apparently, the early onset of baldness did nothing to diminish his appeal but, whatever his secret, when he turned up as a farm servant at Cairnbank estate in 1827 the assistant cook, Jane Brechin, was the next woman to fall under his spell.

With her family's roots delving deep into the local countryside, Jane had been born in August 1788 at Upper Craighill, Kincardineshire, the daughter of farm worker Robert Brechin and his wife, also Jane. At a time when education was generally considered low priority for working-class girls, in common with many others from a similar background she entered employment as a housemaid, working her way up through her efforts to her current post at Cairnbank, a large house and country estate near Brechin which was owned by a wealthy grain merchant, William Smart. Plumpish and plain, it is easy to understand the attraction from Jane's point of view, but for John, standing at a little over six feet tall and fifteen years her junior, we might suspect it was more a case of cupboard love as the cook eagerly topped up his rations in the farm workers' bothy. By then in her late-thirties, Jane was joshed by her fellow house-servants for falling for the charms of a mere 'laddie', though, as things turned out, her dreams of a happy future evaporated when Adam disappeared overnight with no reason given.

What became of Adam in the years that followed his speedy departure from Cairnbank? Details vary between scattered, verifiable facts and material verging on the mythological. He was said to have spent time in Aberdeenshire where he took on casual farm work, supplementing his small income with the proceeds of petty crime. His engagement to a young woman at this time allegedly gave rise to a curious incident, as he would later recount. A few days before the wedding was due to take place, he recalled that he had a dream in which his fiancée hovered over his bed in the shape of a beautiful dove and he heard the following words - 'John, we are not to be married; my time in the world will be very short. You are to die an awful death, but you and I shall be happy in the world to come.' As he approached her house the following evening, he claimed to have heard the singing of psalms and, peering through the window, saw a body laid out on a bed surrounded by mourners. The corpse, he quickly realised, was that of his fiancée. What this bizarre episode, subsequently related in various forms, indicates about Adam's state of mind - or more likely his loyalty to the truth - we can only speculate but undoubtedly the dream (if ever there was one) gave him the excuse he needed to bolt once again and free himself from whatever responsibilities he left in his wake.

A good deal easier to verify, however, is the fact that he had not given up on his amorous ways. Church records testify that he fathered a son, also John, at Chapel of Garioch, Aberdeenshire, in November 1830. Yet again he absconded, leaving the child's mother, Janet Laing, in the lurch, burdened with sole responsibility for her baby son's upbringing. This time Adam fled to Glasgow where early in the new year of 1831 he enlisted as a Private in the 2nd Queen's Dragoon Guards. In an effort to escape his past he cited as his next-of-kin a fictitious brother, Isaac Adam, living at Kirkintilloch, Lanarkshire - though clearly his knowledge of the local geography left a little to be desired since the town in question was in fact located not in Lanarkshire, but rather Dunbartonshire. During the next fourteen months the Dragoons were stationed variously at Manchester, Leeds and York before being ordered north to Edinburgh in spring 1832 where they remained for the following year. In November 1832 Adam was granted leave to visit his family at Craigieloch and it seems he took the opportunity at this same time to call in on his old admirer at Cairnbank. Despite being abandoned four years earlier, we can only assume that Jane Brechin was generous enough to forgive and forget since it is thought that she offered to fund his discharge from the army. Although Adam chose not to accept, the two agreed to keep in contact by letter. On Jane's part it turned out to be a great mistake.

In April 1833 the Dragoons' stay at Edinburgh came to an end and the regiment embarked on a three-week march south to Nottingham where Private Adam was assigned the duty of guarding the Law Courts at Derby, fifteen miles to the west. For convenience he was accommodated at the Red Lion Inn on Canal Street and it was here on Christmas Day of 1833 that he first set eyes on Dorothy Elliott, the teenage daughter of a local lead-miner, who was employed as an assistant cook. Clearly there was an instant attraction and within a matter of weeks romance appears to have blossomed. A mere three months after their first encounter John Adam turned up at the Red Lion, kitted out not in his usual uniform but in civilian garb, and broke the news to Dorothy that he was about to be discharged from the army and had come, so he said, to ask her to marry and return with him to Scotland. In an effort to overcome her natural trepidation, he gave his word that they would stop off at Sheffield, the first halt on their journey north, where their wedding ceremony would take place. Speed was of the essence, he urged Dorothy, and advised that if her parents were to raise any objection to their daughter's abrupt departure then she should tell them that her marriage to Adam had in fact already taken place. What he did not disclose was that he had lied about being discharged from the Dragoons, and the truth was that he had deserted with stolen money to the tune of £60.

When Dorothy agreed to leave Derby she effectively surrendered control of her own life and placed her future squarely in the hands of John Adam. Pressure of time, so it seems, prevented them from being married at Sheffield as they pressed north, conveyed by a succession of stagecoaches via York, Edinburgh and Perth until they were finally set down at Forfar and covered the last twelve miles to Craigieloch on foot. By this stage we may be certain that John had come clean regarding his desertion because Dorothy was introduced to his family as his lawfully-wedded wife whose well-heeled parents, he explained, had bought him out of the army and set up their daughter and new son-in-law with a healthy bank balance to begin their married life. But unsurprisingly his family were not the only ones at Lintrathen to take a keen interest in Adam's reappearance. Rumours circulating concerning his new-found wealth did not escape Betsy Eason's relations and they immediately set their sights on recouping eight years' worth of unpaid alimony. Confronted with the fact of his illegitimate son, Adam refused point-blank to accept responsibility and as a result was placed under arrest by order of the local Sheriff. Effectively backed into a corner, he eventually agreed to make a down payment of £20 to be followed up in due course with regular maintenance payments until his son was old enough to become self-supporting. A meeting was called to conclude the agreement in writing but even before the ink had dried, so the story goes, Adam took the legal document and in a dramatic gesture tore it to shreds. This being Sunday, it was not possible to contact the Sheriff and by the following morning the birds had flown. Adam and Dorothy had fled overnight, it was generally believed on a stagecoach back to England. What his actions say about his sense of responsibility or level of human decency is a moot point.

In the event, they opted not to head south but, in what can only have been an attempt to throw Betsy's relatives off the scent, they trekked north-west, crossing the Grampian hill-passes on foot before dipping down to the valley of the Dee. From here they followed the river upstream to Braemar where they took to the hills once more, bypassing the village of Tomintoul on the very fringes of the Cairngorm mountains. By the time they dropped down to the low country and struggled into Inverness, they had covered one hundred strenuous miles on foot in a matter of eight days. It is perfectly possible that they would have faced stretches of lying snow along the way, and what, if any, accommodation they could find we have no way of knowing. Previously accustomed to nothing more rugged than the thronging streets of Derby, what Dorothy made of it all we can only guess.

By then cash was running low and, out of his original £60, Adam was down to £10 in notes issued by provincial English banks which were not accepted by the wary shopkeepers of Inverness and it took the local branch of the National Bank of Scotland a whole fortnight to exchange these for Bank of England notes. When the money eventually came through, Dorothy and Adam resumed their northward trek, stopping fifteen miles and a ferry-crossing later at the town of Dingwall where, under the names of Mr and Mrs John Anderson, they found lodgings in the home of John Urquhart, a sawyer to trade, and his wife, Christian. The change of surname, Adam explained to Dorothy, was to help him dodge responsibility for yet another illegitimate child. In early May of 1834 Adam was taken on as a labourer at the Craig Quarry, north-east of Dingwall, on a wage of one shilling and sixpence a day. By no means a fortune, it was enough to keep the wolf from the door.

At least for a time. During the autumn work at the quarry dried up and Adam found himself laid off with no source of income. Positive references from his employer, David Sutherland, enabled him to pick up casual work here and there but it was a hand-to-mouth existence and he found himself struggling to make ends meet. Still no marriage took place and, amid (unsubstantiated) rumours of possible pregnancy, Dorothy steadily lost faith until finally she confessed her intention to leave Dingwall and return to her parents' home in England. Some say Adam dangled before her the prospect of their leaving the country together and emigrating to North America as man and wife. He had attempted to borrow money locally to fund the wedding and cover the cost of their passage, he claimed, but without success and now as a last resort he was prepared to return to Craigieloch in the hope that his mother and brother might help out. But if truth be told, there was no shortage of reasons for steering clear of his home turf. For one thing, there was little chance that Betsy Eason's relatives would have forgotten their grudge and, as if that wasn't cause enough, then there was also the unfinished business with Lintrathen Kirk Session. Finally - and probably most hazardous of all - he was well aware that the most likely place for an army deserter to be apprehended was in his own backyard.

So, if not his family, where else to turn? He knew from Jane Brechin's letters that she had left her job at Cairnbank in May of the previous year - 1833 - to open up a small grocery store in Market Street, Montrose - a major step up in the world for a girl from her humble background. Her new business prospered to the extent that within the next year or so she found herself in a position to deposit considerable sums of money in two major banks. Adam was confident that visiting his old flame would prove a profitable move, and all Dorothy need be told when he returned flush with cash was that he'd spent a fortnight with his family whose generosity had allowed him to pay the rent and attend to their immediate needs.

Giving Craigieloch as wide a berth as possible, he made his way south to Montrose where he turned up on Jane's doorstep and confessed his financial woes. Naturally kept in the dark about the existence of Dorothy Elliott, Jane fell anew for his legendary charm and showed willing once again to let bygones be bygones. Taking full advantage of her trust, Adam seized the moment to make a proposal of marriage. A second bite of the cherry was the last thing Jane had expected and her delight can be imagined as she joyfully accepted and the two settled down to plan for their combined future. A stranger to the truth as so often, Adam told her that he was currently in the final stages of establishing a small sawmill in the Inverness district and promised that they would be married once he had found conveniently located shop premises to allow her to carry on with her grocery business. Jane was a plain, stoutish woman in her mid-forties, her complexion scarred by smallpox, and the chances are she thought her time for romance had come and gone. At long last her patience was to be rewarded. Or so she thought.

In the days and weeks following his return to Dingwall, Adam was regularly to be seen haunting the local post office, eager for news from Montrose, but not until early February 1835 did a letter finally arrive which reassured him that his scheme was progressing to plan. The sale of Jane's grocery shop had been successfully completed, he read, and she was ready to join him in the north. As far as Dorothy was concerned, naturally a little explaining required to be done. A letter had reached him like a bolt from the blue, he told her, sent by an unknown solicitor to inform him that he was the beneficiary of a substantial bequest, left to him by an uncle on the West Indian island of Antigua, and that it was necessary to travel south to attend to the necessary legal paperwork. Dorothy was suspicious. Although she was barely able to read or write, the envelope's clumsy lettering did not strike her as the work of an educated professional, coupled with the fact that the envelope was postmarked not with the name of some great city but rather the modest east-coast town of Montrose. In spite of her misgivings, she said nothing.

Around the middle of the month Adam rejoined Jane at Market Street and for the next fortnight or so he shared her accommodation in the back-shop. Conscious that he had left Dorothy sorely in need, one of his first tasks was to send a £1 postal order back to Dingwall - presumably paid for with Jane's money and certainly without her knowledge. He had good reason to be concerned - records show that during his absence Dorothy had been forced to rely on poor relief. Back in Montrose the lease on Jane's shop expired at the end of February so she and Adam flitted to the small town of Laurencekirk, ten miles north, where they were temporarily put up by her (disapproving) mother and where their wedding was planned to take place. But they weren't done with Montrose quite yet. On Sunday, 8 March, they travelled back from Laurencekirk to attend a service at the parish church and hear their marriage banns announced. Although it was customary for banns to be read out on three successive Sundays, Adam paid a fee to shortcut the system and have them all taken care of on the one day. After the service Jane returned to her mother's house but Adam stayed on at Montrose, waiting for the banks to open for business at the start of the week. The task Jane had left him to carry out demonstrated her absolute faith in his integrity - or, maybe more likely, the depth of her infatuation. Either way, such was her level of trust that she was prepared to endorse with her signature the reverse side of two bank deposit slips and, by so doing, grant him access to her savings: £15-odds from the National Bank of Scotland; and not far short of £100 from the British Linen Bank. Astonishingly, all that Adam was required to do was to countersign Jane's two deposit slips. Wealthier to the tune of £15,000 in today's purchasing power, before leaving Montrose he made arrangements for items of her furniture to be transported north to Inverness where they would be placed in storage - a bed, two wooden trunks and a heavy chest of drawers. The truth, of course, was that Jane's furniture was destined not for some fictitious future marital home but instead for John and his common-law wife's use in Dingwall.

With his business satisfactorily attended to, more than likely Adam had a spring in his step as he strode to the premises of master tailor James Valentine to collect his wedding clothes - a splendid outfit consisting of a blue jacket adorned with gleaming gilt buttons; a smart waistcoat with contrasting red buttons; and, to complete the effect, a pair of plush fawn-coloured trousers. When the two men set off for a celebratory drink Valentine could not help noticing that his companion's wallet was amply stocked with banknotes - back pay, Adam explained, which he had been owed for some time. During the evening he returned to Laurencekirk where he presented his banns certificate to the parish minister, Rev. John Cook, who, with no reason to harbour any kind of suspicion, agreed to conduct the marriage ceremony. So, two days later - on Wednesday, 11 March 1835 - John Adam and Jane Brechin were made man and wife. As well as her mother, Jane's sisters and brother were present for the ceremony but none of Adam's relations. The reason is not hard to see: his family had already met his 'wife' at Craigieloch twelve months earlier, a girl more than two decades younger than Jane Brechin and whose accent betrayed her roots on the far side of the border.

The newly married couple left Laurencekirk for Inverness a few short hours after the wedding ceremony and following an overnight stop at Aberdeen they reached their destination the next afternoon after dark. Seeking accommodation, they were directed to Chapel Street where they arranged to rent a room in the home of Janet and Hector MacIntosh. Within hours of moving in there was still no let-up in Adam's schedule. He explained to Jane that he must leave very soon to catch a westbound stagecoach in order to finalise details in connection with their new home and shop premises on the shores of the Beauly Firth. Departing at around 9 p.m., he travelled not west as he had stated, but rather north, catching the Kessock Ferry across the straits linking the Beauly and Moray firths to rejoin Dorothy in Dingwall around midnight. Still wearing his wedding outfit, he explained that his new clothes had been bought with money inherited from his father. Furniture left to him by an elderly aunt, he added, would be delivered to Dingwall in the near future. Hearing of these multiple legacies, Dorothy must surely have smelt a rat, all the more so when the following morning he deposited a sum of £100 in the local branch of the National Bank. For reasons best known to herself she chose not to question him.

In the days and weeks that followed Adam embarked on a strange double-existence based on dishonesty and lies, during which he played off his lawful and common-law wives, one against the other. After a week with Dorothy, he travelled south to Inverness on Friday, 20 March, on his employer, David Sutherland's business, so he said. Arriving at Chapel Street, he told Jane that arrangements for their fictitious new home near the Scuddel Ferry were not yet finalised so she would need to remain in Inverness for a few weeks longer. He left that same evening, ostensibly to supervise the ongoing preparations, but in reality he caught the ferry back to North Kessock before continuing to Dingwall. Jane's landlady, Janet MacIntosh, could not help but notice a clear incongruity between her lodger's homely appearance and her young husband's handsome good looks, and she sensed a coolness on Adam's part and distinct lack of affection towards his new wife. His visits, she noted, were irregular and brief.

At Dingwall, on the other hand, John and Dorothy 'Anderson' had made a positive impression within the local community but, unbeknown to their neighbours, under the surface all was not well. Dorothy had recently detected a change in John's manner. He had grown preoccupied, sullen and morose, even on occasion aggressive - the effect, had she known it, of the stresses and strains of the double-life he was living. Increasingly unsettled, once again Dorothy told him that she wanted to return to England and this time John appeared willing to assent, assuring her that their marriage would take place as soon as he rejoined her in Derbyshire. He managed, however, to persuade her to stay on at Dingwall for a few more weeks until May - from his point of view a satisfactory outcome. He was confident that his circumstances would have changed before the date arranged for her departure.

On Friday, 27 March, he took the Kessock Ferry again, this time south to Inverness where Jane was able to tell him that her furniture had been delivered from Montrose. Adam immediately arranged to have it taken by cart to South Kessock to be ferried from there to the north shore of the firth where it would stored at a local inn, so he told her, until their (imaginary) new home and shop premises were ready to be occupied. In reality he arranged for the furniture to be delivered to Dingwall but before it was loaded on to the cart, he was careful to check for any personal items that were unlikely to have belonged to an elderly lady - his alleged late aunt - and which might have sparked Dorothy's suspicions. On arriving at John Urquhart's house, he gave the carter, Robert Thomson, a dram and paid him a fee of five shillings as agreed.

On Friday, 3 April, Adam crossed the Beauly Firth to Inverness yet again, and broke the news to Jane that their marital home was fit for habitation at last. Their landlord at Chapel Street, Hector MacIntosh, expressed surprise as they prepared to leave at so late an hour - somewhere around five or six o'clock in the evening - but Adam explained that he intended to break the journey and spend a night en route to their new home. Sailing from South Kessock at 7 p.m., they were the ferryman Roderick MacGregor's final passengers of the day and had the boat entirely to themselves. Disembarking at the north shore, they trekked inland, climbing towards the high moorland ridge that divided the Black Isle down the middle and was known to local folk as the Millbuie. The two were last seen fading into the thickening gloom of an early spring night.

A week later, in the morning of Friday, 10 April, two women, Betty Gray and Peggy Stewart, were engaged in the task of replacing small fir trees, frost-damaged during the preceding winter, on a recently established area of woodland on the chilly heights of Millbuie. The women had brought along two children to act as helpers: Jane Stewart, their thirteen-year-old niece, and John Campbell, aged eleven, who, perhaps in an effort to warm up, left off from their work and entered the ruins of an old cottage.

The first thing that caught Jane's eye was a greenish-brown glove of fine kid leather lying discarded on the ground, then what looked like a scrap of black gauze, partly covered over by stones and rubble. Thinking the gauze might come in useful for dressing her toy doll, she bent over and tried to dislodge the material but found that it was stuck fast. She turned and called to the adults outside who, hearing her cries, came across and joined the children inside the ruined walls. One of the women took a turn at trying to tug the black gauze loose but it still refused to budge. A few paces away, a shoe could be seen protruding from the ground so she bent down to try and draw it free from the surrounding debris. Imagine her shock when she looked inside and saw what appeared to be a human foot, pallid and stiff. Horrified at the discovery, the women immediately sent off the two children to alert the nearest neighbour, William Forbes, who lived not far away.

There appears to be a little confusion about what happened next. The children, it seems, found William Forbes at home sitting by his fireside, but when told that scraps of clothing had been found in a ruin nearby, initially he was reluctant to leave the comfort of his home. His lack of urgency, it has been suggested, was down to the children's failure to mention the discovery of a dead body - a curious omission, to be sure, though it is possible that they themselves were not in full possession of the facts at this stage, shielded from the brutal reality by the two adults, Betty and Peggy. Whatever the reason, when Forbes was finally persuaded to leave home he sent for Alexander MacDonald, innkeeper of the nearby Halfway House, to accompany him. What is certain is that he knew enough by then to bring along a spade which, on entering the cottage, he used to remove stones and turf from where one of the four walls had collapsed inwards. As he continued to dig, a leg became visible, dressed in a grey stocking. But there was worse to come. As he lifted a large rock from the mound of rubble, the shape of a female face, battered and bloodied, surfaced from beneath. After replacing the stone, Forbes hurried from the scene to report his gruesome discovery.

Word was quick to spread. Forbes' companion Alexander MacDonald gave details to Colin Young, estate manager at Kilcoy Castle, who suggested that the parish minister, Rev. John Kennedy, be immediately informed. The local schoolteacher, Hugh Mackay, dispatched one of his pupils to carry the news to Dingwall, while Alexander MacDonald intercepted a carriage that happened to be passing, ferrying Sir Colin Mackenzie, the laird of Kilcoy, along the same route. After listening to the innkeeper's grim tale, Sir Colin undertook to notify the authorities on his arrival at Dingwall. Somewhere along the way he overtook Mackay's pupil and was consequently first to break the news. Meantime, back at Millbuie, the estate manager, Colin Young, reached the ruin at around 10 a.m. where he learned that some time earlier a local farmer, Roderick Morrison - with a small band of locals gazing agog - had taken it upon himself to remove the bloody stone to check whether he might recognise the dead woman's face. In the event, his questionable act proved to be wasted effort when he found himself looking down at the face of a stranger. At this point, estate officer Young took charge and ordered the removal of more debris, thus exposing the dead woman's bonnet and veil made from the same black gauze that had originally been spotted two hours earlier by the thirteen-year-old, Jane Stewart. As more rocks and soil were cleared, the dead woman was seen to be wearing on her right hand a green glove matching the one found earlier, while on the third finger of her left hand - often used at the time to denote marriage - there was a gold ring. On her undergarment were what appeared to be the initials IB, embroidered in red-coloured thread, and inside her small handbag - in the parlance of the time a 'reticule'- were fourpence in copper coins and a pillbox marked *J. Mackenzie, Chemist and Druggist, Forres* which contained two pills. Once he was satisfied that no more clues were to be found, Young arranged for the woman's body to be covered over again - 'lest dogs get at it' - pending the arrival from Dingwall of the Procurator Fiscal, Hugh Innes Cameron.

Accompanied by Sir Colin Mackenzie, Cameron arrived at the scene shortly after midday and immediately set about searching the ruin and its surrounding area for bloodstains, footprints or any other evidence but in the event he turned up nothing of any significance. Along with him were two doctors, William Hall and John Jones, who began a preliminary examination of the body while he himself interviewed witnesses. First to be questioned was Colin Young who was able to confirm that three large stones had been earlier removed from where they had been placed, presumably by the attacker, in a crude attempt to conceal the body from view. Next the innkeeper Alexander Macdonald stated that he had neither seen anyone in the vicinity of the ruin the previous evening nor been aware of any disturbance. When William Forbes' turn came to speak, he described for the Procurator Fiscal how the children, Jane and John, had turned up on his doorstep around 8 a.m. and how, accompanied by Macdonald, he had made his way to the ruined cottage where the two men had proceeded to unearth part of the woman's body. By the time the Fiscal's inquiries were complete and he felt free to authorise the corpse's removal, it had already been dark for several hours. While he had encountered no problems in building up a picture of events relating to her discovery, it was clear that he was no further forward in identifying the dead woman. In accordance with his instructions, at around 7 p.m. her remains were placed on a horse-drawn cart and carried the five or so miles to Dingwall where they were laid out in a council building pending further investigation.

In order to pin down the dead woman's identity it was essential to generate as wide a publicity as possible. The best method to achieve this in the early part of the nineteenth century was by using a 'handbill' - a printed notice designed for distribution by hand. Once the Fiscal had authorised a suitable document, he then co-opted the services of Robert Carruthers, proprietor of the *Inverness Courier*, with the result that by the evening of the following day (Saturday, 11 April) handbills containing details of the dead woman's appearance, clothing and the few small items in her possession had been printed and circulated throughout Easter Ross, the Black Isle and Inverness as well as more widely by means of the mail-coach network. Speed being of the essence, an attempt was made to distribute the bills in time for clergymen to read them to their congregations the following morning.

As it turned out, it was a tactic that paid off when Rev. Finlay Cook's service at East Chapel, Inverness, generated what looked like a promising lead. Reading from the handbill, the minister informed his congregation that the unknown woman had 'dark brown hair, mixed with some grey', was 'about forty years of age; 5 feet 7 inches high [and] stout in figure'. Her complexion was 'marked by small pox' and a scar could be seen running diagonally across her left cheek. Her clothing, the minister continued, was very dark in colour. (In fact, the handbill described her various garments as 'black' five times in all.) An exception was her gloves which were 'of green kid [leather]'. As they listened to the minister's words, it struck two members of the congregation in particular, Hector and Janet MacIntosh, that the dead woman's appearance, as described from the pulpit, was a remarkably close match to their former lodger in Chapel Street whom they had known as Mrs John Adam. That same afternoon MacIntosh and his wife approached John Macbean, the Inverness Messenger-at-Arms, to report their suspicions. They were able to correct one small but significant detail. The initials embroidered on the woman's undergarment were not IB, as had previously been thought, but rather JB. Their lodger's maiden name, they had been led to believe, was Jane Brechin. In addition, there were able to give a detailed description of their lodger's husband, the man who had come and gone periodically from their house in Chapel Street.

The information they provided turned out to be crucial in establishing a link between John Adam of Inverness and John Anderson of Dingwall, and the description they gave - echoed by their neighbours, James and Ann Anderson - was enough to enable Sheriff's Officers in Dingwall to identify Jane Adam's husband as John Anderson who lived with his 'wife', Dorothy, in the town's Main Street. Sometime around midnight on Sunday, 12 April, Adam was roused from sleep, handcuffed and summarily marched to be imprisoned in the local tolbooth. Following his arrest, his room was searched and a number of garments were found initialled with the letters JB, and £74 in banknotes that had been stashed beneath his pillow. Questioned further, he maintained that his surname was Anderson, not Adam, and that Dorothy was his spouse.

Taken to view the corpse, he insisted that Jane Brechin was previously unknown to him, let alone his lawfully wedded wife, but his claim was insufficient to stand on its own. As a test of his sincerity, a curious old ritual was put into effect, sometimes known as 'ordeal by touch' or 'bier-right'. As reported in sections of the press, Adam was directed by the Procurator Fiscal, Hugh Cameron, to take Jane's hand in his own and declare whether he had ever held it there before. He stated that he had not. 'Place your hand on that bosom,' the Fiscal continued, 'and say, before these persons, and your God, did your head ever rest on it?' 'No, it did not,' came the unhesitating response. 'Touch those faded lips,' Cameron continued, 'and say did yours ever meet them in a kind embrace?' 'No, no!' Adam cried, sweating heavily by then and showing unmistakeable signs of distress. There is a degree of uncertainty as to how this episode was brought to a close. 'Very well,' the Fiscal was believed to have said. 'We are all in the presence of God, who knows best.' John Adam's ordeal was possibly (but not undoubtedly) the last occasion in Scotland when a suspect was subjected to this harrowing ritual in its entirety, designed to enable those observers present to base their conclusions not only on his words but also his actions and facial expressions.

Among the various potential witnesses brought to Dingwall were Hector and Janet MacIntosh who, shown Jane's body, immediately recognised their former lodger and they had no hesitation in identifying the prisoner John Adam, still under lock and key, as her husband. On Thursday, 16 April, Adam was transferred (via the same Millbuie hill-track, as it happened) to the tolbooth of Inverness where he was picked out in an identity parade by Jane Brechin's cousin, Margaret, and her husband, Colin Munro. Remarkably, they had recognised Jane from her description in Fiscal Cameron's handbill after its content was broadcast at Montrose. Arriving by stagecoach a day later, Jane's brother-in-law, Archibald Gauk, confirmed that he had been present at her wedding to Adam at Laurencekirk a month earlier. Tightly cornered, the evidence continued to pile up against him. The Procurator Fiscal of Montrose, Robert Burness, forwarded two bank slips, each bearing his signature, which he had used to plunder Jane Brechin's accounts. When two of his former army colleagues, Sergeant James Bleakley and Private Joseph Collier, were brought to Inverness tolbooth they instantly recognised him as a deserter from the Dragoon Guards. He appeared relaxed in the two men's company, so it was said, shook hands cordially with each and inquired after his old comrades. (Despite the cheerful familiarity with which he had greeted his guests, he would later assert that never at any stage had he enlisted in the army at all.) A curious anecdote survives from this time telling of an unnamed man who visited Adam's cell, claiming to have been a guest at his wedding. 'Oh John! I am sorry to see you here,' he apparently said - 'Don't you know me?' Adam replied that he did not. The jailer raised the prisoner's cap to give the stranger an unobstructed view of his face but apparently there was no need. 'Dinnae dae that,' said the nameless man - 'I ken him well eneuch.' At that, the wee story fades out, its protagonist never at any stage named.

When Dorothy's turn came to be questioned, she recounted in her statement how late one night in March Adam had arrived home from Inverness, dressed in a new suit of clothes and with £100 in his wallet - his share, he had told her, of his father's legacy. He was 'stiff and tired' from walking quickly and hefting a bulky basket. Among its contents she remembered a tea caddy, an umbrella, a pair of partly-knitted socks (a little odd, she thought at the time) and a number of articles of women's clothing, some embroidered with the letters IB. His late aunt's surname, Adam explained, had been Burns. Though dubious, Dorothy asked no questions, suspecting he had picked the goods up cheap at some or other event such as a pawnbroker's sale. Several pieces of his aunt's furniture were still to be delivered, Adam said, and in the days that followed she remembered him travelling from Dingwall to Inverness more than once to check whether the furniture had arrived. Dorothy had her suspicions, yes, but she had no idea at the time of the grim significance of these objects and events - nor indeed their connection with the shocking news that broke some weeks later in connection with the discovery of a body on the heights of Millbuie. Folk were saying, Adam told her, that the dead woman was thought to have been the wife of a shepherd. Though Dorothy was nominally literate, when she had given her account of events the Procurator Fiscal noted at the foot of her declaration that 'she is at present so agitated that she cannot sign her name'.

During the last week of May Dorothy paid a visit to Adam's cell and, in what must have been a moment of great poignancy, the couple formally shook hands. Dorothy broke down, unable to contain her distress, and Adam attempted to pacify her, expressing confidence in his likely acquittal and assuring her that all would turn out well. After composing herself she suggested to him that it might have looked less evasive if he had admitted his marriage to Jane right from the outset but he replied that the moment for that had passed and there was nothing to be done now. Revealing an unexpected touch of humanity, he asked Dorothy how she was coping money-wise and whether she had anyone she could depend upon. She reassured him that the Provost of Dingwall - the Fiscal, Hugh Innes Cameron, as it happened - had taken it upon himself to ensure that she was adequately provided for. (It seems she chose not to mention the fact that she had also been in receipt of poor relief: Dingwall Kirk Session records list two payments, each for five shillings, which were made to 'Mrs Anderson from the south... in distress'.) Hearing that her circumstances were tolerable, Adam appeared relieved, crying, 'Oh! As soon as the trial is over, I shall join the regiment with which I was connected.' (The regiment, that is, he had denied ever being associated with.) Clearly it was a forlorn hope. Before she got up to leave, Dorothy assured him that she would continue to ensure that he had clean clothes to wear. 'John, I forgive you for what you have done to me,' she told him - 'May the Almighty forgive you.'

But concerning the death of Jane Brechin, his resolve showed no sign of weakening. Despite the accumulated weight of evidence, he still refused to give ground, consistently asserting his innocence and insisting that he had an alibi up his sleeve, a claim that would never be substantiated. The official statements he had made at Dingwall - in legal terminology 'precognitions' - had been a bizarre concoction of half-truth, fabrication and fantasy, and following his transfer to Inverness he continued in the same vein, insisting that his name was John Anderson - and that John Adam, whoever he might be, was a person unknown to him. A razor was found among his clothing, giving rise to fears of suicide, so his legs were shackled, guards posted in his cell and a candle kept burning all night. But ever so gradually things started to change. He was often to be seen poring for long periods over the Bible, and when he complained of the discomfort his iron fetters caused him, by then he had earned sufficient trust for them to be removed, allowing him to stretch his legs and participate in games of pitch-and-toss with fellow inmates. In what looked like a positive step, he indicated that he wished to revise his earlier statements and while the version of events he came out with now was by no means one hundred per cent accurate, undeniably it approximated a good deal more closely to the truth than its predecessor had. For the first time he was prepared to admit to his true identity and acknowledge Jane Brechin as his wife, claiming he had been unable to recognise her corpse in its mangled state. Credible or otherwise, the crux of the matter remained unaltered when he continued to deny any involvement in her killing.

At ten o'clock in the morning of Friday, 18 September, John Adam entered the dock at Inverness High Court: thirty-one-years old, tall and well-dressed but apparently not sporting the wig he was accustomed to wearing. The charge he faced was one of murder and his future would be determined, however long or short it turned out to be, by fifteen male jurors, all prosperous local citizens. In response to doubts regarding the exact date of Jane Brechin's death, the terms of the indictment had been left deliberately vague. Despite her having been seen on Friday, 3 April, by her landlord at Chapel Street and by the Kessock ferryman, Adam was charged with having committed her murder 'on or about the 30th day of March 1835, or on or about the 6th day of April 1835, or on one or other of the days of these months, or of February immediately preceding, or of the May immediately following, the particular day being to the Prosecutor unknown'. Such a sweeping timescale granted the prosecution a generous latitude in marshalling its evidence - not only that but, whether by accident or design, it made cooking up a convincing alibi a good deal trickier for Adam. Asked how he pled, he replied firmly Not Guilty.

The reality was that he had left his lawyer, James Crawford, a major mountain to climb. Despite a degree of haziness concerning specific dates, the prosecution had no trouble amassing a weight of evidence based on the testimonies of an array of witnesses who ranged from the Millbuie tree-planters (who addressed the court in their native Gaelic) to the landlords of Mr and Mrs John Adam in Chapel Street, Inverness, and respectively Mr and Mrs John Anderson in Dingwall. The two doctors, Hall and Jones, who had conducted a post-mortem of the murder victim's corpse were next to be quizzed. The Laurencekirk Church of Scotland minister, Rev. John Cook, took his turn as did the Kessock ferryman, Roderick MacGregor; Robert Thomson, a Black Isle carter; an Angus farmer, Archibald Gauk, and his wife, Margaret; two bank cashiers from Montrose; plus various other witnesses which brought the total to twenty-four in all. In a moment of high drama two stones were displayed before the court which had been found, crusted with dried blood, beside the dead woman's body and whose shapes corresponded precisely with wounds inflicted on her head. One rock in particular was of colossal proportions, weighing some two stones.

For the defence, the best that James Crawford could do was to call upon David Sutherland, Adam's employer at Craig Quarry, who described him as 'a steady, industrious and sober man... harmless and inoffensive'. But, despite Crawford's best efforts, it was simply not enough. At the end of proceedings lasting more than fourteen hours the men of the jury retired at half-past midnight to consider their judgment. Every second of their absence must have been excruciating for the man in the dock until they returned to the courtroom at 1.15 a.m. where, asked by the judge, Lord Moncrieff, for their verdict, the jury's spokesman, Colonel John Munro, replied that unanimously they found the prisoner guilty of murder as charged. Hearing their decision, John Adam understood full well that his fate was sealed and, barring some miraculous intervention, he had only a few weeks left to live. From the bench Lord Moncrieff warned him against pinning his hopes on a possible reprieve. 'The Prince of Darkness took advantage of you,' he told him bluntly.

During his final month in jail Adam was visited by various clergymen, the most regular being Rev. Alexander Clark of the Old High Church, all of whom urged him to confess but, in spite of their appeals, he remained intransigent. Another frequent visitor was the headmaster of Raining's School nearby, Ebenezer Davidson, to whom Adam apparently recounted a lurid version of the dream in which his deceased fiancée in Aberdeenshire had paid him a night-time visit in the form of a dove. The stolid Davidson, it seems, was unimpressed. During his time alone, Adam devoted his energy to putting together his own account of recent events, for the most part yet another assertion of his innocence but also this time an attempt to discredit the witnesses who had testified against him. The phrase 'false oaths' features no fewer than half a dozen times, side by side with a liberal sprinkling of expressions such as 'falsity', 'false evidence' and 'false witness'. The document in its entirety appeared in the *Inverness Courier* on Wednesday, 14 October - two days before the date set for his execution - but it seems unlikely to have convinced many of the newspaper's readers of his innocence.

Adam's two brothers, James and William, had been seen in the public gallery during his trial and when they visited him afterwards in the tolbooth the mood, we may imagine, would have been sombre. Some days after their departure Adam received a letter from Craigieloch in which James urged him to make a clean breast of his crimes and devote what time he had left to preparation for the hereafter. But James was whistling in the wind, no more successful in his objective than the various clergymen who visited his brother in jail. On the same day as his article appeared in print, Adam sent a letter to Dorothy - written, according to town gossip, partly in his own blood - and the following day, the eve of his execution, in an emotionally-charged encounter she visited his cell in the company of Rev. Clark to take her final farewell. In spite of her tearful entreaties, Adam refused to budge. Immediately after she left in a state of great distress, Adam turned to Rev. Clark, saying, 'Oh, tell her to beware of bad company'. Simply good advice? Or perhaps as close to a confession as he would come.

Against the odds Adam slept soundly overnight and disposed of a hearty breakfast the following morning. Before putting on the black coat provided, he arranged for his own clothes, precious items in those straitened times, to be given to a fellow prisoner, John Sutherland, a housebreaker and thief with whom he had become close whilst awaiting his doom. (It has been suggested, albeit without evidence, that Sutherland was the only man to whom he ever confessed his guilt.) When it was time to leave, he indicated to town officials that his preference would be to make his final journey on foot but so thick were the crowds of spectators - an estimated 8,000 in all - that his wish could not be granted and coach travel was the only viable option. Throughout the mile-long journey, he remained calm and composed but continued to deny any involvement in Jane Brechin's death. From the scaffold he turned to face south, prompting some to speculate that he did not wish to die with the prospect of the Moray Firth laid out before him and the dark Millbuie ridge looming beyond, while others, more cynical, suspected instead that he was looking back towards the town, hoping against hope that a last-minute reprieve might be on its way. A psalm was sung and a final prayer offered up. But the seconds steadily ticked away and by the time Rev. Clark's voice fell silent Adam seemed to have become resigned to his fate and turned to the clergyman, asking to be remembered to his mother and family at Craigieloch. Then with total composure, even a shred of dignity, he released the white handkerchief that acted as a signal to the hangman who immediately drew back the bolt and sent him plummeting to his death.

So, his story finally at an end, what are we to make of the murderer John Adam? When his head was examined shortly after death, phrenologists (believers that its shape and form could reveal personality traits) found nothing good to say about him. Irrespective of their methods, who today would disagree with their conclusions? Plausible and predatory by nature, a self-seeking seducer and persistent liar, there seems no doubt that he was deficient in empathy and untroubled by remorse. His crimes were inexcusable, his dishonesty unatoned for, and he died without apology. During the course of his adult life, he had shown no qualms about leaving a trail of female misery in his wake, maybe more than we know: young women, abandoned pregnant and without support in an unforgiving, moralistic age. His greatest victim by far was poor Jane Brechin: a plain, middle-aged woman, conscious that life and happiness were passing her by, whose credulity and insecurity he preyed upon for his own selfish gain. His wickedness knew even greater depths when, in a premeditated act of brutality, he violently took her life on the lonely heights of Millbuie. Her final moments scarcely bear thinking about.

The only possible exception to Adam's heartless callousness was his fondness for Dorothy Elliott - an impressionable girl in her teens, dazzled by his charm and taken in by his lies, but for whom he appeared to feel genuine affection. Be that as it might, the warmth of his feelings did not prevent Dorothy too from being added to the list of his victims, left far from home to cope with trauma, distress and the gruesome outcome of his crimes. Whether she ever returned to England we have no way of telling.

Malcolm Macleod
Bayble, Isle of Lewis - January 1838

There can be no doubt that nineteenth-century Scotland was a devout and God-fearing place, nowhere more so perhaps than the scattered crofting communities on the Isle of Lewis. So, when Isabella Macleod called on her daughter in the village of Bayble during the afternoon of Saturday, 27 January 1838, and found the door locked, she turned away quietly, imagining that Henrietta might be engaged in prayer and prefer not to be disturbed. Returning some time later, however, she grew a little concerned when she found the door still fastened, so, knocking loudly, she called out her daughter's name. When the door eventually opened, it was not Henrietta who answered but her son-in-law, Malcolm Macleod. There was a long moment of silence before he finally spoke up. 'Henrietta has nothing to say now,' he told her, 'she cannot speak.' And in the minutes that followed Isabella would be confronted with the tragic reality that her daughter would never speak again.

When she stepped inside, Isabella found her lying motionless on a bed in the inner room. It was only when she reached out and touched her that the penny finally dropped. Turning to Macleod in shock, she uttered the words - 'Henrietta is dead.' The news travelled quickly through the small community of Bayble and, hearing of the tragedy, Henrietta's brother, Roderick Macleod, hurried to his sister's bedside where he found her still warm to the touch. 'It will be a great loss to me,' he said quietly.

Instantly on the defensive, Malcolm Macleod responded by saying that the greater loss by far would be his own. When Henrietta lay down, he explained, she had appeared perfectly well and everything was as normal. Patting his distraught mother-in-law on the shoulder, he added, 'You know I was good to her.' Roderick Macleod, for one, knew no such thing and, when he examined his sister's body more closely, he noticed scratches on her face and cheeks and around her mouth. Traces of blood were visible on her teeth. The conclusion he drew was instantaneous and damning. Looking his brother-in-law squarely in the eye, he told him, 'As sure as Henrietta is dead, you will die also.'

Malcolm Macleod and Henrietta had been married in the spring of 1829, and in the nine years that followed she gave birth to three children, all of them sons. For a time Macleod worked as a schoolmaster and, in order to be qualified to teach classes in Gaelic, he undertook a course of study at Stornoway where his tutor, Rev. Mackenzie, remarked on his 'mild and gentle disposition'. The minister's assessment of his character was by no means unique: Macleod's neighbours at Bayble recalled 'from his schoolboy days... his patient endurance of injuries', and described him as having a 'temper[ament] quite the reverse of irritable'. Within the local community he was noted for great piety, and certain individuals were in the habit of coming to him for private religious instruction. On the face of it then, Macleod came across as a dedicated family man who worked hard at the fishing and in the harvest field to support his wife and sons. Unfortunately, though, there was a good deal more to his character than that and, with the passage of time, it became increasingly obvious that something had gone badly wrong.

For a start, deep divisions opened up between Macleod and his wife. He detected what he interpreted as her growing coolness towards him, while, for her part, Henrietta confided in her sister, Catherine, that Macleod had begun to ill-treat her. She voiced deep concern about what the future might hold and, as if to confirm her fears, a series of bizarre incidents followed soon after. On one occasion Macleod forced her on to her knees to swear on the Bible that she had never been unfaithful to him. Another time she had been using a knife to peel potatoes - an ordinary, everyday task - when he laid hold of her, demanding to know who the knife belonged to. She warned him to stay back or he might cause himself an injury - but his reading of the situation was different entirely. By his way of it, Henrietta had brandished the knife and threatened to stab him and, so strong was his conviction, that he insisted on summoning two church elders to act as witnesses. Known for her good character and gentle nature, Henrietta's denial was accepted without question, and it was left to the elders to convince Macleod that his wife had meant him no harm. Their efforts, however, met with limited success when sometime later he claimed that he had been wakened in bed by the pressure of his wife's elbow, pushing down against his chest. Convinced once again that she was trying to kill him, he ejected her and her youngest child from the house. Upset and bewildered, Henrietta sought refuge with her father where she remained for several days. Eventually she returned, bringing her sister for moral support, and - on the surface at least - she and her husband were reconciled.

On top of his marital problems, Macleod experienced a growing alienation from the church. This came to a head one Sunday when he rose to his feet during the sermon to lambast a visiting minister, Rev. Finlay Cook of Caithness, crying, 'I am tired of you, you devil!' He claimed later that his utterance was directed, not at the clergyman, but at Satan who had recently been tormenting him, and that in reality the words he spoke had been 'I am tired of you, you devil that is in me!' Either way, his outburst caused uproar and embarrassment, and it seems likely that Henrietta would have felt a degree of relief when he took the decision to absent himself from church altogether, reportedly through doctrinal differences with the minister. One of his objections was to a stone cross in the church which, in his eyes, smacked of Roman Catholicism. Refusing to be influenced by his opinions, Henrietta herself continued to attend. Meanwhile, his eccentricities grew ever more pronounced. He was observed one day working in the fields totally naked, an event that sent shockwaves through the rigidly Calvinist community of Bayble. On another occasion he wrapped himself up in a blanket that had previously been steeped in cold water, and wore it like a cape for the rest of the day as penance for the sins of his neighbours which, to his way of thinking, made the Isle of Lewis 'very dark'. His former teacher in Stornoway, Rev. Mackenzie, received a letter from him which the clergyman was startled to see had been written in blood. And as if that wasn't enough, Macleod constructed for himself his own wooden pulpit. Most peculiar of all, however, was an object that he also made from wood and took the form of a cartwheel within which he habitually knelt to pray. Studded around the rim were ten vicious spikes, each pointing upwards, and should he fall asleep and lean to one side while praying those particular spikes that injured his skin, he took to represent which of the Biblical Ten Commandments he had recently been guilty of breaking. Scars on his body corresponded with the positioning of the spikes.

Even outwith the sphere of religion, Macleod's behaviour grew ever more curious. He told his brother-in-law, Roderick, that he was on the verge of inventing a machine capable of perpetual motion; that is to say, able to operate indefinitely without an energy source. In this connection, he contacted Rev. Mackenzie at Stornoway, asking him to petition the local Member of Parliament on his behalf with a view to procuring a quantity of lodestone - magnetic iron ore - which he believed was essential to the success of the project. This lodestone, he argued, was the final component required to construct a boat that was able to sail, independent of wind or tide. 'It is a machine of such utility,' he told Mackenzie, 'I think it is the greatest loss that it should remain concealed, since it is so plainly discovered to me, and that as from the Lord.' It would later be alleged - albeit without much evidence - that he had been heard expressing the belief that, until such time as he had committed a murder, the success of the project would elude him.

Given the strained nature of Macleod's marital relations and his widely-known far-fetched beliefs, there was never any doubt in the minds of Henrietta's family as to who was responsible for her death. The sharp words that her brother, Roderick, directed at Macleod had made that perfectly clear. Realising the position he was in, Macleod slipped quietly out of the house and into the thickening darkness, travelling fifteen miles to his aunt's house at Shader on the west coast of the island. Soon after, he learned that he was being pursued so he fled then to the moor where he spent a cold and miserable night, hidden within a peat stack. The following evening he managed to creep into a hayshed where he passed a more comfortable night, but by morning he had come to accept the inevitable. After praying for a while, he set out for Stornoway with the intention of giving himself up. Six miles from the town, he caught sight of someone coming towards him and, ashamed to be seen, he turned aside and squatted in a gravel quarry, turning his back to the road and pulling his cloak over his head. Drawing alongside, the walker - Donald

Mackenzie, a local gamekeeper - paused and called out, 'Who are you? Are you asleep?', to which Macleod replied and said that he had been walking from Shader. 'Let me see your face,' Mackenzie told him, 'for I should know every person at Shader.' Following a brief further exchange, it emerged that the gamekeeper had come in search of Macleod and bearing a warrant for his arrest. Fatalistic now about his future, Macleod made no effort to resist and accompanied Mackenzie to Stornoway where he was duly passed into the hands of the authorities.

During the time he spent in jail he consistently appeared depressed and in low spirits. He showed great contrition for what he had done, saying that if he was in possession of a thousand worlds, he would sacrifice them all to bring Henrietta back to life. In time the whole sorry tale spilled out. On the morning of 27 January, Macleod recalled, an argument had flared between himself and his wife after she vented her frustration when he refused to go out to work. Hard words were exchanged until finally he capitulated, took up a creel and made his way to the hill to gather peats. The peat stack in question was a quarter of a mile from the house and, as he walked there and back, his mind was consumed with the premonition that tonight would be the night when Henrietta would strike to end his life. His belief was bolstered yet further when he arrived home to find that the tense atmosphere had not eased. He retreated to the barn where he thrashed corn to feed to the cattle and, his job complete, returned once again to the house where he found Henrietta unwell and taking medicine she had been given by a neighbour. Unable to settle, he went back to the barn and, when he came inside a third time, he saw Henrietta sitting by the fireside. Macleod explained that by then his mind was in a state of turmoil, and it came into his head that if he were to have any chance of living, then the plain fact was that Henrietta must die. With none of his children at home, he knew he would never have a better opportunity.

This was the point when Henrietta's fate was sealed. After making sure that the door was jammed shut with a stick, he seized hold of her, gripping her head with one hand while clapping the other over her mouth. All she managed to gasp out was a helpless plea - 'Let me alone!' - before he pushed her face-down on the floor. To prevent her from struggling, he pressed his knee against her back while at the same time twisting her shawl tighter and tighter around her neck until he saw blood oozing from her nose and mouth. Only once he was certain that all signs of life were extinguished did he relax his grip. The entire grisly operation, he estimated, had been completed within five or six minutes. Then, lifting Henrietta's body from the floor, he laid her flat on her back on top of the bed and, soaking a cloth in a pot of water, he used it to rinse the floor-dust from her face before drying it with a towel. He had only just finished when he heard Isabella's loud knocking at the door, so he tucked the pot and towel out of sight beneath the bed before answering. Although he was fully aware at the time of the attack that Henrietta was expecting their fourth child, he would later claim that in the heat of the moment the thought of this had never entered his head.

The two surgeons who carried out the post-mortem examination of Henrietta's body, Roderick Miller and Alexander McIver of Stornoway, were able to confirm that her injuries were consistent with Macleod's account of her death which had, they concluded, resulted from both suffocation and violence. The doctors further confirmed that she was six months pregnant. During the time that Macleod spent in jail awaiting trial, he sent two letters, both in Gaelic. The first was to his brother, Angus Macleod of Port Vallon, Stornoway, and from its style we might suspect it was the work of a man perhaps unaccustomed to writing letters. As well as containing a candid admission of guilt, it consisted largely of requests for his brother to settle a number of debts on his behalf of small sums owed to various local merchants and other individuals - including, rather poignantly, the thirty shillings due to 'Mr. Kenneth C. Shadder [sic] for the cow.' He finished by expressing the hope that the Lord would take care of his children, and signed off as 'Poor, poor, poor Malcolm Macleod'. The second letter was addressed to his brother-in-law, Roderick Macleod, tenant of Bayble. Again, he expressed great contrition, describing himself as 'a lost sinner, even the chief of the blackest of sinners'. 'I now confess with sorrow and shame,' he continued, 'the thing for which I am deserving of being in chains of darkness till the great day of judgment.' His principal focus was the welfare of his three children: 'I pray thee from the brink of Jordan, that you nor any other will impute my sins to my poor children; but that you will shew them mercy for the sake of the Lord, and that you will set a godly example before them in the days of their youth.' The letter specifically requested that the children should not in future be reminded of their father, and he asked Roderick to distribute his clothes among them: 'Send one of the blankets to each,' he wrote, 'and make use of the other few clothes according as they will suit.' He also told his brother-in-law that 'You may sell the crop and potatoes', and 'regarding the barley we bought at Aignish, you have the most part of it for the meal you sold.' The letter was signed by 'The poor wretch, Malcolm Macleod'.

After his frank and seemingly heartfelt confession, it may have come as a surprise when Macleod pleaded not guilty at his trial in Inverness on Saturday, 14 April. The reason was quite simple. Much of his defence's argument was to suggest that Macleod was subject to episodic bouts of insanity, and therefore at such times could not be held to account for his actions. Examples were cited such as his unorthodox religious practices; a letter written by him in blood; the fear that haunted him of his own wife. His cousin, it was revealed, was known to suffer similar periods of insanity which raised, the defence suggested, the possibility of heredity. The jury, however, was unconvinced. When the trial ended at nine o'clock in the evening, its members took a mere five minutes to return a unanimous guilty verdict. Before passing sentence, the judge, Lord Cockburn, addressed Macleod in sonorous tones. 'You have been guilty of murder in its last and most aggravated form,' he told him. 'You did not murder a male enemy in the heat of blood, or from the passion of revenge; you did not murder a stranger to your habits, your home, or your heart. You have taken away that life which you vowed before God and man to cherish and protect. You have taken away the life of your wife.' Regarding Macleod's future prospects Lord Cockburn pulled no punches: 'I have to tell you plainly - I would be your worst enemy if I concealed it - that you can have no hope of mercy from man. You stand doomed to death.' Urging Macleod to devote what time he had left to consideration of his place in the afterlife, the judge announced his sentence in the standard form of words: 'In respect of the foregoing verdict, I discern and adjudge you, the said Malcolm Macleod, to be carried from the bar back to the tolbooth of Inverness, therein to be detained and fed on bread and water only, till Friday, the 11th of May next, and upon that day, between the hours of eight and ten before noon, to be taken from the said tolbooth to the common place of execution of the city of Inverness, and there, by the hands of the common executioner, to be hanged by the neck upon a gibbet, until you be dead - which is pronounced for doom, and may the

Lord have mercy on your soul!' Hearing his fate spelt out, Macleod appeared unresponsive and rested his head upon his hands as he had throughout much of the trial.

As it turned out, Lord Cockburn's gloomy prognosis was a little premature. Following petitions to the Home Secretary, Lord John Russell, Macleod was granted two successive stays of execution pending further inquiries, during the course of which several doctors - including Alexander McIver - stated their conviction that he had been of unsound mind at the time of the murder. The Society for the Abolition of Capital Punishment, a small association based in London, became involved in his case and exerted what pressure it could. When various of his neighbours on the Isle of Lewis were questioned by an Inverness lawyer, they described Macleod as a mild-mannered man, easy-going under normal circumstances but who, they added, was 'of a visionary and abstracted turn of mind'.

The decision to establish an inquiry was vindicated when its findings were deemed to have raised sufficient doubt concerning Macleod's mental health for his case to be reviewed at the highest level. Following due process, a letter dated 1 June 1838 was received by the provost of Inverness, John Ferguson, from the Under Secretary of State in the Home Department in Whitehall. 'Following representations from various quarters which have raised considerable doubt as to [Malcolm Macleod's] state of mind,' the letter informed Ferguson, 'Lord John Russell has thought it right to recommend that the prisoner's life should be spared.' Given the weight of evidence - and in spite of Lord Cockburn's pessimism - it seems likely that many at the time would have viewed the Home Secretary's decision as the correct one. Instead of facing the rope, Macleod was ordered instead to be transported for life to New South Wales. In November 1839, he left his three small sons and the old Hebridean way of life behind when, along with 289 other convicts - nineteen of them Scots - he boarded the *Mangles*, with the prospect of a five-month voyage ahead of him and an uncertain future at the end of it.

David Patterson
Dolphinton, Lanarkshire - May 1838

When the General Assembly of the Church of Scotland convened in Edinburgh in May 1838, members of the Education Committee were addressed by Rev. Dr John Aiton of Dolphinton, Lanarkshire. The kirk had a legal responsibility, he told his audience, for monitoring the running of 'parochial and burgh schools' throughout the length and breadth of the land. Unless churches exercised a 'vigilant superintendence,' he warned, 'great evils might arise from their negligence.' Aiton's remarks were met with general approval but, as he returned to his seat, he could not have known just how prescient his words would prove to be. A mere two months later David Patterson, the parish schoolmaster at this same Dolphinton, was placed at the bar of the High Court, faced with a charge of culpable homicide. It was claimed that on Wednesday, 16 May, Patterson had seized an eleven-year-old pupil, James Forrest, and dragged him by the hair before throwing him with great force against a wooden bench and on to the floor. Grievous injuries to the child's head, spine and elsewhere on his body were believed to have been responsible for his death ten days later. If proved to be true, a more striking example of Rev. Aiton's 'great evil' would be hard to imagine. Patterson pled not guilty.

James' mother was the first witness called. In her opening evidence, she recounted events of 16 May, when James arrived home from school complaining of feeling unwell. He seemed weak and lethargic, she told the court, and showed no appetite for food. He took to his bed at seven o'clock that evening but woke up during the night, distressed and in a state of confusion, repeatedly begging her to keep Mr Patterson away from him. During a lucid interval he described for the first time the assault he had been subjected to, and told his mother bluntly that he believed his teacher had killed him. When his turn came to give evidence, the dead boy's father - also James Forrest - told the court how before 16 May his son had been in a normal state of health, had shown a good appetite, and had always been physically active. To demonstrate his point, Forrest described how the day before the alleged assault James had energy enough to give him a hand to load up a cart. Twenty-four hours later, he continued, his son had become frantic, agitated and barely coherent. During one of James' calmer interludes, Forrest told how he had sent for David Patterson to hear the schoolmaster's version of events, and he recounted the ensuing conversation for the court. Patterson had started off, he said, by claiming that he had 'only' taken hold of his son's head and 'given it a twist.' Listening from the sidelines, James was having none of that: 'That was on Monday,' he interrupted his teacher, 'but on Wednesday you took me by the hair of [my] head, and swung me around.' 'Whisht, boy,' snapped Patterson, 'tell no falsehoods.' But James was not to be silenced and immediately repeated his accusation. 'What state was I in?' demanded Patterson. 'Was I in a passion?' 'Yes,' replied James, 'but you know that best yourself.' Forrest explained to the court that, when his son showed no sign of improvement by Friday, 18 May, he had called in Dr Kelloe of Biggar and Dr Dickson of Edinburgh, but despite the two men's best efforts James passed away a week later on Saturday, 26 May.

Next to take the stand was a succession of James' classmates - three girls and two boys, ranging in age from eight to twelve. Asked to recall what had happened on 16 May, the children's accounts differed in some minor particulars, but all five were consistent in describing the teacher's treatment of James as violent, harsh and severe. His punishment, they said, had been meted out for the most trivial of reasons - one scarcely credible today. They told the court how, after reading a passage from *The History of England* (an odd choice, perhaps, for Scottish children in a Scottish school), Mr Patterson had begun to teach a lesson on spelling. When James Forrest was asked to spell the word 'stupefaction' - hardly a term in everyday use - he had begun to answer with the letters *'s-t-i...',* thus prompting Patterson's facetious response - 'You are a stupefaction!' - a puerile jibe that I am certain he did not expect to travel outwith the four walls of his classroom. Inexplicably, the schoolmaster had then lunged at James, grabbed him by his fringe and forced him down upon his back against a bench. Pressed for more detail, none of the schoolchildren could be sure of whether James had been lifted clear of the floor, but there was no doubt in any of their minds that he had been struck on the head and knocked down more than once.

The best defence that Patterson could muster took the form of the testimony of a seven-year-old child, Thomas Smith. The boy told the court how, a few days before James Forrest took ill, the two of them had gone to a nearby wood in search of beech nuts. As James clambered up through tangled foliage, a branch beneath him gave way with an alarming crack and he plunged to the ground, landing on top of a bare tree root where he lay in pain, according to Thomas, for the next half hour. Questioned about the height James had fallen from, the boy replied - with a suspiciously high degree of precision - that the branch was eight feet and nine inches above the ground, and went on to insist - unprompted - that he had never heard the matter discussed, seen the tree in question being measured nor been told its height. What the members of the jury made of the seven-year-old's reliability as a witness we might wonder. After the boy left the witness stand, the defence called upon two local ministers, Rev. John Wilson of Walston and - as luck would have it - Rev. John Aiton of Dolphinton, both of whom alluded to Patterson's 'mild disposition', and stated that in their opinion a violent act such as this was entirely out of character.

Dr. Kelloe, who had examined James on Friday, 18 May, testified that he had found swelling at the point where the spine met the pelvis, and he believed that such an injury was likely to have been caused by the assault as described by the preceding witnesses. He was willing to concede the point that a recent injury might be expected to display bruising but, more important than that, if it had been sustained any time earlier James could not have carried on with his everyday activities, never mind help to load a cart. Responding to a request from the Sheriff of Lanarkshire, two local doctors had carried out a post-mortem examination and, when questioned in court, both agreed that it was quite possible for the assault as described to have been responsible for the child's fatal injuries. They hedged their bets, however, when they accepted that these injuries might equally have been caused by a fall from a tree. Concluding their evidence, the two doctors made a point of ruling out the defence's suggestion that the inflammation detected on James Forrest's lungs could have resulted from exposure to the cold.

Once the jury had heard the testimony of all of the witnesses, its members retired and took a little more than half an hour to come to their conclusion. Returning to the courtroom, their spokesman announced that, by a large majority, they found the prisoner guilty of culpable homicide but, in acknowledgement of his previous good character, they recommended him to the mercy of the court. Prior to passing sentence, Lord Medwyn addressed the convicted man, highlighting the seriousness of his crime and its grievous impact on parents who, seeking to give their child the benefit of an education - not yet compulsory in Scotland - found his life cut short by the very person to whom he had been entrusted. The judge went on to say that, but for the jury's recommendation, he would have considered imposing a sentence guaranteed to prevent the prisoner from future offending *in this country* - an unmistakeable reference to transportation overseas - but in the circumstances he had settled instead on the more lenient punishment of an eighteen-month prison term in the jail of Edinburgh. And if Lord Medwyn's words were greeted with relief by the convicted killer, it seems equally likely that James Forrest's parents would have viewed his sentence as pitifully inadequate.

There are times, such as this, when nineteenth-century attitudes to crime and punishment are hard to fathom. The previous month - June 1838 - another prisoner tried at the High Court had been treated a good deal more harshly than David Patterson. The man in the dock in that case was one Thomas Brash who, convicted of 'stealing a handkerchief out of a gentleman's hat, in the upper gallery of the Theatre', found himself banished overseas for a term of seven years.

Christina Gilmour
Inchinnan, Renfewshire - December 1842

Thirty-year-old John Gilmour, farmer at Town of Inchinnan, had been married little more than a month when his health took a sudden downhill turn and he died in mysterious circumstances in January 1843. In the local area tongues wagged and, although in the weeks that followed suspicion fell increasingly on his young widow, it took Renfrewshire Rural Police until April to act on the rumours. Following initial inquiries, Superintendent George McKay secured a warrant for Christina Gilmour's arrest on April the 21st but it soon became clear that the bird had already flown.

A little over two months after her husband's death Christina Gilmour (née Cochran) had left her marital home and returned to her father's farm at West Grange near Dunlop, Ayrshire, where she stayed for some time until, seeing the shape of things to come, her family decided that drastic action was called for. By her own later account, she was taken from home against her will and, after a few days holed up in a house near Fenwick, passed from person to person as she was conducted on a lengthy journey to an unknown destination. Following her trail, Superintendent McKay's investigations led him first to Carlisle, then on to Liverpool where he learned that, after posting a letter to a former lover, she had embarked for New York aboard the sailing ship *Excel* in the company of an unknown man, travelling in separate cabins under the assumed names of Mr and Mrs John Spiers. A less determined officer might have conceded defeat, but not McKay. Booking a passage on a faster vessel, the Cunard steamer *Acadia*, he succeeded in overtaking Mr and Mrs Spiers mid-Atlantic and, after securing a warrant from the US authorities, boarded their vessel immediately before she docked at Staten Island on 21 June. When intercepted and challenged, Christina made no attempt to deny her identity and was taken into custody. In leapfrogging the *Excel*, Superintendent McKay had undeniably pulled off an impressive feat - yet, had he but known it, it was only just the start of his trans-Atlantic mission. For the record, the slippery Mr Spiers - a cash-strapped Ayrshire shoemaker by the name of Simpson - showed a clean pair of heels and vanished into the USA without trace.

Now turn the calendar back ten months to Christina Cochran's marriage to John Gilmour. The following account of events leading up to that occasion has been pieced together from newspaper reports of the time plus a number of other contemporary sources. As the eldest daughter of Alexander Cochran and his wife Margaret, prosperous farmers who owned their own land, it was evident throughout her early years that Christina's parents had ambitions for her future. She began her education at Dunlop parish school, an establishment attended by those possessing sufficient means, before moving on to attend boarding-schools at Glasgow and Paisley where she acquired among other skills the art of dressmaking. Her performance as a scholar was reported to have been satisfactory if not distinguished. During spells at home, she was by no means treated as a lady of leisure. Despite their comfortable circumstances, the Cochrans employed no house servants and Christina was expected to carry out her share of domestic chores - a custom she continued into her own marriage, as we shall see. Slim and fair-haired, she was generally viewed as attractive and, in terms of manner, she was described as being 'of a very mild, gentle deportment, with no violence of any kind about her'.

Though admired by several affluent young men in the district, Christina's preference was for a certain John Anderson, ten years older than herself and the son of a neighbouring farmer. He gave her reason to believe that her feelings were reciprocated but before he was financially in a position to formalise their relationship another farmer's son stepped forward. A few years closer to Christina's age, this second John - John Gilmour - was well educated and generally thought to have excellent prospects. He won her father's approval, and some have suggested that she only accepted his marriage proposal in the hope of forcing John Anderson to declare his hand. If indeed so, her ploy was singularly unsuccessful. When Anderson learned of her engagement it appears that he received the news surprisingly casually.

Christina reportedly went off the rails a little at this time. Her personality underwent a drastic change, it was said, and whereas formerly she had been of a bright and cheerful disposition she withdrew into herself and became gloomy and morose. She rose from her bed at strange hours and roamed throughout the house and, previously fearful of the dark, she wandered into the fields late at night. She began to neglect her appearance and allowed herself to overeat, driving her mother to place her on a strict dietary regime. It appears that she was still in correspondence with her first love and her marriage twice had to be postponed. Strangely, her spirits appeared to rise during her fiancé's visits and on two occasions she accompanied him to Paisley and Glasgow to purchase what were known to the country folk of the area as 'the braws', i.e. her wedding clothes.

It was assumed that once all communication with Anderson had ceased Christina's low mood would gradually pass, and indeed it was ultimately she herself who appointed the day for her wedding - Tuesday, 29 November 1842. Following the ceremony in Dunlop Kirk the newlywed couple, accompanied by one of Christina's sisters, left by carriage to take up residence at their new home - the farm of Town of Inchinnan, fifteen miles or so to the north, on which her new husband's father, Matthew Gilmour, had taken a lease. The wedding day had passed off smoothly and without incident, but when the farmhouse went quiet that night and the couple were left alone together things took a more unsettling turn. Nothing it appears could convince Christina to undress and come to bed and she reputedly spent the entire night huddled in a chair by the fireside. Trying to make sense of her actions, her new husband could only put her anxieties down to shyness or modesty. But, so we are told, it continued and it seems that the nights that followed saw no improvement. During daytime relations between husband and wife were courteous and respectful but, despite this, there must surely have been a great deal of tension bubbling below the surface. It was rumoured indeed that the marriage remained unconsummated. How these intimate details became known is unclear.

Twenty-one-year-old Mary Paterson had worked as a dairymaid at Town of Inchinnan since moving from John's father's farm at Dunlop at Whitsun 1842. On Boxing Day of that year John had been married for nearly a month when, just as Mary was preparing to leave on an overnight visit to her sister at Dunlop, his new wife buttonholed her and asked her to stop off on her way through Paisley to run a message on her behalf. Handing her a small sum of money, she asked her to call at a certain address where the inhabitants would send a 'callant' - a boy - to a chemist's shop nearby to buy arsenic for poisoning rats. (If Mary thought it a convoluted arrangement for making a simple purchase, then she chose not to mention it; as a humble farm servant it wasn't her place to question why.) As she passed through Paisley, however, the plan did not work out as intended. Mary didn't have her instructions in writing - she had never been taught to read - and when the address slipped her memory she decided to postpone her errand till the following day.

On her way back from Dunlop, she called at a chemist's shop in Paisley where she explained to the proprietor, Dr Vesey, the purpose of her visit. When questioned, she told him that the arsenic was for Mrs Gilmour, Town of Inchinnan farm, and was required for the purpose of killing rats. She was asked also to give her own name. Apparently satisfied, the druggist took Mary's money and wrapped the white powder in a small paper package which he marked clearly with the two words - 'Arsenic, Poison'. Back at the farm, Mary handed the packet over to Christina, explaining as she did so the reason why she had not followed her instructions to the letter but had bought the poison in person from Dr Vesey's shop in the town. When she went on to tell her that she had been required to provide the purchaser's name and address, Christina went silent. The following day something happened which Mary thought a little strange. She met Christina in the farm's boiler-house where she produced what appeared to be the same small paper package and immediately dropped it into the furnace directly in front of Mary, giving as her reason the fact that she was inexperienced in the use of poisons and had grown afraid that she might mishandle it and make some grievous mistake. When viewed with hindsight, it looks very much as though Christina made a deliberate point of ostentatiously destroying the packet in Mary's presence and, of course, there was no way Mary could have told whether or not it still contained the deadly powder.

Hitherto hearty and robust, John Gilmour's health took a sudden dip the following day - Thursday, 29 December - and New Year celebrations must have been distinctly muted at Town of Inchinnan while he remained unwell over the weekend. First thing in the morning of Monday, 2 January, he was violently sick but later in the day his spirits rallied sufficiently to allow him to fit out the horse and gig and drive his wife to Ayrshire to pay a New Year visit to their relatives. Passing through Paisley, John spotted one of his workers in the street - another Dunlop man, John Muir, currently making his way back to Inchinnan - and he pulled over to have a word with him. He told Muir about his illness, how he had been forced to endure bouts of painful retching with no clue as to the cause. Despite the date, Muir did not suspect for a second that his boss's ailment was the self-induced outcome of seasonal excesses since he 'knew him to be a sober man'. By the time John and Christina reached Dunlop, John's condition had worsened once again. Before travelling on to spend the night with his parents-in-law, he called at his own parents' home where his father could not help noticing that he was 'all swelled up about the chest'. Matthew Gilmour would later recall his son 'throwing up' several times during what was a relatively short visit. John returned for a couple of hours the following morning and again was overcome by 'a fit of vomiting'. Once he had adequately recovered, he and Christina left in the afternoon and drove back to Inchinnan.

At this stage he was not yet confined to bed. The next day - Wednesday, 4 January - he had a conversation with John Muir in the stable. His face, according to Muir, was 'a kind of swollen ways' and his eyes appeared watery: the result, Muir assumed, of his constant retching. He saw him later in the day, this time sitting at the kitchen fire and bringing up what Muir described as 'a kind of brownish stuff'. It was obvious to him that John's condition had deteriorated since their chance encounter in Paisley two days earlier. Muir was uneasy. Who could say what was taking place within the four walls of the farmhouse? Granted, John's younger brother, Matthew, came and went at intervals, lending a hand on the farm, and from time to time one of Christina's sisters would spend a few days at the farmhouse, but it had not gone unnoticed that the lady of the house kept no cook or maid and that she alone attended to cooking and preparation of food. The truth, in fact, was that in the week since ill-health had descended on John Gilmour a dark cloud of suspicion had steadily been forming over Town of Inchinnan. Sometime earlier, during a moment of indiscretion, Christina had given Mary Paterson reason for profound disquiet when she let slip that she had agreed to marry her husband only under duress and had then gone on to name John Anderson as the man she would have chosen if left to her own devices. Inevitably Mary's story had spread throughout the small community of farm servants though at this stage no-one felt in a position to speak out openly about his or her suspicions.

Friday, 6 January, was a day of comings and goings. Smartly dressed and carrying a small silk bag or 'reticule', Christina left the farm in darkness before 7 a.m., telling Mary that she intended to walk the two miles to Renfrew as 'she was wanting something to see if it would do any good to her husband'. She added that Mary need not mention to anyone else that she had gone. She did not spend long in the town and was back shortly after breakfast-time. Also out early was John Muir, thrashing (threshing) corn before daylight. Taking a break for breakfast somewhere between eight and nine o'clock, he passed through the boiler-house on his way to the kitchen but when he returned the same way after eating, something that had previously gone unnoticed caught his eye. Lying in a dark corner of the boiler-room was a black bag which he bent down to examine. When he lifted it up and looked inside, he saw a 'wee phial', stopped with a cork, filled with a liquid resembling oil but whose sweetish scent he did not recognise. What the liquid was he did not know but he was certain it wasn't turpentine with which he was familiar. Beside the phial was a small package, tied at the neck with thread and wrapped in paper clearly marked with a single word: 'Poison'. He handed the black bag to Mary Paterson, telling her what was written on the package inside, and she in turn passed it on to her mistress and asked if it belonged to her. Christina took it from Mary but did not respond to her question immediately, though later in the day she told her that the phial contained turpentine which she had bought that morning to apply to her husband's skin in the hope of relieving his pain. She offered no explanation for the word 'poison' - given Mary's illiteracy she presumably felt no need to.

In the early evening she left home for a second time, on this occasion to be driven to Paisley by another of the farm labourers, Sandy Muir. En route she explained to him that, because her husband would not agree to being seen by a doctor, the purpose of her outing was to visit her uncle,

Robert Robertson, who had, she said, experienced 'a heap of troubles' himself in his time. She hoped, therefore, that he might be persuaded to come to the farm and apply the medical knowledge he had gained in order to help John. On their arrival at the house, Sandy Muir was invited to make himself comfortable in the kitchen while Christina was ushered into the parlour where she found her uncle busy writing. They had not been in one another's company for some three or four years and until his wife introduced Christina he failed to recognise her as his niece. He had heard she was married, he said, and knew they were now almost neighbours, living as they did only a few miles apart, but her reaction to his opening remark must surely have taken him aback. In a virtual repetition of her confession to Mary Paterson, she confided in her uncle - a virtual stranger - that she was not living at Inchinnan by choice, that she had been pressurised into the marriage against her will and that her preference would have been for John Anderson of Dunlop. Attempting to smooth things over, her uncle - good soul that he was - preached a short homily, saying that many people found themselves unable to spend their lives with their first choice of companion but, by spending time together and learning to appreciate one another's good qualities, a deep fondness between husband and wife would frequently blossom. His words appeared to soothe her and, with calm restored, she proceeded to bring up the reason for her visit. As her husband was averse to receiving treatment from a doctor, she explained, she wondered if he would be willing to visit the farm to see whether he might be able to help. Mildly alarmed, her uncle's first impulse was to propose calling out a doctor straight away but she said no, telling him she would prefer if he came and assessed the situation for himself before taking that step. After a little more discussion, he agreed. As Sandy and Christina left Paisley to ride home, we might find ourselves wondering what exactly it was that prompted her to pay her uncle a visit that night - an uncle, we should not forget, with whom she had not been in contact for several years. Given the situation, the reason she gave - that she was seeking his medical expertise - seems implausible. If we think back to her pre-marital depressive state, not long before, it seems far more likely that her visit was the reflection of a troubled mind - possibly the help she was seeking was less for her husband and more for herself. Questioned later, John's workers reported that she generally appeared calm and in control of her emotions at the farm but, similar to the time when she gave voice to her unhappiness when speaking to Mary, maybe this was another occasion when the mask dropped and her cool-headed veneer fragmented and cracked.

Back at Inchinnan, John Muir had taken advantage of the mistress of the house's absence to go 'ben the hoose' shortly after eight o'clock and speak to John Gilmour in private. Muir's loyalty to the Gilmour family was beyond question. He had worked for Matthew, senior, at Dunlop; he had accompanied son John to Renfrewshire to help establish him at Inchinnan; and he had watched his health plummet within a matter of weeks. There was no doubt he was able to put two and two together. Entering the farmhouse, he found the patient in bed where he had spent the entire day. When he complained to him of severe aches in his side, Muir recommended that a doctor should be sent for. Gilmour replied, yes, if there was no improvement by morning, he would agree to that but he felt it was too late that night. Mindful of the black bag and its contents, Muir was persistent until finally Gilmour relented. Asked to name the doctor he preferred, he opted for McLaws at Renfrew, two miles closer than Paisley. Before Muir left his bedside, Gilmour said to him, 'John, this is an unco thing.' Muir was uncertain what lay behind this remark but did not press him. The poison bag in the boiler-house was never mentioned.

As it turned out, McLaws was not the optimal choice. Accompanied by ploughman, William Arthur, Muir set out for Renfrew but part-way there the two men came across the doctor at Inchinnan toll-house. It was obvious that he had been drinking and was hardly likely to be on top of his game. He agreed, nonetheless, to return with them to the farm and they arrived back sometime between ten and eleven o'clock. Hearing Gilmour's symptoms - internal pain, high temperature and insatiable thirst - McLaws diagnosed his complaint as being inflammatory in origin and proceeded to bleed him, virtually a default treatment in the earlier part of the nineteenth century, and recommended that turpentine be applied to his skin. Probably because of McLaws' own alcohol-impaired state, he failed to register that his patient had spent much of the last week vomiting. When Christina and Sandy Muir returned from Paisley between 11 p.m. and midnight Mary Paterson was in the kitchen and the doctor's horse was still tethered at the door. Christina did not speak but went directly to her husband's room. What conversation took place in the bedroom we do not know but, by McLaws' own account, he left after undertaking to pay a return visit the following day - a promise, incidentally, he failed to keep.

For many years Alexander Wylie had traded with the public in drugs, medicines and other similar items. Regarding sales of poison, he was scrupulous in questioning customers and his record-keeping was meticulous. On Saturday, 7 January, it was not quite daylight when a well-dressed lady entered his shop in Renfrew shortly after 8 a.m. and explained that she wished to buy poison 'for killing rats in the field'. She identified herself as Miss Robertson and, when asked for the name of the purchaser, replied 'John Ferguson' but claimed to be unable to remember the name of Ferguson's farm. The druggist proceeded to work his way through the names of local farms, listing them one after another, but without success. His customer explained that she was new to the area and none of the names he had mentioned sounded familiar. Not yet defeated, Wylie called upon a local grocer, James Smith, for assistance who was 'an old inhabitant of the place'. Did he, the chemist asked, happen to know a farmer by name of John Ferguson? Smith too was stumped and, looking for a clue, asked Miss Robertson whereabouts his farm was situated. In response she described its location in the vaguest of terms as 'up by Paisley, in that direction'. Despite his misgivings, Wylie finally conceded the point and sold Miss Robertson tuppence-worth of arsenic which he wrapped up in two separate paper 'pokes', one inside the other, marking the outer one clearly: 'Poison, Arsenic'. Before handing the package over, he made an entry in his poisons register: 'January 7, 1843. For John Ferguson per Miss Robertson, for killing rats in the field. James Smith, witness.' Still suspicious of her intentions, before Miss Robertson left his shop, he made a point of warning her not to attempt to take arsenic herself or give it to anyone else. 'Here is James Smith,' he told her, 'who will be a witness against you.' These were words which in the fullness of time would prove to be prophetic. As the shop door closed behind her, the chemist's wife watched Miss Robertson walk away, her steps leading in the direction of Inchinnan.

Two days earlier John Gilmour's younger brother, Matthew, had ridden to Dunlop bearing the bad news that his condition continued to slide downhill and Matthew Gilmour senior responded by travelling to

Inchinnan, arriving at the farm on Saturday mid-morning. He found his son in bed complaining of near-constant sickness, pain and raging thirst. He was nursed by Christina but when she was absent the two men spoke alone. When John asked his father to stay overnight Matthew Gilmour found himself in a quandary: if he failed to return home that night, he told his son, the members of his family at Dunlop would be worried about his safety. Torn by divided loyalties, eventually he arranged that word was to be sent to him if there was no improvement in two days' time. He waited until shortly after nightfall before leaving - roughly 4 p.m. in midwinter Renfrewshire - and in a state of deep anxiety he travelled home in the dark.

Just before Matthew senior left for Dunlop, true to his word Christina's Uncle Robert had arrived at Town of Inchinnan where he spent more than an hour at John's bedside. During much of this time, he observed John bringing up green and yellow bile and listened to his complaints of constant pain in his right side. John told Robertson about Dr McLaws' visit the previous night and how he had bled him but that he had not been entirely sober at the time. As a more dependable alternative, Robertson recommended Dr Robert McKechnie from Paisley and offered to call him out when he returned to the town, but characteristically John expressed reluctance and it was finally left that Christina would send for McKechnie if his condition worsened yet further. As Robertson was preparing to leave, he and his niece found themselves briefly alone together and yet again she returned to the subject of her unhappy marriage. She shed tears and seemed full of regret. It struck her uncle as odd that this should be her focus at such a critical time. Despite her openness about her feelings, some would later suggest that John himself was never aware of the depth of her fondness for her first love. Others thought this unlikely.

At nine o'clock on Sunday morning Robertson received a message to say that John's condition had gone down overnight. As previously agreed, he immediately contacted Dr McKechnie and then rode to Inchinnan himself. When the doctor arrived in the early afternoon he found the patient in bed, suffering cruelly from fever, thirst and a racing pulse. He prescribed calomel powder, a popular remedy for upset stomachs, and recommended that a blister be applied. This involved placing a hot plaster on the patient's skin with the intention of raising a blister which could then be drained - the mistaken belief being that his system could thus be purged of impurities. As Christina was unfamiliar with how to administer the process, Robertson agreed to wait with her to demonstrate the correct method. Before leaving, Dr McKechnie instructed her to keep samples of her husband's vomit and urine for examination when he returned the following day. Meanwhile John Muir was sent to Alexander Wylie, the druggist at Renfrew, for tartaric acid and soda. Off his own bat Wylie added magnesia to the order, telling him it helped when a patient was persistently 'throwing [up]'. Arriving back at Inchinnan, Muir passed the medicines to Christina, repeating the chemist's instructions for their use. Even from the farm kitchen he could clearly hear his master's violent retching. Robertson offered to stay overnight and he and his niece took turns to sit by John's bedside. When he relieved her at 3 a.m. John told him that he felt that the blister had benefited him. It offered the first glimmer of hope since he had been stricken down eleven days earlier.

Sadly, it turned out to be a false dawn. Admittedly McKechnie found Gilmour's pulse rate had dropped a little when he examined him the following day, but it transpired that Christina had retained no samples of urine or vomit for him to examine: there was so little, she explained, she did not think it worth saving. The doctor prescribed effervescent powders and what he called simply 'blue pills'. As the day wore on, it became increasingly clear that any improvement in John's condition had proved short-lived. At one point he sent for John Muir and the two men spent a few minutes alone in one another's company. John asked Muir for a drink of porter or ale, requesting that he heat the bottle in the fire before pouring the liquid into a glass. What conversation passed between them is not known. More and more the downhill track of John's illness was growing to look irreversible, and it was decided that evening that word should be sent to his father to come to Inchinnan as a matter of urgency.

Accompanied by Christina's sister, Mary Cochran, Matthew Gilmour made an early start on Tuesday, 10 January, and reached Town of Inchinnan at 10 a.m. where he found his son distressed and in pain. He waited with him throughout the day and remained at his bedside all night. By morning John was no better - if anything worse, as by then the pain had spread through his upper abdomen and into his throat. In the early afternoon he was attended by Dr William McKechnie - son of Robert McKechnie - who quickly realised that his situation was growing precarious. Throughout his visit John was sluggish and drowsy and the doctor was told that his mind had started to wander, though he did not see evidence of this for himself. He found him reluctant to speak but when questions were put to him, he was able to answer coherently. McKechnie bled him again and left more effervescent powders. In the early evening John rose unexpectedly from his bed and sat on a chair but, too weak to support himself upright, he tumbled to the floor and his father had to help him back into bed.

It was clear by now that time was running short and various of John's friends and relations assembled around his bed. As well as Christina and his father, Mary Paterson and Sandy Muir were both present but, sadly, not his loyal and devoted servant, John Muir. Christina's sister, Mary, came and went from the room as did John's fourteen-year-old cousin, Andrew, who had been living at Inchinnan since November. It was what Andrew Gilmour heard that would later cause a stir. At some point before John's death - Andrew was unsure exactly when - he heard him utter the words - 'Oh! if you have given me anything, tell me before I die,' and express a wish to be 'opened' after death, that is, examined internally during a post-mortem investigation. Sandy Muir was later able to corroborate that he had spoken these words but was unable to say to whom he had addressed them. Suffering from deafness, John's father heard nothing. Were they simply the disordered thoughts of a dying man? Or had a deeply suppressed suspicion worked its way to the surface? Whatever the explanation, what was beyond doubt was that John Gilmour's story had reached its conclusion and, after fourteen days of suffering, he finally gave up the ghost between six and seven o'clock in the evening of Wednesday, 11 January 1843.

A coffin was made by Inchinnan undertakers, McKeans, and five days later John Gilmour's corpse was taken by coach for burial at Dunlop kirkyard. A coffin-plate inscribed with his name was screwed to the lid and after the coffin was lowered into the grave a heavy iron grille known as a mortsafe was secured on top, a legacy from the days of the bodysnatchers not so long before. The key to the mortsafe was then handed over for safekeeping to the dead man's uncle. Once the funeral was over, it cannot have been easy for Matthew Gilmour to return to Town of Inchinnan to wind up his late son's affairs. Christina stayed on at the farm for nearly two months after John's death before returning to live under her parents' roof at West Grange. However, it soon became obvious that there was little chance that the gossip surrounding John's death had been laid to rest alongside his earthly remains.

Alexander Cochran would later claim that it was at his daughter's own instigation that her late husband's body was exhumed as a means of quashing once and for all the rumours that were swirling around his death. It seems improbable. By his own account, Cochran then raised the matter with Christina's father-in-law, Matthew Gilmour, and the two men approached the Procurator Fiscal whose authorisation was needed to allow the grave to be opened. On Saturday, 22 April, the mortsafe was unlocked, the turf sliced open by undertaker, Archibald McKean, and the coffin raised. Three surgeons were in attendance - Drs McKechnie, McKinlay, and Wylie - as well as Superintendent McKay of Renfrewshire Police and, at the request of the Gilmour family, their local doctor. The coffin was borne to the nearby session-house where a dissection was carried out on the corpse. Based on their initial examination, all three participating doctors agreed that there was evidence of arsenic in John Gilmour's internal organs, samples of which they retained for chemical analysis. These were subsequently sent for testing to one of Europe's pre-eminent toxicologists, Professor Robert Christison of Edinburgh University (a prominent witness fifteen years earlier at the notorious Burke and Hare trial), who concluded that Gilmour's death had indeed been caused by arsenic poisoning, most likely administered in repeated doses.

If, as her father claimed, the exhumation was intended to clear Christina's name, then why had he rushed to coordinate her flight from the country in the last few days before it was due to be carried out? Clearly the timing looks more than a little suspicious. Whatever the truth of the matter, he might well have been successful in helping her evade Scottish justice but for the doggedness of Superintendent George McKay who, even before the *Excel* had docked at New York harbour, had secured a warrant from the US authorities for her arrest. Her American lawyer, Thomas Warner of the New York bar, argued the case against extradition on the grounds that his client was insane, and in the series of hearings that followed various medical experts were called upon to offer assessments of her mental state based on their observations of Christina while in custody. She was regularly to be seen sitting on the floor of her cell, they reported, engaged in private conversations with herself. She appeared to have partly lost the ability to count. She was unwilling to sleep in the bed provided because it was already occupied, she stated, by her (deceased) grandmother. At times she claimed no recollection of having been married, while on other occasions she acknowledged the fact but was willing to admit to an attachment to another man whose identity she refused to divulge. She had been coerced into leaving Scotland, she said, and, when asked if she would be prepared to return, she replied, 'Oh! I dinnae like a ship - it is so long - so long in crossing - I would rather go in a coach.' More than once her conversation came around to her troubled relationship with her father. She wept as she recounted the ill-treatment she had received at his hands: how he had 'confined her in a garret' and 'thrashed' her during her childhood, and yet, for all that, she still expressed affection towards him and appeared keen to see him again. Alarmingly, her wrists had to be bandaged after she self-harmed using scissors, explaining that 'it was amusing to see the flies come and lick up the blood'.

Although admitting to not being one hundred per cent certain, the doctors' overall opinion was that her claim of insanity was bogus and that she had effectively been shamming. As evidence they stated that her behaviour changed when she was conscious of being observed and they noted that intermittently her actions were those of a perfectly sane person. They claimed that she was guilty of overacting and her skill in evading questions was over-ingenious for someone whose reason was impaired. (I can't help wondering what a modern-day psychologist might make of Christina's case. Our understanding of the workings of the human mind has come a long way in the last two centuries.) Next up, Superintendent McKay was invited to set out the evidence from Scotland that would justify her extradition. Protracted legal wrangling followed, occupying the space of several weeks and culminating in Thomas Warner's last-ditch petition to U. S. President John Tyler, but ultimately to no effect. A warrant was issued by the American authorities authorising Christina Gilmour's removal to Scotland and on Wednesday, 16 August, she was escorted by Superintendent McKay aboard the packet-ship *Liverpool* in the company of an elderly Scotswoman, apparently keen to return to her hometown of Paisley, who had been enlisted to act as her companion during the voyage. And so began Christina's long and arduous sea crossing to Britain - reportedly 26 days of non-stop gales - travelling via

Liverpool to Greenock and whatever fate might await her there.

Four months later her trial came before the High Court in Edinburgh on Friday, 12 January 1844 - a year and a day, as it happened, after her late husband's death. Such was the level of interest that her case had generated that there was considerable pressure for seating in the public gallery from both men and women. Christina Gilmour stood at the bar, 25 years old and dressed in widow's weeds. When the charges were read out - that on repeated occasions during December 1842 and January 1843 she had poisoned the food and drink of her husband, John Gilmour, and had thus murdered him, then, conscious of her guilt, had absconded in order to defeat the ends of justice - she replied 'in a low but firm voice, "Not guilty".' Among the witnesses called by the prosecution were the druggists from whom arsenic had been procured: an assistant of Dr Vesey (the latter having passed away since Mary Paterson's visit to his shop in Paisley) and Alexander Wylie of Renfrew who presented his poisons log for scrutiny in which a sale had been recorded on 7 January to 'Miss Robertson' whom the pharmacist identified as the woman at the bar. The main thrust of the case for the defence was that John Gilmour's death could have resulted from suicide, either intentional or otherwise. His workers confirmed that arsenic was routinely kept at Town of Inchinnan for use as rat poison if and when required, and Christina's lawyers argued that it was impossible to rule out the possibility that an accident could have taken place. Alternatively, they put forward the theory that deliberate suicide might have been prompted by Gilmour's unhappiness in his marriage. A point they chose to sidestep, however, was the medical experts' unanimous opinion that death had most likely resulted not from a single dose, but from repeated doses of poison. No attempt was made to deny that Christina had acquired arsenic but it was argued that her intention was to administer the poison to herself as a desperate means of escaping a loveless marriage. The defence rested its case without calling any witnesses and the court was adjourned at 7 p.m. until the following morning.

The second, concluding day of the trial - Saturday, 13 January - began with addresses to the jury, first from the Lord Advocate, Duncan McNeill, representing the prosecution, followed by Thomas Maitland, former Solicitor General, on behalf of the defence. One of three judges at the bench, Lord Hope, then proceeded to charge the jury with a lengthy series of observations on the case occupying no less than four and a half hours. Retiring at 8 p.m. to consider the evidence - persuasive, albeit circumstantial - it took the fifteen members of the jury, presumably by this stage fairly battle-weary, only an hour to reach a verdict that took some by surprise: 'The Jury,' announced their spokesman, 'after a mature and careful consideration of the evidence brought before them in this case, are unanimously of [the] opinion, that John Gilmour died from the effects of arsenic; but find it Not Proved against the prisoner at the bar.' The outcome was greeted with noisy approval in some areas of the public gallery, prompting a rebuke from the bench, as Christina Gilmour was dismissed from the bar, a free woman. Was she surprised? Quite possibly. Relieved? Almost certainly. In the meantime, crowds had gathered outside, eagerly anticipating her appearance. In order to preserve her privacy a hackney carriage was driven up and brought to a halt outside the front of the building so, while their attention was distracted, she slipped unobserved out of a rear door in the company of one or two friends.

'The Scottish verdict' - or in Sir Walter Scott's memorable phrase, 'the bastard verdict' - Not Proved is a controversial legal oddity, pretty well peculiar to Scots law and dating back several centuries. Neither guilty nor not guilty - fish nor fowl - the not proven verdict is often interpreted as signifying that a jury is sceptical of the innocence of the accused yet unconvinced that the evidence presented by the prosecution has placed his or her guilt beyond doubt. In the aftermath of Christina Gilmour's trial, this was the cloud under which she returned to her parents' home in Ayrshire and under which she was to spend the rest of her life. In the years and decades that followed she lived quietly and never remarried. In a small rural community, it was inevitable that her path would have crossed with that of her first love but clearly nothing came of it. In February 1894 John Anderson died at the age of 88, still single, in the village of Dunlop. Following the death of her parents, Christina lived on with various relations, provided for by income earned from an annuity which was presumably her share of her parents' legacy. On Thursday, 14 December 1905, at the age of 87 she died in the small town of Stewarton, three or four miles from her childhood home. It is recorded that following her husband's death she spent more than sixty years dressed in the black clothing of a widow in mourning.

Darby Furie & Theodore Dowd
New Cumnock, Ayrshire - March 1851

It could, of course, have been put down to simple coincidence but in the eyes of many the sight of seven unfamiliar men breakfasting in style at the Coalburn miners' rows looked more than a little suspicious - especially given the previous day's break-in at a grocery store a handful of miles away at Coalhall. Virtually the shop's entire stock had been cleared out with the exception of a ten-gallon cask of ale, presumably too heavy and unwieldy to be manhandled off the premises. Not just that, but the strangers - by their voices Irishmen - were offering various items for sale: bread, eggs, sugar and tea, all at knockdown prices. Before breakfast that morning - Wednesday, 19 March 1851 - they had been heard amusing themselves, firing off pistols and targeting an old hat, but no-one had ventured to approach too closely. Despite the bargains on offer, it seems likely that the residents of the rows heaved a sigh of relief when their visitors departed in the direction of the Nithsdale Iron Works where they stopped off for refreshments at the Bankglen Inn, a couple of miles from the small town of New Cumnock. The Bankglen was not what you might call a genteel establishment. A virtual outpost on Ayrshire's upland fringes, New Cumnock was for the most part a settlement of coal miners and iron workers - hard men doing a hard job - but in spite of the public house's rough-and-ready clientele it was ably managed by a feisty forty-year-old widow, Elizabeth Watson, a local born and bred.

Even so, after a drink or two things grew a little boisterous. One account described how a quarrel broke out during which one of the strangers' hats - described as a 'fur bonnet' - was launched into the fire and singed before it could be retrieved from the flames. That was the point when one of the company decided he'd had enough, rose to his feet and made his exit. The others waited until early evening to leave the comfort of the fireside and continue to the village itself where they soon located a lodging house. Although the landlady, Janet Pearson, could not offer them accommodation, she agreed to boil a kettle and allow them to come inside to brew a pot of tea. At around seven o'clock one of the men went out to a small shop where he exchanged a few coppers for matches and a candle, but by then their coffers were sorely depleted and their money largely squandered. Times were tough, work not easily come by, so what was to be done? Based on previous form, these were men with few scruples about stepping outwith the limits of the law in order to fill their pockets, but the scheme they came up on this occasion was more than usually vicious. One man dropped out, not wishing to be part of it.

At first glance the moorland farm of Robert McNaught might not have seemed the most obvious choice. The 1850s Ordnance Survey Name Book described Craigshiel as 'a poor looking farmhouse, on the Earl of Dumfries' property', but for the men's purposes the principal source of its attraction was its isolated location. Situated more than 1,200 feet above sea-level alongside a cart track used for transporting coal and lime, the steading was a full four miles from New Cumnock, hunkered down in a hollow north-east of Corsencon Hill and more than a mile adrift of its nearest neighbour. Shortly after 7 p.m. the strangers started out for Craigshiel in pitch darkness, buffeted along the way by a series of squalls that seesawed between rain, sleet and snow. Bad and bad enough, you might think, but for the farmhouse's occupants, most already asleep, the men's arrival would prove more tempestuous by far than the wild March weather outside.

It was between nine and ten o'clock when the strangers reached Craigshiel. The only member of the household still active was one of the two housemaids, Mary Wilson, who was carrying out her final duty of damping down the fire in the grate. Sharing a bed in the kitchen were Robert McNaught and his wife, Susannah - nearly 35 years younger than himself - with their baby son alongside, born just a few months earlier. In a room adjacent, the farmer's grown-up son, John, was an overnight guest, having come to Craigshiel to help his father with an early sowing of oats. The two housemaids, Mary Wilson and Grace Murdoch, also slept in the kitchen side by side. The first suspicion Robert had of anything untoward was when he heard a loud knocking at the farmhouse door. Holding a lighted candle aloft, Mary Wilson approached and called out 'Who's there?', to which an unknown male voice replied, saying he had become lost on the road and wanted permission to come inside to light his pipe from the remains of the fire. As Mary knew full well, it was a common ruse to gain entry and, as soon as she refused, a second voice spoke out: 'Damn your soul - why ask for a light? Look about for what we want!' And, at that, there was a mighty bang as the door burst open and a band of men forced their way inside, wielding pistols and heavy wooden cudgels. Straightaway one of the ruffians made a lunge for a shotgun he saw hanging from one of the ceiling joists and, fearing that his own weapon might be turned against him, Robert rose from his bed and managed to wrest it from his grip, disabling the gun in the process by twisting the barrel from the stock. In the fist-fight that followed, the doughty 65-year-old was initially holding his own until he heard a voice cry 'Fell the old bugger!' which acted as a clarion call for his opponent's companions to wade in and overpower him by force of numbers, hurling him to the floor and savagely beating him. When one of the men stamped on his head with the heel of his boot, he lost consciousness. Although Mary Wilson's candle had been snuffed out and the house was in near-darkness, she could see enough to know that blood was running from his wounds - in her own words - 'like a loch'. In an effort to defend the house, McNaught's dog leapt at one of the attackers, gripping him by the trouser-leg, and received a savage kick for its pains. In desperation and distress the younger servant girl, Grace Murdoch, pleaded for the creature's life to be spared.

It had all happened in seconds. Panic-stricken, Mary Wilson shouted to Robert's grown-up son to hurry from the room next door, crying, 'Come fast! Come fast! Or they'll hae your faither killed.' Still groggy from sleep, John McNaught stumbled along the lobby to the kitchen door where a pistol was thrust in his face. Someone barked out the words 'Stand back!' and when he failed to comply the unknown gunman squeezed the trigger but by sheer good fortune the weapon misfired. Just like his father, John too was thrown to the ground and beaten into submission. The terrified maids were warned not to attempt any moves, but amidst the chaos and commotion fourteen-year-old Grace Murdoch slipped out of the farmhouse door unnoticed. Fearing for her baby son, Robert's young wife, Susannah, attempted to follow suit but was forced back when she found her way barred by one of the attackers. With the men of the house effectively incapacitated, the raiders felt free to ransack cupboards and cabinets, trunks and presses, unhindered in their frenzied search for money. But when their backs were turned, Susannah seized the opportunity to escape outdoors through a window opening, carrying her child in her arms. One of the robbers gave chase but mercifully he was thwarted by wild weather and unfamiliar surroundings. With no other option, Susannah had left the house in her nightclothes which she was forced to remove and wrap around her baby for warmth. Struggling over the mossy uplands, at one point she sank into a bog and extricated herself and her son only with the greatest of difficulty, and by the time she arrived around midnight on the doorstep of her nearest neighbours, the Riddel family at Lethans, she was in a state of near-collapse. To cover a mile had taken her all of two hours.

Back at Craigshiel the thieves were left frustrated at their failure to turn up anything of significant value. The small sum of money that McNaught kept in the house had been hidden well. Their haul consisted of modest items, most notably three checked shepherds' plaids, two pairs of boots, an incomplete fowling-piece (shotgun) and small items such as a penknife and comb. A number of papers and documents were also taken in the hope that they might be of value. In their haste to be gone, the housebreakers left behind them a fur cap and a candle, both of which would later help to link them with the men seen drinking at New Cumnock earlier in the day. It was the fourteen-year-old housemaid, Grace Murdoch, who brought news of the attack down off the hill to Midton of Corsencon where the farmer, John Spence, roused one of his workers and sent him on horseback to New Cumnock to raise the alarm and call out the local doctor. Then he and his son set out for Craigshiel where another moorland farmer, John Ferguson of Clocklowie, had likewise come to offer support when he got wind of the raid. When news spread to Old Cumnock, ten miles away, the local constable, James Johnston, assembled a posse of men who hurried to the farmhouse as quickly as possible but, arriving at 5 a.m., they were too late to capture the robbers. From his bed, Robert McNaught was able to update Johnston on Grace Murdoch's earlier account of events. He had regained consciousness, he said, while the housebreakers were still in the process of ransacking his home so, despite his injuries, he had managed to inch his way across the kitchen floor and into the adjoining stable. From there he had crept outside into the kailyard and concealed himself behind a corn stack until he was certain they were gone. When it was his son John's turn to be questioned, he recounted how he had avoided further injury by slipping underneath his chaff bed where he lain motionless and unseen. Neither of the men was able to pin down definitively how many raiders there had been - five? maybe six? - but given the clamour and confusion their visit had unleashed, a degree of uncertainty was forgivable. One thing was beyond doubt. When the attackers fled, they had left behind them a scene of shock and horror where two of their victims were grievously injured and fighting for their lives. Examined by Dr Thomas Hunter, Robert was found to have three broken ribs and six head wounds, some two inches deep and cut into the bone. John had seven wounds to the head and a fearful gash on the rear of his left leg.

After hearing the various accounts, Constable Johnston backtracked to New Cumnock where he set about interviewing witnesses who had encountered the raiders at various times throughout the preceding day. News of the atrocity was met with shock: Robert McNaught was a well-respected figure in the locality, a devout man and one of the co-founding elders of New Cumnock Free Kirk. Johnston ensured that information concerning the attack was communicated by rail to the neighbouring towns of Cumnock and Muirkirk as well as the county town of Ayr, twenty miles west. The following afternoon - Friday, 21 March - the Procurator Fiscal arrived from Kilmarnock to conduct investigations. That same day news of McNaught's ordeal crossed the county boundary into Dumfriesshire, and when five shady characters turned up in the evening at a farm on the Buccleuch Estate known as the Kiln, once again asking for a light and brazenly demanding an old cap to replace one that had been lost, the farmer's wife, Agnes McCall, was instantly on the alert. She took a bold step: 'I doubt you have been at Craigshiel last night at that robbery,' she stated bluntly. They denied it, of course, and claimed they were travelling west after completing a job in Edinburgh, but Agnes was not fooled. A search party was got up at Sanquhar but, once again, to no avail. The fugitives appeared to have melted into the ribbon of woodlands that flanked the River Nith.

But, amateurish as ever, they left clues in their wake. The next morning a police officer picked up a handkerchief near Sanquhar which turned out to have been stolen during the raid. A checked shepherds' plaid was found among a cache of clothing, abandoned in a burn in the woods. A scrap of paper, discarded after being used to light one of the men's pipes, was identified as part of a letter, handwritten by Mary Wilson, dated the previous day and taken before it could be posted. But of the robbers themselves there was no trace. Rumours abounded. Back at New Cumnock a story did the rounds that the entire gang had been captured and was due to be escorted back to the village by rail. A large crowd gathered at the station who whooped and cheered as the train pulled in - but their celebrations proved short-lived. Only two suspects stepped out on to the platform, both of whom were quickly cleared of any involvement in the crime.

The consensus was that by now the gang was most likely to have scattered. Two men were arrested near Sanquhar only to be released a short time later and an alleged sighting was reported ten miles farther south in a wooded glen near Drumlanrig Castle. A third suspect was apprehended near Moniaive who apparently bore a strong resemblance to one of the descriptions given to police but the evidence was too thin to hold him. Two Irishmen were picked up at Carsphairn on the borderlands of Galloway, giving credence to the theory that the robbers might be aiming for one of the Wigtownshire ports with a view to setting sail for their native land. Police were deployed to the area but ultimately to no effect. The task officers faced was far from easy. Descriptions of the men they were seeking were for the most part sketchy, so when it came to the crunch none of the arrests made so far had stood up to scrutiny. Every one of those taken into custody was eventually freed.

In the absence of any significant progress, a notice was posted in the *Ayr Advertiser* on Thursday, 10 April, by Archibald Bell, Sheriff of Ayrshire, offering a £50 reward 'for the apprehension and conviction of [the suspects] and a proportional sum for any one of their number'. Descriptions of the wanted men - six, not five - followed, of whom four were named with varying degrees of certainty. First came Edward McGill:

age twenty or twenty-one, slim build, medium height and clean shaven. He was believed to be dressed in a white hat and boots which were tied with green laces. The second suspect was named as Michael McDonald - of a similar age and height to McGill, but heavier in build and with a pockmarked complexion. He was last seen wearing a 'broad blue bonnet, with blue ribbon'. The third man sought was 'supposed' to go by the surname of Doolan: 'light and delicate-looking'. It looked as though he was not the original owner of the shoes he was wearing which were described as 'cut in front [with his] toes projecting'. One of the three remaining men 'might' be Theodore Hughes, a colliery worker, but no attempt was made to name the final two. All were thought to be wearing similar moleskin garments - 'very dirty' - with the exception of one of their number who was believed to be dressed more formally in a 'frock-tailed coat with narrow stripes' - quite possibly stolen. In an effort to avoid being recognised, they were believed to have exchanged articles of clothing amongst themselves. The offer of a reward, it was stated, was to hold good for a period of three months and Sheriff Bell's advertisement concluded by stating that all six suspects spoke with Irish accents.

Striking a more cheerful note, it was reported around the same time that, despite their dreadful injuries, both Robert McNaught and his son were responding positively to medical treatment. Healing, of course, was a slow process; likewise, police investigations. Not until the second half of July, four whole months after the raid, was there an important breakthrough when several credible suspects were taken into custody in Dumfriesshire. Stationed at Bowholm near Canonbie, the local policeman, James Underwood, had been approached by a certain Bernard Williamson who tipped him the wink that two men of his acquaintance had recently confessed to him in detail their involvement in the Craigshiel raid. Known to Williamson as Jeremiah Haggarty and Peter Friar, it seemed all three had known one another for some considerable time. Several years earlier they had been workmates during construction of the Edinburgh to Hawick railway and, since their paths recrossed three weeks earlier, they had been travelling together in search of employment. It had been a lean time, Williamson said, Haggarty had complained bitterly of painful feet and, with no work to be had, they were forced to beg from farmhouses by the roadside. After their descriptions had been circulated in newspaper reports, apparently they'd had a narrow escape when pursued by men with dogs near Edinburgh.

You might think that such shared hardships might have bred a sense of loyalty but, no, certainly not on Williamson's part when he made the choice to betray his former friends. For whatever reason, he revealed that they were currently to be found camping at the Scotsdyke Plantation, a short distance from Canonbie on the English side of the border. Clearly, he had given some thought to how the situation might play out. He advised Constable Underwood to enter the woods and lie low and in the meantime he would return to Scotsdyke and under some or other pretext lure his associates away from their camp. Backed up by three colleagues, Underwood did as suggested, concealing himself amongst the trees, until a short time later Williamson reappeared on cue with his unsuspecting former friends in tow to deliver them, Judas-like, into the policeman's hands. Reportedly neither of the two resisted arrest.

While they were jailed at Canonbie overnight, a curious episode took place. From outside their cell Constable Underwood eavesdropped on a conversation during which Haggarty suggested that it would be a good thing if they were taken to Dumfries, rather than Ayr, because he believed the authorities there had no information that could be used against them. He was worried, however, in case 'old Craigshiel' might be brought down from Ayrshire. 'I wonder if the old bastard would know us,' Underwood heard him say. When the policeman revealed his presence and accused them of being the Craigshiel raiders, Haggarty remained silent but, dropping his guard, Friar responded by saying that he believed 'his harvest was shorn' - or put another way, his goose was cooked. He was said to have admitted his guilt later and in private to William Thomson, the Sheriff Clerk of Dumfriesshire.

It emerged in due course that Friar had been convicted of burglary at Dumfries the previous year. He and two fellow 'vagrants' had entered the stable of a local farm where they had used a skeleton key to open a 'kist' - a large chest - they found inside. They then proceeded to help themselves to its contents of men's clothing and other small items, one of which - with consummate irony - was a copy of the Bible. Unlike the raid at Craigshiel, there had been no suggestion of violence: on the contrary, three farm workers occupying the loft above had slept on throughout the entire episode. Friar and his two companions' luck, however, soon ran out. Captured and convicted, they spent the following three months behind bars.

Friar for one had not learned any lessons. After a night in the cells at Canonbie fifteen months later, Haggarty and he were taken to Dumfries where, questioned before Sheriff Napier, they abandoned all pretence and gave their names respectively as Darby Furie - nineteen years old, 5' 9" tall and unmarried - and Theodore Dowd - age twenty-three, nearly six inches shorter and likewise unmarried. Neither could read or write. Regarding the raid at Craigshiel, both men flat-out denied any part in it. Furie declared that he had never met Dowd and Williamson until the previous day, and added that he was not familiar with the Ayrshire countryside. Despite Dowd's earlier confession to the Sheriff's Officer, he insisted that he had been 120 miles away at the time of the robbery, living and working at a property in Dundee - a claim subsequently discredited when the address he gave was found not to exist. In the meantime, another arrest was made when Police Superintendent John Sabbage of the Carlisle force received information that a third possible Craigshiel raider, Charles Doulan [sic], was working as a farm labourer near the hamlet of Bewcastle, Cumberland. Doulan was captured, escorted back to Carlisle and duly sent on with Furie and Dowd to answer to the authorities at Ayr. All of the men, it emerged, were originally from County Tipperary. When the manner of their arrests became known, the rumour gained ground that their informant, Williamson, had possibly had a hand in the Craigshiel robbery himself but it was a suggestion that appears not to have been pursued. What, we might ask, could he have hoped to gain by his treachery? Perhaps the squaring of an old, unknown grudge? Alternatively, a free pass in exchange for turning Queen's evidence? Certainly, there appears to have been no suggestion that he ever picked up any share of Sheriff Bell's reward - though whether or not he was aware of the three-month time limit may be a moot point. However obscure his motives, the upshot was that two of those interviewed at Ayr, Furie and Dowd, were charged with the crime of stouthrief - theft by housebreaking coupled with assault to the danger of life - and remanded in custody pending trial. The third suspect, Doulan, claimed to have been the individual who opted out when the plan to raid Craigshiel was conceived at New Cumnock and his story appears to have been accepted. (Notably, neither of the two men charged was among those named in the *Ayr Advertiser* of 10 April, while the whereabouts, involvement or even the very existence of the three others who featured

- Hughes, McDonald and McGill - remained unknown. The use of aliases was, of course, widespread.)

While locked up at Ayr, for just over a week Darby Furie shared a cell with George Dunsmore, a miner from the Ayrshire village of Lugar who was serving a three-month sentence for assault. By Dunsmore's way of it, Furie gave him a detailed account of the Craigshiel burglary without any attempt to shy away from his own involvement. Robert McNaught, he had told Dunsmore, had been subjected to a thoroughgoing 'belltinker' - that is, an out-and-out thrashing. The version of events he gave implicated Theodore Dowd but effectively exonerated the informant, Bernard Williamson. In the aftermath of the crime Dowd and he had taken to the hills, he continued, planning to travel down through the border country and cross into Northumberland. They had bought their food from shepherds they met along the way, but finally the forces of the law had caught up with them a short distance over the border. While Furie's cellmate might not have been the most trustworthy of witnesses, the level of detail he could pass on about the Craigshiel robbery gave his story a definite ring of truth.

The trial did not take place until June of the following year, 1852, at the High Court in Edinburgh. The indictment was read before the court: 'in the company with others and your confederates to the prosecution unknown [you did] wickedly and feloniously, break into and enter the farmhouse of Craigshiel... by forcibly bursting open the door thereof [and] you did, wickedly and feloniously, attack and assault... Robert McNaught and John McNaught'. Both accused pled not guilty. During the following trial, the necessity of categorically identifying those responsible for the Craigshiel outrage was central to the prosecution's case and although there was a degree of uncertainty about Dowd and Furie's participation in the actual mêlée itself, there were enough solid witnesses from Bankglen, New Cumnock and Sanquhar who were prepared to testify that the two accused had been among those who left New Cumnock by the coal road on the evening in question, and who subsequently fled into Dumfriesshire once their pillaging was complete. Interestingly, both Charles Doulan and the informant, Bernard Williamson, were among those called upon to give evidence. Emphasis was placed on the strong circumstantial evidence that existed - a fur cap abandoned at the scene of the crime; a candle bought at New Cumnock and later found at Craigshiel; and, possibly most damning of all, the signed fragment of Mary Wilson's letter, picked up near Sanquhar, which conclusively linked the fleeing men with the robbery. On top of that, there were Furie's incriminating remarks overheard by Constable Underwood at Canonbie as well as Dowd's confession in confidence to the Sheriff's Officer at Dumfries. And finally, there was the account of the raid as recounted to George Dunsmore while Furie and he shared a cell at Ayr. At the trial's conclusion the verdict, of course, was guilty and the newly-convicted men were each sentenced to banishment overseas for a period of twenty-one years. It could have gone a lot worse for them. The fact that they had a future to look forward to at all was down to nothing more than the McNaught men's resilience and powers of recovery in overcoming their life-threatening injuries.

Placing the crimes of Dowd and Furie in their historical context, there is no question that the years following the potato famines of the 1840s were anything other than tough for Irish men and women, forced from their homeland by poverty and starvation and not universally well received in their new host countries. That said, it would be hard, if not impossible, to justify the murderous brutality meted out by the Craigshiel raiders, three (or four) of whom were ultimately never brought to justice. Before departing British shores, the two men convicted appear to have spent time aboard the hulks that stood at anchor off the south coast of England, awaiting their full complement of transportees. First to set sail was Theodore Dowd (convict number 3511) who left in April 1855 and arrived at Fremantle, Western Australia, after a three-month voyage aboard the *Adelaide*. Strangely, it would be more than two years before Darby Furie (4649) followed on aboard the *Nile* which finally docked at Fremantle on New Year's Day of 1858.

On the surface at least it looks as though Dowd settled well to his new existence down under where he was assigned to work as a groom. He was granted his ticket-of-leave in April 1858 which allowed him greater freedom though he remained subject to a form of probation. Three years later he was recommended for a conditional pardon which entitled him to travel more widely but still within fixed parameters. Ultimately, he did not enjoy a long life and was only in his early forties when his body was found lying by the roadside in 1871. He had never learned to read and write and remained unmarried. Despite the trust placed in him by the

Western Australian authorities, the fact that he still chose to operate at times under an alias - Peter Theobald - leaves a lingering aftertaste of suspicion.

His old companion, Darby Furie, outlived Dowd by a considerable margin though he was not, it seems, totally successful in turning over a new leaf. Initially assigned to work underground in the mines, he earned his ticket-of-leave within months of arriving but from time to time he was still inclined to stray from the straight and narrow. In April 1861 a gentleman by the name of Rearden was walking back to Perth after a race meeting at Guildford, a few miles east of the city, when he heard horses and carts approaching from behind. As he stepped aside to let them pass a voice cried out, 'Are you going to Perth?' to which he replied 'Yes', then the next thing he knew he was struck a mighty blow below his left ear that felled him to the ground. Despite his shock he was conscious of a hand rifling through his inner pocket and, once he had sufficiently regained his senses, he realised that his wallet was gone. He spotted his assailant making off at speed.

The runaway thief's flight from justice did not last long and, caught in a matter of moments, he turned out to be none other than Darby Furie. A cut-and-dried case of assault and robbery, you might think, but it wasn't that simple. First, no wallet was found about Furie's person. Not only that, but it emerged that, conscious that Rearden had been celebrating a little too heartily, one of his racing friends had removed the contents of his wallet - £30 in total - for safekeeping. The fact was that whoever had pickpocketed Rearden - Furie or indeed anyone else - had got away with nothing more than an empty wallet, therefore the case was not pursued. He received his conditional pardon in January 1862 and in the years that followed he appears to have gravitated south and east until 1894 found him at the gold-mines of Ballarat, Victoria, where he is recorded as having been fined forty shillings for using obscene language with the alternative of fourteen days in jail. An additional five shillings was added for being drunk at the time. By then Furie would have been more than sixty years old and, like Theodore Dowd, remained illiterate and unmarried. A case for sympathy? Most probably not. There is no getting away from the fact that Dowd and Furie had no regard for the victims of the crimes and their misfortunes were undoubtedly of their own making. Whether the two men's paths ever crossed in the sun-baked land down under is not known.

Were their nights ever troubled, we might wonder, by thoughts of an isolated farmhouse, 10,000 miles to the north, where lives were changed forever? It seems unlikely. The chances are that the demands of their new lives would have dominated their existence and memories of a wintry night in a far-off land retreated into the distant past.

Catherine Beaton
Claddach Kyles, North Uist - June 1856

Despite her straitened circumstances, for a woman approaching her eightieth year, Margaret Maclean was unquestionably spry and active. Dependent for her existence on poor relief, she lived alone in a humble stone-and-turf dwelling in the scattered crofting township of Claddach Kyles, fifteen miles west of Lochmaddy on the wild, western rim of the Outer Hebrides. For all her perceived fitness, members of this remote North Uist community were in the habit nonetheless of keeping an eye on their elderly neighbour and when there had been no smoke seen coming from her chimney for several consecutive days in June 1856, and she herself had not been seen for the best part of a week, it was initially assumed that she was simply enjoying a spell away from home. By Thursday, 26 June, however, alarm bells had started to ring. Arriving to investigate, a group of locals found Margaret's door closed, chained and padlocked and, despite attempts to peer through a window, they were unable to see inside. What happened next is a little unclear as the recollections of the various people involved do not tally exactly, but it appears that a local shopkeeper, Norman MacDonald, was first to grasp the bull by the horns when he broke apart the chain attached to the padlock, swung open the door and entered the house. What he saw was Margaret's lifeless body sprawled out across the bed and he quickly realised that this was no accident but rather the result of foul play.

Perhaps surprisingly, Margaret Maclean's death wasn't the only event of its type to take place in the Highlands in 1856. Four months earlier a similar loss of life occurred near the east-coast town of Alness in Ross-shire. Somewhere in her sixties, Margaret Munro was an unmarried woman who lived alone in a tiny house in the hamlet of Obsdale, twenty miles or so north of Inverness. By no means isolated, her home was situated within a few yards of neighbouring cottages, one of which was occupied by her married sister and her husband. Although Margaret earned no more than a modest income from working in the fields and picking up whatever casual employment became available, it was rumoured locally that her frugal lifestyle had allowed her to build up a considerable nest egg, estimated by some at upwards of £10. How exactly that figure was arrived at is anybody's guess, the outcome most likely of the flimsiest of local gossip.

For Margaret, 23 February 1856, had passed off much like any other Saturday. After finishing her day's work at Dalmore, she walked the short distance to Alness where she bought a few groceries before returning home in the evening. Not until the following morning was there suspicion of anything amiss. Seeing no smoke rising from Margaret's chimney, her sister came across to check up on her and, to her horror, found her lying among bedclothes that were saturated with blood. She realised immediately that Margaret was beyond help, with all traces of life long departed. An investigation was launched which soon revealed that if her reputed savings had been her attacker's goal - what else? - then his objective had not been met in full. On a shelf alongside the groceries she had bought the previous evening were a few scattered shillings and some odd coppers - a small sum, for sure, when compared with what turned up a few moments later. Concealed within the cuff of a dress belonging to Margaret was cash to the value of £3 and fifteen shillings - the equivalent of several hundred pounds today. How much money her killer got away with, of course, could never be known.

Forty-eight hours later - on Monday 25 June - a party of local officials descended on Margaret's cottage. It didn't take them long to see how anyone with malicious intent could have easily forced his way into her home: she was in the habit, they learned, of securing the outer door with nothing more substantial than a light wooden log to jam it closed from inside. Among the group were three doctors from the nearby towns of

Alness, Tain and Invergordon whose post-mortem examination concluded that Margaret's death had resulted from a severed windpipe, though both the jugular vein and carotid artery remained intact. Both of her arms bore marks where her attacker's fingernails had gripped and held her down but, despite this, she appeared to have been overpowered quickly and the doctors indicated that they were unable to identify signs of a struggle. Death, they suggested, had been well-nigh instantaneous. The murder weapon - the victim's one and only household knife - had been discarded a few feet from her bed, its blade encrusted with dried blood. The visiting officials were told that Margaret had been similarly robbed three years earlier, but on that occasion when it became known that she had gone to consult a local 'spaewife' - a woman with clairvoyant powers - the stolen money (roughly £3) had been mysteriously returned by its superstitious thief. But this time round the brutal actions of whoever was responsible had ensured that the same thing could not happen twice. No-one, it seems, was ever brought to book.

For longtime residents of Obsdale, Margaret Munro's violent death brought to mind an earlier outage that bore striking similarities to the present case. In March 1830 another single woman also in her sixties, Helen MacKenzie, was brutally murdered and her cottage on the Invergordon estate, a short distance from Obsdale, ransacked during the hours of darkness. Globs of melted candle wax had solidified on the floor throughout her house which indicated to investigators just how thorough the murderer's search had been. Suspicion fell on the dead woman's nephew, Hector Munro, who was arrested a fortnight later at Oldmeldrum, Aberdeenshire, still in possession of some of his Aunt Nelly's cash.

Fast forward now a little over a quarter century to June 1856 when Norman MacDonald forced his way into Margaret Maclean's home at Claddach Kyles, and found his elderly neighbour's body slumped to one side on top of her straw mattress. Her body was swaddled head to toe in a tangle of bedclothes and, as the scene before him sank in, MacDonald saw that her head was resting on a petticoat that doubled up as a pillow and partially overhung the wooden headboard. Her right leg was twisted beneath her at an unnatural angle. Lifting the bedclothes to uncover the old lady's face, MacDonald's eye was immediately drawn to a stripe of livid bruising, a finger's width across, that extended partway around her neck. Her mouth gaped open, allowing her bloated tongue to protrude, and her lips were swollen. Spatters of dried blood could be seen on her face. Near the bed, shards of broken pottery lay scattered and two wooden chests appeared to have been piled one on top of the other. MacDonald speculated that fragments of broken shellfish that littered the floor were likely to have been the remains of the old lady's last meal. Eager to see for themselves, some other neighbours followed him into the house - though one woman turned away immediately, unable to stomach the gruesome sight that confronted her. MacDonald knew enough to ensure that everything was left undisturbed, just as he had found it, and as he hurried off to raise the alarm it struck him that the person responsible for this atrocious act had taken time to secure the door before fleeing, presumably in an effort to delay discovery of the crime for as long as possible. When the local Inspector of the Poor was informed of Margaret's death, he visited the house a short time later and compiled a list of its contents to be forwarded to the Procurator Fiscal at Lochmaddy.

Two days later, on Saturday, 28 June, a post-mortem examination was carried out by a local doctor, John MacDonald, who found the old lady's internal organs to be sound and in good order and this, plus the fact that he could detect no sign of disease, led him to rule out any possibility that death was by natural causes. On the contrary, bruising to be seen around Margaret's neck suggested that asphyxia, interruption to breathing, had been responsible - the result, he inferred, of violent strangulation. Epileptic convulsions or any similar event would have resulted in much less regular and well-defined markings, and the head's own weight overhanging the headboard would, in his opinion, be insufficient to account for the bruises, all of which led him to conclude that considerable external pressure must have been applied, thus confirming that Margaret was the victim of murder. The fact that her teeth had been loosened and thrust back into the cavity of the mouth pointed to the same conclusion. From the degree of putrefaction evident, MacDonald estimated that death was most likely to have occurred eight to ten days previously. A second doctor, Roderick Maclean of Dremisdale, agreed with his colleague's findings and similarly formed the opinion that Margaret Maclean must either have died through strangulation or as a result of being smothered. He specifically rejected outright any possibility of suicide. Had she suffered some kind of seizure, he believed that the marks on her neck could only have been produced had her windpipe been pressed down heavily on the headboard of the bed, and this he considered improbable. The weight of her head alone, he thought unlikely to have produced such deep-seated bruises.

With murder now established, in as small and close-knit a community as Claddach Kyles it didn't take long for a suspect to emerge. A thirty-two-year-old spinster who lived with her mother at nearby Balemore, Catherine Beaton had already acquired for herself a reputation for dishonesty. Convicted at Inverness four years earlier of having stolen a quantity of coloured wool from Alexander MacDonald of Knockline - less than a mile across the fields from her home - it was noted during her trial that even then she was already regarded as 'by habite [sic] and repute a thief' and was duly sentenced to twelve months' imprisonment. Given her record, then, it was only natural that Beaton should have come under the spotlight and, as her movements around the time of Margaret's death were steadily pieced together, suspicion increased and intensified.

It emerged that five days earlier, on Friday, 20 June, Catherine Beaton had paid a visit to a local acquaintance, Mary Stewart, at around half-past seven in the evening. During the course of the two women's conversation Margaret Maclean's name had cropped up and Beaton told Mary that she had encountered the old lady some days earlier and that she had seemed very poorly. At the time of their meeting Margaret had been in the process of making her way to the seashore, Beaton continued - a statement that prompted Mary Stewart to comment that surely, then, she couldn't be as unwell as all that. But Beaton was not to be swayed and maintained that the old woman's appearance gave the distinct impression that she had no more than a short time left to live. Beaton left for home just over an hour later, her most direct route passing virtually within hailing distance of Margaret Maclean's front door.

The North Uist folk were habitually early risers - never more so perhaps than on mornings such as Saturday, 21 June, when the steamer from Glasgow was expected at Lochmaddy. Donald Maclellan was no exception, on the move well before daybreak as he accompanied his brother on the first part of his fifteen-mile trek to meet the boat. Even at that early hour, the roads were already busy. The brothers stopped off at Norman MacDonald's house where they found the merchant busy packing a cart-load of eggs for transportation to the port to be loaded aboard the steamer. Shortly after 3 a.m. Maclellan left to return home and, even though it was not yet fully light, he made out the form of a woman, maybe one hundred yards distant, following a footpath that led towards Margaret Maclean's cottage. She was dressed, he could see, in a blue dress and a coloured headscarf with a black shawl drawn around her shoulders. It did not occur to him at the time to pay any heed to who she might have been. A little later Mary MacInnes had been herding her father's cattle for an hour or so when she saw a woman she did not recognise appearing at the gable-end of Margaret's house and walking downhill towards the road. The unfamiliar woman was likewise dressed in a dark blue gown and a brown headscarf which Mary could see was decorated with red and white spots. She had a black shawl wrapped around a bundle which she carried on her back. Even though the morning was dull and wet, from the position of the sun behind the clouds Mary was able to estimate the time as being somewhere between five and six o'clock, making it some two to three hours since the woman had been seen by Donald Maclellan.

After he returned from Norman MacDonald's house, Maclellan spent the next few hours indoors before heading out into the fields at about 6 a.m. Before getting down to work, he spotted this same woman walking a short distance ahead of him. When she paused to sit down for a chat with Catherine MacKinnon, an employee at nearby Dusary Mill, he was able to catch up with her and recognised her then as Catherine Beaton of Balemore. It struck Maclellan that he had not previously noticed the large bundle concealed beneath her shawl, nor indeed the smaller one she had resting on her lap. Once he had moved on, Beaton divulged to Catherine MacKinnon that the larger of the two bags contained wool - an assertion she would trot out more than once throughout the day. When the two women were joined by another neighbour, John MacBean, Beaton went on to describe how she had just newly crossed back to the Uist mainland from Baleshare, a tidal island accessible only at low water, and so hazardous were the conditions, she said, that she had come close to drowning. In spite of her purported ordeal, she came across as remarkably calm and composed and MacBean could not help noticing that her clothing seemed quite dry.

Five days later, on the day Margaret's murder was discovered, Beaton was walking along the high road when she happened to meet one of the Baleshare islanders, Donald MacDonald of Illeray, and when they paused to exchange news, it was only natural that their conversation should turn to the shocking discovery at Claddach Kyles. In line with her story to Mary Stewart a week before, Beaton proceeded to tell MacDonald how not long ago she had accompanied Margaret back from Lochmaddy and, during the course of their walk together, the old lady had confided that she knew full well that her time on earth was running out, and she had gone on to say that she would not need as many peats cut for winter fuel as in previous years since she was certain she would not live long enough to use them. There was more. Steering the conversation in a new direction, Beaton told the Baleshare man that suspicion had fallen on a woman living at Claddach Kirkibost named Penny Cameron and that she had approached Beaton earlier that day asking to borrow a blanket - as instructed, so she claimed, by the Inspector of the Poor. Wary of cooperating, Beaton had refused for fear that any blanket returned to her later might be one stolen from the dead woman and subsequently implicate her in the crime. Instantly MacDonald smelt a rat. How, he asked, was she so sure that a blanket was among the items stolen from the dead woman's house? Thrown on the defensive, Beaton had no ready answer and blurted out that her remarks could not be used to incriminate her without corroboration. Donald MacDonald, we may be sure, drew his own conclusions. But if all this wasn't fishy enough, there was worse still to come.

Beaton must surely have felt under increasing pressure as she watched the evidence pile up against her. When Sub-Inspector of Police Archibald MacDonald conducted a search of her home he unearthed a woman's cap, concealed inside a box within a chest, which he identified as having belonged to the murder victim. A parcel of wool and various bobbins of thread he likewise believed to be stolen. Adding to the weight of evidence, a distinctively-cracked teapot in Beaton's possession was identified by Norman MacDonald as one he had sold to Margaret Maclean. And, on top of all that, a boy called Neil MacDougall added to her woes when he came across two pairs of grey stockings jammed into a narrow cleft of rock no more than twenty yards from her home. Wisely, he left the items untouched but when his father, Charles, learned of the discovery he removed the socks to be passed on to police. Before he had time to do so, however, Beaton approached him and offered various gifts in exchange for the stockings' return - 'as much cloth,' he would later recall, 'as would make [him] a suit'. With surprising openness, she said that these stockings were liable to prove her undoing. Charles' wife spoke up, telling her that her situation would be much less serious if she had simply robbed Margaret Maclean but had not taken her life. 'Lord, help me,' implored Beaton, 'although mankind will not.' Perhaps it was a little too late for prayer.

When Sub-Inspector MacDonald returned to Beaton's house for a second visit, he quickly became aware of the smell of burning. When questioned, her mother told him with inexplicable honesty that she had destroyed Margaret Maclean's plaid (a long woollen garment worn over the shoulder) in the fire for fear of the disgrace that would descend on her house should her daughter be charged with murder. Hearing her mother's words, Beaton turned to her and snapped, 'If there was no-one else to condemn me, you would do it yourself!' Deciding that the time for firm action had arrived, at this point MacDonald informed Beaton that she was under arrest and confined to the house, then he resigned himself to a long wait until he could summon assistance the following morning. Making use of the time on his hands, he extracted a sample of ashes from the grate which he then wrapped in a handkerchief to be passed for examination to the authorities at Lochmaddy. A short time later, just as what passed for midsummer darkness descended, Catherine Beaton quietly took him into her confidence. Were he not here, she told him, she would take herself away to Bawlaggan - a notoriously dangerous stretch of coastline not far away. There was no need to say anything more. Taking pity on her despite himself, MacDonald asked, 'Poor creature, what will you do now?' Her answer, if she gave one, is not on record.

If things weren't gloomy enough for Beaton already, a spell in jail pending trial dampened her spirits still further. More than once she knocked on her cell door and asked the jailer, Duncan Matheson, to convey to the sheriff the deep regret she felt for her actions. And yet, for all this apparent show of remorse, when the charges of theft and murder were read out at Inverness three months later, she entered a plea of not guilty - her words translated from the Gaelic by John Fraser, an interpreter engaged to assist those in need of his services. Possibly it was the trial's dual character - proceedings conducted largely in Gaelic, but subsequently reported in English - that accounted for an inexplicable little episode that featured in the press. A couple of days before her arrest, the story was recounted of how Beaton had arrived at Lochmaddy where she apparently presented the jailer, Matheson, with the surprising gift of two hens complete with their clutch of chicks. Presumably aware of Beaton's status as prime suspect and alert to the possibility of attempted corruption, without hesitation he handed the birds over to Sub-Inspector Macleod who, for whatever reason, returned them later that same day. At no point, it seems, did money change hands. As to what lay behind these puzzling events, the *Inverness Courier* ventured no theory. We can only conclude, I suppose, that something got lost in translation.

Turning to weightier matters, what was undeniably in Beaton's favour was the fact that no smoking gun had materialised during the course of the police investigation but, that said, countering the weight of circumstantial evidence that was stacked up against her was always going to be a mammoth task: her movements on the morning in question looked highly suspicious, plus the fact that the dead woman's possessions, found within and around her home, were going to be more than tricky to explain away. And as if that wasn't enough on its own, her previous convictions, as confirmed by the Depute Sheriff Clerk of Lochmaddy, would hardly have done her any favours either. No witnesses were called for the defence and although she remained unshakeable in proclaiming her innocence, ultimately Beaton's protestations fell on deaf ears when the jury were unanimous in finding her guilty of theft.

All well and good, but making the more serious of the two charges stick proved a thornier proposition. As confirmed by the post-mortem examinations, a murder had been committed but by whom? The proposition that the thief and murderer were two separate individuals might have stretched credulity, but in the absence of concrete proof it was a suggestion that the jury were not entitled to dismiss out of hand. And it may well be that their deliberations were dogged by just such a possibility because, following an absence of twenty minutes, they returned to the courtroom where their spokesman announced that by a majority decision, they found the charge of murder Not Proven. Hearing his words spoken, the prospect of dying at the end of a rope was lifted from Beaton's shoulders but, of course, her troubles were not at an end. It fell now to the judge, Lord Cowan, to pass sentence in relation to her conviction for theft and when his sonorous tones fell silent Beaton was led from the dock facing the prospect of six years' penal servitude to come. Daunting enough to be sure, but at the end of the day we might wonder whether she had been successful in avoiding the just and proper consequences of her actions and evading the full weight of the law. Common sense might suggest so. But if her case demonstrated anything, it was this: that for a jury to be wholly convinced of a prisoner's guilt can take something more solid than mere suspicion, however strong that might be.

Well, Catherine Beaton's trial was done and dusted - even if its outcome was controversial - but it had raised a disturbing question that remained unanswered. What, we might ask, drove a woman in her early thirties to put an elderly neighbour through an ordeal - probably fatal, undoubtedly traumatic - for the dubious prize of a bundle of wool, a length of cloth, a few pairs of socks and a cracked teapot? Contemporary reports leave us no clue, and today, more than a century and a half on, we can do no more than simply speculate.

Thomas Ross
Kirkoswald, Ayrshire - January 1859

In the last week of March 1826, a horrific event took place on the Earl of Home's country estate in the eastern borders. A twenty-five-year-old poacher, John Guthrie of Coldstream, was prowling through the Hirsel woods under cover of darkness when his foot triggered a thread-like wire, set in place some time earlier by the Earl's gamekeeper, James Craw. The consequences were both instant and catastrophic. A deafening bang rang out accompanied by a sudden flash of light and Guthrie collapsed to the ground, clutching one of his knees in agony.

He had, it transpired, fallen foul of a 'spring-gun' - a species of mantrap in widespread use at the time whereby a shotgun was primed to fire automatically in the event of a tripwire attached being disturbed. The aims of the device were clear and unambiguous: first, to deter individuals from trespassing or poaching on private land and, secondly, to wound or kill those who carried on regardless. Regarding Lord Home's victim in 1826, Guthrie's fate was a deeply unpleasant one when he died a fortnight later as a result of lockjaw, a complication arising from his injury. Scant comfort though it might have been to his family, his death contributed to an ongoing debate regarding the legality - and morality - of spring-guns. As far as this particular case went, gradually the publicity petered out until the story went quiet - under the aristocratic influence, one might suspect, of whom else but His Excellency the Earl of Home?

By the middle years of the century mantraps were a thing of the past but face-to-face confrontations between poachers and gamekeepers continued unaffected. Thirty years after Guthrie's death and well over one hundred miles to the west, two keepers on Bargany Estate, Ayrshire, settled down for a wait. Christopher McCarfrae and James Anderson chose their place with care, positioning themselves in the lee of a dyke where a gateway - known at the time as a 'slap' - opened on to Laggan Hill. Clear moonlit conditions offered excellent visibility. They had been waiting in silence for an hour and a half when three shadowy figures came into view, descending from the hill in their direction. Realising they were being watched, the three strangers made an abrupt halt so McCarfrae rose to his feet and walked towards them. As he drew closer, he saw that the men were accompanied by a pair of fierce-looking lurcher dogs and that each was armed with a stout 'skull-cracker' club. He recognised one as a local man, Matthew Snedden, who had a rolled-up net tied around his waist and he could not help noticing that Snedden's two companions' coat pockets looked suspiciously full.

When challenged, the men denied being poachers but claimed instead that they had lost their way in the darkness. Asked to explain their possession of a net and hunting dogs, they had no ready answer so they opted for a different tack, appealing to the keepers that surely in difficult times a hare or two might be spared for poor men like themselves. Pressed for their names, neither of Snedden's associates was willing to cooperate and the mood turned distinctly darker when one of them - later identified as Thomas Ross, a weaver in his thirties from Maybole - revealed that this was not by any means the first time he had trespassed on Bargany lands after dark. He added menacingly that on certain previous occasions he had stood close enough to McCarfrae as to have reached out through the darkness and touched him with his hand. Outnumbered and faced with the men's sturdy cudgels and ferocious dogs, the keepers decided against attempting an arrest and convoyed their unwelcome visitors instead to an old cart-track that snaked across the hills from Laggan farm towards the town of Girvan, several miles away. Once the suspected poachers were off their hands, the gamekeepers breathed more freely and returned to scour the slopes of Laggan Hill where two wooden pegs quickly turned up of a type commonly used when hanging a net between gateposts into which a fleeing hare was intended to become entangled.

Of course, in the small community of Girvan the men's identities were bound to leak out and it took less than twenty-four hours for the third alleged poacher, William Stevenson, to be identified at the town Cross, while his mate, Thomas Ross, was found drinking in a nearby pub. Matthew Snedden was also rounded up and soon all three were in police custody. After a struggle Ross eventually allowed himself to be searched by duty officers who found concealed about his person a heavy bludgeon, a kind of bag that was regularly used by poachers, and finally a bloodstained net with soft down adhering that the policemen believed was traceable to the coat of a hare. All three men were charged with trespassing and carrying offensive weapons before being released on bail.

When their trial took place at Ayr several months later - in April 1858 - the evidence against them seemed damning. Their presence on Laggan Hill during the hours of darkness was tricky to explain, no less the poaching paraphernalia found in their possession. Speaking from the witness box, Snedden's mother, Agnes, made a last-gasp effort to account for the bloody net, relating how her son and his two co-accused had called on her during the early hours of Monday, 30 November, bringing with them a bag containing a dead rabbit which they said had fallen victim to a weasel and then abandoned by the roadside. Her testimony cut little ice in the courtroom, as did various minor technicalities raised by the defence.

With one crucial exception. Up until now the outcome of the trial must have seemed assured but there was a single issue - trifling perhaps on the face of it - that remained to be settled. For a trespass conviction to be secured it was necessary to determine whether the three men had, or had not, been intercepted on enclosed private land or alternatively on an area of ground generally viewed as a public pathway. The first essential, then, was to pin down exactly where routes existed near Laggan farm to which local people had traditionally had right of way. Testifying before the court, the farm's tenants, John Arthur and his brother David, confirmed that a well-trodden path ran north and south through their steading which was routinely used by their neighbours on journeys to and from Girvan. All fine and good but more to the point, however, was the need to determine whether a similar right-of-way existed that descended from Laggan Hill where Ross, Snedden and Stevenson had been intercepted by the Bargany keepers.

Opinions varied. On the one hand, gamekeeper McCarfrae insisted that no such road existed on Laggan Hill - the implication, of course, being that the three accused had indeed been caught in the act of trespassing. On the other hand, a local farm worker, James Cox of Troweir, contradicted McCarfrae's statement when he suggested that an old, ill-defined track ran down the hillside which was routinely used by farm carts. One of the Laggan tenants, John Arthur, sided with Cox but went on to complicate matters by adding that at times when the hillside had been ploughed the route in question effectively ceased to exist. Hearing this, the defence was quick to pounce in an effort to sow seeds of doubt in the minds of the jury and, as things turned out, their efforts brought success. Following a short recess, the jury members returned to the courtroom where their spokesman announced that by a majority verdict they found the case against the three prisoners not proven. Hearing that he was off the hook, so great was Thomas Ross's relief that he turned towards the jurors and thanked them effusively for their kindness, declaring himself unable to find the words to express the warmth of his gratitude. No wonder he was relieved: it had been a pretty close shave and he'd dodged conviction by the tightest of margins. He'd have been grateful, you might think, to have been granted time to ponder the error of his ways.

Although Ross and his companions' brush with the law was common knowledge in the area, it turned out to have little or no impact as a deterrent. Less than a year after their acquittal, confrontation flared once again between poachers and gamekeepers, this time on the Culzean Estate, eight miles or so north of Laggan Hill as the crow flies. Faced with a recent upsurge in poaching, the Marquis of Ailsa had beefed up his counter-forces in response and shortly before midnight on Saturday, 15 January 1859, gamekeepers patrolling near the village of Kirkoswald heard gunshots coming from Park Glen, an area of woodland stocked with the Marquis' pheasants. They immediately hurried to the spot and moved forward through the trees, fanning out in an attempt to flush out any intruders. Other than the sticks they were carrying, all were unarmed though one man held a large dog at the end of a leash. As three of the group - Hugh Connell, Thomas Harvey and Richard Jones - picked their way through the moonlit forest, the forms of two men broke cover from under their feet and fled, threading swiftly through tree limbs, brush and branches. Sprinting in their wake, the three gamekeepers matched them stride for stride and, as Jones ran, he realised that this was not the first dealings he had had with them. He cried out, 'It's no use your running - we know you!' Hearing his words, the poachers knew that flight was futile so they brought up short and wheeled around to face their pursuers. They weren't quite out of options yet but had one final card to play.

Cornered and at bay, each of the men raised his rifle, took careful aim and fired. No more than four or five yards away, Jones took the full brunt of the blast as shot entered his chest before passing directly through his heart. Death was well-nigh instantaneous. His companions heard no more than a muffled gasp - 'Oh!' - before his body crumpled and fell to the ground. He wasn't the only casualty. A collateral victim of the brutal attack was the gamekeepers' dog which was also shot and collapsed, apparently lifeless. One of the poachers, James Withers - a man who went by the nickname of 'Tanderagee', a small town in Ireland - was seized and held fast by Connell and Harvey and when the shocking sight of Jones' motionless corpse was pointed out to him his first instinct was to deflect the blame. 'I did not take his life - I shot the dog,' he whined in self-pity. A short scuffle followed as he made a half-hearted bid for freedom but he was easily overpowered and restrained. In the meantime, his slippery accomplice had managed to make his escape by plunging into a narrow ravine and melting away into the darkness. This second man was a shady character with whom the Culzean keepers were already well acquainted: no other than a Maybole weaver in his thirties by the name of Thomas Ross.

The body of Richard Jones was carried to the nearest farmhouse at Ballochneil, then even before dawn broke the machinery of the law swung into action. At 7 a.m. a Maybole magistrate, William Hannay, accompanied by three police officers turned up at Ross's home at Allan's Hill where they found their man in bed, stretching and yawning theatrically as he made a show of rousing himself from sleep. When questioned about his movements the previous evening, Ross claimed he had been at home all night but his story convinced no-one. When his boots were examined, they told a different tale: still wet and muddy, the pattern of their 'tackets' - or hobnails - corresponded closely with footprints found in Park Glen which led directly towards Maybole. Not far from the scene of the shooting, his shotgun was recovered from the place where it had been discarded in the fields. Described in the press as a 'rickety piece', it had proved lethal for all that. While being handcuffed, Ross offered no resistance and a short time later he was transferred in the company of James Withers to the county town of Ayr where the two were lodged behind bars pending trial. In a poignant footnote to the tragedy, the gamekeepers' dog, left for dead on the forest floor, was reported to have crawled home during the early hours and, against all the odds, looked likely to survive.

When the resulting trial took place at Ayr three months later - precisely a year after Ross's previous acquittal - it threw up one or two surprises. First, there was only one man in the dock after James Withers had agreed to turn Queen's evidence in a blatant attempt to save his own skin. And, more dramatically still, the charge to which Ross pled guilty had inexplicably been downgraded from one of murder to the lesser crime of culpable homicide. As baffled as anyone else, the judges themselves - Lords Cowan and Ivory - were caught unawares by the fiscal's change of mind. Pondering the matter, Lord Ivory stated that he was willing to accept the possibility that, in the darkness and confusion at Park Glen, Ross might have discharged his firearm in the heat of the moment with no intention to kill. But be that as it might, the judge continued, the fact could not be dismissed that he had been engaged in illegal activity at the time while his victim by contrast was carrying out his lawful duties as a gamekeeper. 'Your crime falls the very smallest shade short of [murder],' he told Ross, and 'it must be followed by a sentence only short of capital punishment.' The court's decision, he pronounced, was that he 'be subjected to penal servitude for the whole space of [his] natural life'. What this meant in effect was his embarking on a one-way ticket to Western Australia with no prospect of ever seeing his wife or children again. So, for the second time in a year Ross had sidestepped the full weight of the law but what a price he had paid by so doing.

No doubt his outlook seemed bleak but he was certainly not alone and there was more than enough suffering to go around. In a shady corner of Kirkoswald's ancient kirkyard, amid graves that span the centuries, a grey-coloured headstone marks the resting-place of Richard Jones. The memorial was 'Erected by the Most Noble the Marquis of Ailsa', we are told, and its legend recounts how Jones lost his life while protecting the Noble Marquis' pheasants - he was 'shot dead,' it continues, 'by Thomas Ross, a noted Maybole Poacher'. Sadly, there is more to come. The stone also records that Margaret Jones, a seamstress to trade, survived her husband by only three years and passed away aged 34 in December 1862. And last to be commemorated is Catherine, Richard and Margaret's daughter, tragically orphaned while still a toddler. Catherine herself did not live to see old age but died, not yet forty, a few miles from her parents' grave. Of her brother John, three years older, no mention is made.

At the end of the day, though, who must bear responsibility for the clashes that blew up at Laggan Hill, Park Glen and in other locations up and down the country? Trespassers and poachers themselves? Yes, of course, though we surely must concede that these were men living through tough times with families to support and homes to maintain like anyone else. Their opposite numbers, the gamekeepers, were no different: ordinary folk too, dependent on the great estates for their jobs, their livelihoods and the feeding of their families. But a third group of players was also involved, operating for the most part from behind the scenes but who should arguably shoulder the bulk of the blame. Secure, well-heeled and snug in their homes, the lairds and the landowners stood as representatives of an unequal society that pitted ordinary people one against the other in circumstances well-nigh guaranteed to lead to conflict and violence. Regrettably, the death of Richard Jones would not be the last incident of its type to take place in the Girvan district and beyond before the end of the century.

Edwin Salt
Juniper Green, Midlothian - November 1859

Deriving from the Roman goddess *Iustitia*, Lady Justice is normally depicted as an elegant, robed figure, blindfold so as to ensure that the law is apportioned fairly and bearing a set of scales to signify impartiality in weighing up opposing arguments. Her sword serves as a symbol of her authority and the weighty powers of enforcement she has at her command. All to the good, most would surely agree, but turn back the clock to February 1860 when the outcome of an Edinburgh murder trial raised questions about whether the goddess's mask might have slipped just a little or her scales of justice tilted a mite to one side. The man perhaps benefiting on that occasion was one Edwin Thomas Salt.

Relocating from the English Midlands, Edwin Salt and his wife, Mary Anne, settled in Juniper Green, a prosperous small community outside Edinburgh, where he worked as an excise officer at a local paper mill with responsibility for oversight and collection of government taxes - a steady, secure and well-paid position. Both in their early thirties, the couple had been married for twelve years and had four young children and, in theory at least, you might imagine that everything in the family's garden would have been rosy.

Sadly, not. A regular visitor to The Old Ship public house at Curriemuirend, drink had the effect of loosening Edwin Salt's tongue and during a memorable bout of temper in autumn 1859 he blurted out that his wife was lying on the floor drunk and that he intended to go home and kill her. Although the landlady, Janet Wallace, was reasonably sure that it was drink that was doing the talking she thought it safest to take his threat seriously just to be on the safe side. 'You must not do that,' she warned him, 'or you will be hanged.' At that he fell silent but it wasn't by any means the only incident of its kind. The Salts' problems with alcohol were an open secret in the village and no-one could have been unaware of the violent rows that frequently blew up as a result.

Given the circumstances, it was possibly inevitable that matters would escalate and, when they did, they developed into an extremely ugly affair. In the early afternoon of Thursday, 17 November, Edwin Salt, visibly under the influence of drink, called at John Macdonald's butcher's shop in Juniper Green. Finding Macdonald absent, he left a brief, strange message to be passed on by his fourteen-year-old delivery boy, Robert Leishman, when his employer returned. In what comes across as an expression of self-loathing, he instructed Robert to tell his employer that he (Salt) was nothing more than a worthless drunk. His message delivered, he then turned on his heel and walked out, leaving the teenage boy speechless and taken aback.

Unusual behaviour, no doubt, but Robert Leishman knew full well that Salt had been drinking and therefore he was not unduly troubled. Ten minutes or so later, however, he heard something far more alarming when William Caldwell, an employee of Janet Wallace at the Ship, visited the butcher's shop bringing an addition to the story. He had come directly from Salt's house, he said, where he had been sent, as many times previously, to deliver bread. 'What rows they have there!' he exclaimed. He continued with his story, telling Robert that when he stepped into the kitchen through the side door a shocking scene had been playing out before him. Mary Anne Salt was lying sprawled on the floor, weeping gently and with blood running down her face, while her youngest child, less than a year old, lay partly beneath her, crying sorely. Edwin Salt was standing by the fireside. 'Damn you,' Caldwell heard him snarl, 'Get up!' but he made no effort to help her to her feet. Laying the bread down, Caldwell slipped away quietly without interfering. Perhaps typical for most fourteen-year-old boys, Robert Leishman was curious to see for himself, so he crossed the road to the Salts' house where he found the scene unchanged. Neither he nor Caldwell took the matter further. At the time intervening in what was viewed as a private domestic dispute was not the done thing.

In the end it was Edwin Salt himself who sought the involvement of a third party. Jane MacKenzie was a widow who was in the habit of carrying out occasional duties such as housework for himself and his wife. At around three o'clock she was working for the farmer of Woodhall Mains, harvesting potatoes in a field alongside the Water of Leith, and when she saw Salt approaching it was immediately obvious to her that he was showing the effects of drink. Offering no explanation why, he asked her to accompany him home but the farmer, John Clephan, was unwilling to release her from her work straightaway, therefore Salt had no option but to turn back without her.

During his absence from home another of Clephan's workers, John Neill, had turned up on Salt's doorstep bringing a delivery of potatoes from the farm. He knocked on the open door but there was no answer. Hearing a sound of moaning, he craned his neck around the jamb and was startled to see Mrs Salt stretched out across the kitchen floor with her head closest to the door and with blood leaking down her cheek. He ran for a neighbour but the closest, a man by the name of Forrester, was wary of becoming involved. Still pondering his next move, he spotted the figure of Edwin Salt approaching on the path that ran alongside the Water of Leith so he hurried forward to meet him. Like everyone else, Neill was already quite well aware of the Salts' stormy relationship but he was unsure how to broach the subject of what he had seen so he started off by telling him matter-of-factly about his delivery of potatoes. Salt replied, directing him to leave them in a nearby outhouse but, just as Neill was turning to leave, he summoned his nerve and spoke up. 'There is surely something wrong with Mrs Salt,' he said. Salt shrugged. Most likely, he said, she would be lying drunk on the kitchen floor, then brought the conversation to an abrupt close by stating that he must excuse himself now as he needed to go to bed. The time, Neill noted, was 4 p.m. He left feeling awkward and ill at ease but was at a loss to know what more he could do. Like both William Caldwell and Jane Mackenzie before him, there was no doubt in his mind that Salt himself had been drinking and what contribution he had made to his wife's sad state he could only suspect.

After Neill's departure, it was the best part of an hour before Jane MacKenzie came in from the fields and made her way to the Salts' home. She was fearful of what she might find. Questioned later, she would state that in her previous nine months of working for the Salts it had been perfectly obvious to her that Mary Anne was dependent on alcohol and when assailed by cravings she found herself near powerless to resist. Mary Anne herself was under no illusions: on one particular occasion she had confided in Jane that 'her whole life and heart was [sic] given to drink,' and she had fallen into despair - 'lost all heart', she had said - and regularly experienced suicidal thoughts. Stepping into the kitchen in the evening of Thursday, 17 November, Jane found her flat out on the floor - feeble, scratched and bleeding.

She was unable to rise to her feet so Jane enlisted the help of Albert, Mary Anne's eldest child, in manoeuvring her, still fully dressed, on to a shakedown bed which she had laid out in a small side-room. Edwin Salt was already in bed a few feet away but he took no notice. Mary Anne recovered herself enough to ask for a drink of water but these were the only words she uttered in the five hours that followed. Once Jane had made her as comfortable as she could, she set about preparing a meal for the children then, before leaving at twenty-past ten, she put them to bed - with the exception of Albert whom she instructed to lock the door from the inside after she had gone. During this entire time Edwin slept on undisturbed.

Was Jane troubled by unvoiced suspicions regarding the part he had played in Mary Anne's sorry state? It seems likely. What we know for sure is that she was sufficiently concerned to return before eight the following morning. She found him up and about, preparing to leave for work, but Mary Anne appeared not to have moved overnight. 'I am dying,' she told Jane. 'No fear of that,' Jane replied - 'You will get the better of it.' Mary Anne did not answer, but before Edwin left for the paper mill she asked him for a glass of whisky which he poured and handed to her. After he had gone Jane opted for a different approach, hoping to comfort her with a warming cup of tea, but to no avail. Even after a night's rest Mary Anne still seemed dog-tired so she undressed her, washed her, and helped her into the 'big bed' that Edwin had recently vacated. When she complained of acute chest pain, Jane's concern grew so she sent Albert to fetch a local doctor, Peter Gordon, but the boy returned a short time later saying he had been unable to find him. Was it a pang of guilt that prompted Salt to reappear from work at 11 a.m. and give her a second glass of whisky? Or simply to ensure her silence? Whatever the reason, the alcohol did no good for by the time the doctor eventually turned up in the early afternoon she showed no sign of improving nor her pain of easing.

Dr Gordon instantly smelt a rat. As he probed into possible causes of Mary Anne's illness, his questions were initially met with silence. He refused to let the matter drop, however, and asked Salt straight out what responsibility he bore. A tense exchange followed. 'So help me God,' came the reply, 'I never touched her.' This prompted Mary Anne to cry out, 'Oh, Edwin, how can you say so?' Dr Gordon turned next to Mary Anne. 'Has your husband struck you or ill-used you in any way?' he asked. 'I think he has,' she replied. At this Salt spoke up. 'No, Mary Ann, I never struck you,' he protested, 'but I gave you a slap... to get you to be quiet.' Seemingly oblivious to any contradiction in his words, he gave the impression that he considered such behaviour perfectly reasonable. Mary Anne concluded the conversation by saying simply - 'You know different.' When asked by Dr Gordon to pinpoint the exact source of her pain, she indicated that it was located deep inside, somewhere in the area of her internal organs or lower back. Before leaving, he prescribed medicinal powders, a mustard poultice and that a hot iron should be placed at her feet.

Once the doctor had gone, Jane turned to Salt and confronted him about his violent behaviour but he appeared to feel no need to excuse his actions. 'I will not deny that I gave her two or three punches,' he stated blandly and, regarding the scratches on her face, his explanation was that she had been drunk and obstreperous and that in his attempts to calm her his nails had inadvertently grazed her cheeks. Under Jane's repeated questioning, his temper started to fray. 'It is too bad of Mary Anne to lay the blame on me,' he said - 'She is a liar.' At that, he turned away and entered the bedroom. 'I am done with you now, Mary Anne,' Jane heard him say and with that he left the house in an obvious ill-temper. Left to carry out the doctor's instructions, Jane went ahead and administered the powders, applied the poultice, then, at Mary Jane's request, she poured her another glass of spirits. No more was said about Edwin's abusive behaviour. During the hours that followed Jane could see her condition steadily sinking until it was clear that her life was drawing to a close and a few minutes after five o'clock her breathing finally ceased. By then Salt had returned home and he was present at the time of his wife's death.

Clearly there would be consequences, and the following day - Saturday, 19 November - a post-mortem examination of Mary Anne's body was carried out by Drs Peter Gordon and Henry Littlejohn, the Edinburgh police surgeon. What the men found was utterly shocking. Her death, they discovered, had resulted from four internal wounds in the areas of the diaphragm, liver and womb which had been caused, they believed, by the violent insertion into her vagina of some blunt instrument - never specifically identified but described as being the size and shape of a walking-stick or poker - which had been withdrawn and reinserted several times to a depth of some eighteen inches. The doctors made a point of ruling out any possibility that the injuries could have been self-inflicted. Given the horrifying nature of her injuries, why, oh why, did Mary Anne choose to remain tight-lipped during Dr Gordon's home visit, and even conceal the truth from Jane MacKenzie whose concern for her could not be doubted? It seems astonishing. When push comes to shove I suppose the most likely explanation for her silence is that, living in an age of excessive female modesty, her embarrassment and feelings of humiliation were simply too great.

Facing a charge of murder, Edwin Salt's trial was heard in the Edinburgh High Court four months later on Monday, 13 February 1860, before a packed public gallery. Asked how he pled, he replied without hesitation 'not guilty'. One of the principal witnesses was Jane MacKenzie whose commitment to Mary Anne at her time of need was unquestionable but whose evidence under cross-examination did not always reflect well on her friend. Regarding Mary Anne's alcoholic binges, Jane had no option other than to admit she had neglected her children's welfare at such times and that it was not unusual for them to leave for school on an empty stomach. Her habits had grown slovenly, personal hygiene went by the board and her family's clothing went unwashed and unmended, sometimes for weeks at a time. Salt, paradoxically, emerged from Jane's testimony in a relatively positive light. He and Mary Anne, she stated, had appeared a devoted couple - at least at times when their relationship was not soured by misuse of alcohol - which he supplied her, Jane added, 'against his will'. She recalled that on

Wednesday, 16 November, he had returned from Edinburgh bringing essential provisions, a gift for the baby and a new dress for his wife. Two days later - the day of her death - Jane recalled Mary Anne's telling her how Edwin had kissed her before leaving home for the paper mill that morning. Jane did not offer an opinion whether she believed this to have been an expression of fondness or, what seems more likely, one of contrition. Areas of potential interest - Edwin's own relationship with alcohol, his history of abusive behaviour and its possible link to his wife's addiction problem - were skated over surprisingly lightly. Throughout much of the trial her perceived failure as a wife and mother was emphasised, the implication being that somehow or other responsibility for her own death lay with Mary Anne herself.

But when it came to the crunch facts were indisputably facts and, despite the defence's desperate attempt to moot the possibility that her death had resulted from suicide, a guilty verdict was pretty much inevitable. Given Salt's history of domestic violence, however, and the cruel and unnatural murder he was convicted of, what might have been less easy to predict was the jury's unanimous recommendation that mercy be shown in view of 'the great provocation' to which he had been subjected. Based on the judge's remarks moments later while pronouncing the death sentence, it may be that even Lord Cowan himself was a little taken aback by their plea for clemency. 'With all [your wife's] faults - and they were many,' he told Salt, 'you ought not to have forgotten that but a few short years ago you had vowed in presence of God and man to love and cherish her.' Salt showed no emotion in response.

What the jurymen chose to interpret as 'admissible provocation' was chewed over widely in the days to come as various parties weighed in with their opinions. A few days after the trial an article appeared in *The Scotsman*, penned by an unnamed correspondent who started out by expressing his view that there was much to be taken from Salt's case 'on which the wise may moralize, and from which the foolish may take warning'. Naturally, his choice was to moralize. 'When a man such as Salt marries a woman for love,' he mused, 'is for years a fond husband, until her conduct drives [him] to drown his sorrows in intemperance [and he] seizes some weapon and kills her in a manner which a lunatic, rather than a murderer would choose, how much of the guilt of this woman's death attaches to her husband? how much to herself?' There's no mistaking which side of the fence the anonymous correspondent comes down on. Any possibility that it might have been Salt's abusive behaviour that drove Mary Anne to seek solace in drink is not for a second considered.

He continues along similar partisan lines. 'Long years of reprimands, and caresses - hopes for amendment on the faith of promises that were broken - the tears of ragged, dirty children, miserable from cold and hunger - all that can madden any man,' he laments, conveniently sidestepping the fact that Salt's 'reprimands' routinely involved slaps, kicks and punches and implying that caring for his children is not a man's responsibility. According to the writer, a matter which ought to have halted the trial in its tracks was the question of looks: '... in appearance Edwin Salt is very far from like a ruffian,' he declares. 'His clear, honest eye, as he sat at the bar, seemed to say for him, "Surely I was not born to sit here and die on a scaffold!" (This decent, upright appearance, it may be recalled, hadn't stopped Salt from pleading not guilty at the outset of the trial.) By the letter writer's way of it, what Salt was - i.e. a comfortably-off middle-class male - mattered more than what he had done.

It was a classic case of vilifying the victim but, that said, Salt's anonymous defender was far from being alone in supporting the convicted wife-murderer and a variety of like-minded articles appeared in the press. In the same issue of *The Scotsman* a letter appeared sent by John M. Ross, Assistant Chaplain at Edinburgh Prison, whose language may have been more measured but whose sympathies were very much in line. The object of Ross's letter was to invite the citizens of Edinburgh to sign a petition, copies of which were to be placed in public places throughout the city, urging Her Majesty Queen Victoria to commute Salt's death sentence, the terms of which, according to Ross, were 'of such a moderate and reasonable nature that it can hardly be conceived that any one can have any scruples of conscience whatever signing it'. He reminds readers of the unanimity of the jury in calling for clemency and (predictably) goes on to highlight 'the great provocation which the prisoner received' - namely, his deceased wife's 'unparalleled drunkenness'. Perhaps, though, Assistant Chaplain Ross's wording betrays him a little when he alludes to Salt's love for her 'in his sober moments'. Not only that, but the details he chooses to omit are interesting too - such as his behaviour towards Mary Anne during moments when he was not sober, plus the cruel nature of his actions that brought her life to such an agonising end.

An unsolved puzzle remained, namely - why Salt chose to kill Mary Anne in the vile and heartless manner he did. Seeking a possible reason, my first impulse was to put his actions down to some form of sadistic pleasure or perverted sexual gratification, but then I wondered if the explanation might be rather more mundane (if no less cruel). Through naivety - or in his drink-befuddled state - it seems at least possible that Salt mistakenly concluded that, internal injuries being invisible to the outward eye, his wife's death would automatically be attributed to unidentified natural causes and for that reason suspicion of foul play would, he hoped, be deflected. Who can tell? The fact of the matter is that any theory can only ever be speculative.

Not everyone contributing to the press agreed with Salt's numerous defenders. Two days later a vigorous riposte appeared in the letters column of the *The Scotsman*, courtesy of an Edinburgher who took deep exception to Assistant Chaplain Ross's canvassing in support of the convicted murderer. His letter proceeded to depict Edwin Salt as 'a notoriously immoral man, and himself a drunkard' and claimed that he himself had routinely plied his wife with alcohol. Alluding to the abhorrent manner of Mary Anne's death, the writer does not mince his words. Why should a reprieve be granted, he demands to know, to 'so frightfully depraved a character' - indeed 'a monster in the shape of man'? Such a course, he insists, would effectively be to excuse a cruel and barbarous murder, an action that would serve no-one's best interests other, perhaps, than the 'life-at-any-price party' - that is, that growing sector of the population who objected to capital punishment in principle (of whom quite clearly he is not one). This incensed correspondent concludes that 'The execution of Salt is a terrible necessity', and, having said his piece, he signs himself off in upper-case Latin: '*AUDI ALTERAM PARTEM*' - translated roughly as 'Take Heed of Other Points of View'.

But in spite of his best efforts the contrary argument would be the one to prevail. At 10 p.m. on Thursday, 1 March, a telegraph message was received in Edinburgh from the Home Secretary, Sir George Cornewall-Lewis in London, to say that a decision had been taken to commute Edwin Salt's death sentence to a life term of penal servitude. On reading the telegram, Russell hurried immediately to the Calton Jail where he informed the prisoner of his reversal of fortune. Not surprisingly, it was reported that Salt received the timely news with gratitude and relief - but for this decision, he had faced a public appointment with the hangman a mere five days hence. Instead, he now found himself facing the prospect of eighteen months' detention on the south coast of England until late September 1861 when, in the company of 306 fellow convicts, he stepped aboard the frigate *Lincelles*, bound for Western Australia. After a brief stopover at the Cape of Good Hope, South Africa, the ship docked at the end of her 115-day voyage at the port of Fremantle near Perth on 28 January 1862.

You might expect that a near brush with death might inspire an individual to reassess, re-evaluate and perhaps set his life on a new course - so, once settled in his new homeland, did Edwin Salt resolve to wipe the slate clean, remorseful for past sins and grateful for his escape from the noose? Well, no, as it happens - not exactly. Move the calendar forward sixteen years to the late 1870s. By then he had married for a second time since his arrival down under. What had become of his first Australian wife, Katherine O'Neill, is not entirely clear but in September 1877 he had married Annie Frances Edwards, a woman some 20 years younger than himself. Marital bliss - if it ever existed - was set not to last. According to the Western Australia *Police Gazette* of 16 October 1878, Salt appeared in court little over a year later charged with having assaulted his new young wife. His description in the *Gazette* provides us with a glimpse of Salt's appearance sixteen years after setting sail from Britain, now in his early fifties: he is of stout build, readers are told, and of medium height; blue-eyed and round-faced. His hair, once brown, is turning grey and he has the 'florid complexion' that is sometimes the mark of a drinking man. Who knows what might be the explanation for the scar on his left hand and a second arching over his right eye? In any case, when Salt made his appearance before the Police Court on Friday, 11 October, he was quickly found guilty of assaulting Annie Frances and was bound over to keep the peace for a six-month period on payment of sureties amounting to a total of £40. For several days after the hearing, he remained under lock and key in Perth gaol until the money - a considerable sum - could be scrambled together to secure his release.

In the years that followed his behaviour showed no sign of improving. On the last day of May 1880, a warrant was issued for his arrest, once again for 'assaulting and ill-treating his wife, Annie Salt'... and so their fractious relationship rumbled on... and on... until nearly thirty years later it finally rose up to a climax that would have been hard to predict. In June 1907 a civil case was raised by Annie in the Central Police Court in Perth but the problem this time was not domestic violence but money. She recounted to the two presiding magistrates how her octogenarian husband had become seriously ill in the early months of the year and, her own health being similarly fragile, she had been incapable of nursing him by herself, therefore she had no choice but to have him admitted to hospital. Difficulties had arisen shortly after he was discharged when he had been taken to live with a daughter by his first Australian wife and her husband, Agnes and George Johnson - the latter a notoriously unsavoury character. From that point on Edwin's mind grew increasingly unhinged, Annie said, and to all intents and purposes he had deserted her and left her with no means of support.

As he stood before the court, it was clear that old age and infirmity had changed Salt virtually beyond recognition. Barely mobile and well-nigh deaf, communication between him and the two presiding magistrates was far from easy. Asked initially whether an amicable settlement might not be reached without the need for formal proceedings, he reacted wildly, claiming - with no apparent sense of irony - that he 'had lived for years in dread of his wife who had threatened to take his life'. Annie, for her part, was having none of it. 'He was sent out here for a terrible crime,' she retorted, 'and has led me a terrible life.' Undismayed, the judges made a second attempt at peace-making but once again to no effect. 'I was told at the hospital not to go near her,' Salt whimpered. 'Three surgeons said that if I went back to her they would lock me up.' Realising any further attempt at conciliation would be futile, the magistrates called it a day and brought matters to a close by imposing what they regarded a fair division of the couple's goods and ordering Salt to pay his wife a weekly allowance of ten shillings.

The exchange that took place during the hearing had been, to say the least, a bizarre reversal of roles and it seems almost certain that by then some form of dementia had Salt firmly in its grip. During the course of his long lifetime, tragedy had finally morphed into farce and the two met head-on that day in the Central Police Courtroom in Perth. Even afterwards, however, the financial wrangling continued until it finally came to an end three years later when Edwin Salt died, aged 85, at the Johnsons' home in Fremantle on Wednesday, 31 August 1910. With palpable irony, at the close of such a disruptive life as his, Salt's death notice placed in local newspapers concluded with the words - 'His end was peace.' Annie followed him four years later, having achieved the distinction (so far as we can tell) of being the only one of Salt's three wives to have succeeded in outliving him.

Setting to one side for the moment the rights and wrongs of the death penalty per se, events down under clearly showed how mistaken the 1860 Edinburgh jurors had been in their assessment of Edwin Salt's character, likewise the many who echoed their appeal for clemency in the aftermath of his murder conviction. How, we might reasonably ask, could all of these individuals have made such a collective error of judgment? Well, for one thing, it seems almost certain that Victorian gender bias influenced their thinking, disposed as it was to depict Mary Anne as the architect of her own misfortunes rather than blame the man who was known to mistreat her and who ultimately took her life. Not only that but probably social snobbery also played its part as the Edinburgh public noted Salt's middle-class position in society and the presumed respectability that went along with it. Today, more than a century and a half on, it is impossible to pinpoint their reasoning for sure but, no matter what, the fact remains that Edwin Salt was and remained a violent, abusive and unrepentant man long after he departed from British shores.

Robert Watt & James Kerr
North Atlantic Ocean - April/May 1868

On Tuesday, 7 April 1868, the sailing ship *Arran* left the port of Greenock, bound for the far side of the Atlantic and the Canadian city of Quebec. A wooden vessel with a registered tonnage in excess of 1,000, her 22-man crew was captained by 28-year-old Robert Watt of Saltcoats, Ayrshire, assisted by his 31-year-old brother-in-law, James Kerr of Lochranza, Isle of Arran, who occupied the position of ship's mate. The *Arran* was loaded with a cargo consisting principally of oakum - a fibre used for plugging cracks in the hull of wooden ships - and coal. Though her outward voyage was expected to last some thirty to forty days, she had been provisioned with enough food to sustain the crew for a good deal longer - sufficient, it was said, to cover the entire 6,000-mile round trip if necessary. Highly regarded by the ship's owners, it was Captain Watt's fifth voyage.

It came as no surprise to the crew when, shortly after leaving Victoria Harbour, two stowaways were found - a common enough occurrence at the time - and were immediately off-loaded on to the accompanying tugboat to be returned to dry land. Once the tug had departed and the *Arran* entered the open sea, the ship's carpenter, John Edgar, began the routine task of battening down the hatches, but just as he was about to hammer home his final nail, he heard a sound of knocking from below. When he removed the planks to investigate, two teenage boys appeared - the forerunners, as it turned out, to no fewer than seven stowaways who had slipped quietly aboard and gone undetected till then. First to materialise were James Bryson and David Brand - both sixteen - followed soon after by four younger boys: Peter Currie, Hugh McGinnes, Hugh McEwan and John Paul, all aged eleven or twelve. Last to surface was Bernard (or Barney) Reilly, a young man in his early twenties. All seven were thin, ragged and undernourished, but they had timed their appearance to perfection, now that it was too late for them to be returned to port. None of the boys had come well prepared - Bryson alone had any food, enough for one meagre meal - and none had clothing beyond the tattered garments they stood in. Two of the smaller boys - Paul and McGinnes - had no shoes. Straightaway they were ushered into the presence of the captain and invited to explain themselves. 'Please, sir,' John Paul is supposed to have said, 'we want to be sailors.'

The fact of the matter, of course, was that Captain Watt was left with little choice, so he allocated basic tasks to the boys as was customary in similar situations, but a few days out in the ocean all seven went down with acute seasickness. Ailing right from the start, Hugh McEwan was seen to be coughing up blood. Their bout of seasickness turned out to be no more than the start of the boys' problems and, as the *Arran* continued west, their ordeal began in earnest. As the vessel picked her way through ice-strewn waters off the coast of Newfoundland, James Bryson provoked the ire of the mate, ostensibly because of his poor personal hygiene. Forced to strip down to his underwear, Bryson was flogged with a 'lead line' - a length of rope used for depth-sounding - and when Captain Watt heard the boy's cries of pain, not only did he fail to intervene but he chose instead to exacerbate matters. Ordering Bryson to strip naked and lie flat, Watt instructed another crewman, Robert Hunter, to throw pailfuls of cold seawater over his body, then, bending over him, used a 'kyar broom' - a stiff-bristled brush - to scrub him both front and back. Even once he had finished, the boy's ordeal was not yet over. It was now the turn of the mate to scrub Bryson viciously, and any time the unfortunate boy tried to wriggle free Kerr threatened him with more of the lash. When he finally let up, he passed the brush to David Brand and ordered him to take over while yet more bucketsful of icy water were flung over the hapless Bryson. Scrubbed till his skin was red-raw, he was then made to get to his feet and stand by the fo'c'sle-head, shivering and dripping, for an hour or more. What could it be but an act of pure sadism that left Bryson naked, chilled to the bone and in agony from bloody weals that scored his back? We would be hard pushed to come up with any other explanation.

As the *Arran* continued westward towards Quebec the sea-ice steadily encroached and by early May she was one of several ships that became totally ice-bound. The consequences for the stowaways were grave. At the start of the voyage, Captain Watt had seen to it that sufficient food was apportioned among them by the ship's steward, John McLean, but ten days into the voyage James Kerr had taken charge of food distribution and he gave instructions that the stowaways be placed on little more than starvation rations. Very soon they reached the stage of scavenging for scraps. Driven by hunger, John Paul was forced to clamber over the side to recover turnip peelings that the cook had tossed on to the ice. When the captain and mate disembarked to examine the hull of the boat, David Brand seized the opportunity to slip into one of the cabins and fill his pockets with ship's biscuits. Following his example, the best James Bryson was able to come up with was a handful of currants but, unluckily for him, Kerr had already climbed back on board and caught him red-handed. Once again, he became the mate's whipping-boy. First, Kerr gave orders for the boy's hands to be securely bound and, next, for his pockets to be ripped open. As a means of taunting him, the currants found inside were then distributed among the other stowaways. Forced to strip, Bryson was flogged once again by Captain Watt who administered somewhere between fifteen and twenty lashes before making the boy sweep the decks completely naked in the intense Canadian cold. More fortunate than Bryson, David Brand escaped punishment when a search of his pockets turned up nothing - the chances are that he had devoured the biscuits already. Perhaps the last straw for the captain and mate was when the store of oakum was found in a filthy state: used, we might guess, by the boys as toilet paper. As the *Arran* sat at a standstill, the stowaways' story went from merely brutal to one of abject horror.

Seen from the ship, a grey haze stretched along the horizon which, by the crew's various estimates, might have been anything from eight to twenty miles away. To the naked eye, it was impossible to tell whether the dark line was the Newfoundland coast or maybe nothing more solid than a long-drawn-out streamer of cloud. Peering through his telescope, Captain Watt claimed that he could see houses and other buildings, strung along the shoreline, and even the figures of people going about their daily business. The boys could tell that he was leading up to something and, setting his spyglass to one side, he turned and spelled it out: there was not enough food on board to take everyone to Quebec, he announced, so the long and the short of it was that they would have to leave the ship. Already on the verge of starvation, Barney Reilly for one was willing to take the risk but, even so, the mate made doubly sure: 'Bugger you,' he told Reilly, 'You will have to go.' Abused and reviled throughout the voyage, James Bryson had few qualms about throwing in his lot with Reilly and taking his chances on the ice, but when David Brand gave voice to his reservations, the response was swift and unambiguous. 'Damn the bite of grub' he would get, the captain told him, if he stayed aboard. The younger boys were equally fearful of leaving. John Paul hid in a seaman's chest but was forcibly removed and, as the child clung to the rails in a last-ditch effort to stay aboard, Watt struck him on the shoulder with a length of wood in order to dislodge him. Ailing from the start, Hugh McEwan was told bluntly that he might as well die on the ice as starve on the ship. Realising that resistance was futile, the boys did their best to equip themselves for their ice-trek, wrapping themselves in scraps of discarded canvas, but the results of their efforts were totally inadequate in light of the extreme cold they would have to face. Other than a breakfast of boiled fish-heads, the boys had eaten nothing since midday the previous day and all they were given for their forced march was half a dozen ship's biscuits, thrown down on to the ice. Could it be that Captain Watt was troubled by a pricking of his conscience? Certainly, just as the boys were leaving, he gestured towards where another ship, the *Myrtle*, lay trapped in the ice, and called out to them that they would be given food there. It would later be claimed that he told them to turn back if they felt themselves in danger. (How else could they have felt?) Two hours later he climbed the rigging to check on their progress through the telescope. 'Had we not better send some men after these boys?' he called down to the mate. 'No fears of them,' came Kerr's callous reply - 'They will be back for their dinner.' Alone among the stowaways, Peter Currie was allowed to stay on board - his father, it was said, being a friend of the mate's.

Making their way towards land, the six boys' ordeal steadily worsened where the ice showed signs of cracking and gaping holes had opened up. In areas of broken ice, they fanned out, each plotting his individual course in order to spread their total weight. As they leaped from ice floe to ice floe, at one time or another all of the boys without exception slithered and slipped into pools of meltwater, and as soon as they hauled themselves clear their dripping clothes instantly froze solid. The first time that the youngest of the group, Hugh McEwan, broke through thin ice, Bryson was there to help haul him out. When the same thing happened a second time McEwan managed to cope without help, but his luck finally ran out around midday when soft ice parted beneath him yet again. Even though they were a matter of yards away, Bryson and Brand were powerless to intervene, and as they looked on in horror the small boy slipped below the surface and the ice closed over him. They waited a few moments, more in hope than in expectation, then hurried on. They did not look back.

Some hours later another of the eleven-year-olds, Hugh McGinnes, reached the limit of his endurance and slumped down on the ice, the rags he was dressed in frozen solid and his bare feet torn and bleeding. The others urged him to get up or else he would surely freeze to death, but the small boy had nothing more to give. He begged his companions not to leave him but they had to carry on, and his pitiful cries accompanied them until he was nothing more than a tiny speck in the distance. How exactly the end for McGinnes came about is impossible to know. Close to exhaustion themselves, the four remaining boys were forced to scramble over troughs and ridges of serrated ice, until eventually they reached their final hurdle. On the far side of a wide channel of open water the houses of a village could be seen. Using wooden battens they had brought from the *Arran* as makeshift paddles, Brand and Reilly tried to guide ice-rafts towards the shore but they made heavy weather of it and soon gave up. In sheer desperation, Reilly offered to swim ashore but, just before the onset of the dark, the boys were spotted by a local woman, Catherine Ann Gillies-MacInnis, and a short time later a small boat left the shore and made its way towards them. The boys' relief, we may be sure, must have been intense. Once on dry land, they learned from the local fisherfolk that they had crossed the ice-clogged Bay of St George and had reached 'The Highlands' - a small settlement of expatriate Scots on the western rim of Newfoundland. All four were in poor shape. After twelve hours on the ice John Paul's feet were ulcerated and bleeding, too tender even for socks. Two of James Bryson's toes were frostbitten and all four boys suffered from ice-blindness for some time to come. At The Highlands they were provided with the necessities of life by a farmer-cum-fisherman, also a MacInnis. A search party was got up but, in spite of its members' best efforts, no trace of the two lost boys, McEwan or McGinnes, could be found. Sometime later, once the surviving four had recovered from their ordeal on the ice, they were put to work at a place called Sandy Point, on the far side of the bay, where locally-caught fish was regularly traded for items such as salt and flour brought in by boat. Here the boys stayed - happily, so we are told - for the next four months. As for the *Arran*, when the sea-ice finally relaxed its grip, she continued across the Gulf of St Lawrence and reached Quebec within a fortnight.

A short time later a letter arrived at Greenock which created quite a stir. Dated 10 June 1868, it had apparently been posted from Quebec by an unidentified member of the *Arran's* crew, and the picture it painted of the stowaways' treatment aboard ship was a shocking one. Their clothing, the writer recalls, was pitifully inadequate for extreme cold that even the suitably-dressed crew themselves 'could hardly stand'. The boys were near-starved, he continues, and often incurred the wrath of the ship's mate who administered 'a walloping' at every opportunity; singled out for special mention were the savage beatings meted out to James Bryson. 'It would take too long to tell you how [the stowaways] were used,' the crewman had written. And at the end of this abuse, six out of the seven had been left to fend for themselves on the frozen sea off Newfoundland.

As the story spread throughout Greenock, it sparked outrage and indignation and soon the whole town was alight with anger. When word went round at the end of July that the *Arran* had been seen, making her way up the Firth of Clyde, an angry mob, both men and women, gathered on the quayside to await her arrival. There had been a rumour that, anticipating a hostile reception, Watt and Kerr had already disembarked, either at the Cloch Lighthouse or at Gourock, but it was found to be false when the two officers were recognised on deck and greeted immediately by a barrage of catcalls, curses and threats. As soon as the ship was moored, a number of local men leapt aboard with revenge in mind, forcing the captain and mate to hastily withdraw and barricade themselves below deck. As the situation escalated, the harbour master, Captain Millar, sent an urgent message to the local police station and officers arrived in numbers to quell the disturbance, though the crowd on the quayside did not disperse till nearly midnight. Policemen remained posted until morning when Watt and Kerr were escorted by horse-drawn cab to the town's courthouse. All along the route their vehicle was dogged by a baying mob who yelled and jeered and pelted it with stones. In the court offices the two men were interviewed by Greenock's Procurator Fiscal and, based on the answers they gave, both of them were charged with assault and with 'cruelly and maliciously compelling one or more of Her Majesty's lieges to leave a ship while said ship was embedded in ice at a considerable distance from land to the imminent risk and serious and permanent injury of their persons.' Neither man was granted bail but, had they but known it, their current situation was about to become a good deal worse.

As Canadian seamen came and went at the port of Greenock, rumours grew rife concerning the fate of the boys on the ice, but only when the Procurator Fiscal for Renfrewshire established telegraph contact with St John's, Newfoundland, was definite information received. The reply from Canada indicated that four of the boys - at this stage unnamed - were alive and well at St George's Bay, but it was another three weeks before the St John's police chief confirmed that McEwan and McGinnes were the two who had lost their lives. Based on this new information, both Watt and Kerr had the charge against them increased to murder, and it was now more essential than ever that the four rescued boys be brought back from Canada to act as witnesses in the forthcoming trial. As it happened, Greenock's provost and local MP, James Grieve, was the owner of a shipping company, Baine and Johnston, whose vessel, the *Hannah and Bennie*, was on the point of leaving Newfoundland, so he offered the boys free passage home. Said to have been reluctant to leave Canada, in the end only three of them sailed from St John's on Saturday, 12 September - Barney Reilly had already left to find work at Halifax, Nova Scotia, as was always his intention. Three weeks after leaving Newfoundland, in the evening of Thursday, 1 October, the *Hannah and Bennie* docked at Greenock where the three well-fed and decently-clad boys disembarked to be greeted with a warm and sympathetic reception on the quayside. William Brand would later recall that he hardly recognised his brother, kitted out as he was 'in sailor fashion', and that the family home was bustling with friends and neighbours until the early hours of the morning.

For reasons that are unclear, while awaiting trial the charge against Watt and Kerr was reduced from murder to the lesser crime of culpable homicide. Their appearance at the High Court in Edinburgh took place on Monday, 23 November, and the case stretched out over three days. Such was the level of public interest that throughout the entire proceedings the courtroom was full to bursting, and when the charges were read out both men pled not guilty. Naturally the principal prosecution witnesses were James Bryson, David Brand and John Paul - this last so small, it was said, that 'he had to be mounted on a stool in the witness-box so that he could be seen'. There was amusement in the courtroom when, cross-examined by the defence, he said that he had run away from home 'for a pleasure sail.' Questioned about their voyage, all three gave corroborative accounts of the barbarous treatment they had been subjected to. When the time came for members of the crew to testify, none could deny that the boys had been abused - Bryson in particular - or that they had left the ship under anything other than duress. Asked why no-one had intervened, the rather limp reply was that it was not a seaman's place to question his officers' decisions. A main plank of the defence was an attempt to convince the jury that food aboard the *Arran* was in short supply, an argument easily demolished when John Hendry, the vessel's owner, stated that she had been amply provisioned for a period of four months at sea. Hendry's testimony was endorsed by the ship's cook, William Saltoun.

It seems probable that James Kerr saw the way the wind was blowing when, part-way through the trial, he opted to change his plea. He was prepared to plead guilty to assault, his legal counsel intimated, on condition that the charge against him of culpable homicide be dropped. Inexplicably, the Solicitor-General on behalf of the Crown was prepared to accede to this proposal and Kerr's sentencing was deferred till the end of the trial. It was made clear that no similar concession would be extended to Captain Watt. During its final summing-up, the best arguments the defence could muster all sounded rather feeble. Captain Watt, it was stated, had been under no obligation to feed and cleed stowaways - 'of the very worst class' - aboard the *Arran*: an argument, of course, which ignored completely the dictates of common humanity. It was claimed that when the ship became ice-bound, the boys had left of their own volition, on the understanding that they were free to return should their ice-crossing become dangerous. There was no definitive proof, the defence continued, to confirm that McEwan and McGinnes were unquestionably dead: all that was known for sure was that McEwan had 'plumped into the water and was lost sight of for three seconds [and] it would surprise no-one if both McEwan and McGinnes were to turn up alive and well'. In the absence of a body, the defence argued, it would be unsafe to convict the captain of culpable homicide. Watt's own declaration stretched credulity no less than his lawyer's had. He had, he claimed, 'invited' the boys to step down on to the ice and 'have a fine run ashore'. Regarding the question of coercion, his response was, to say the least, equivocal. 'I cannot say I forced the boys to leave the ship,' he said, 'but, of course, I told them to go.'

Called by the defence, various witnesses were prepared to vouch for Watt's sound character. Two members of the *Arran's* crew, Steward John McLean and Boatswain Lawrence Thomson, described their captain as 'a kind, quiet man', and responsibility for discipline aboard ship, they said, was delegated to the mate. Watt's minister at Ardrossan and four fellow-parishioners all praised his fine personal qualities, and the chaplain of the Seaman's Friend Society of Greenock went so far as to suggest that stowaways deliberately chose ships he captained because of his known kindly disposition. In the final analysis, of course, the judgment of the jury was the one that counted and its members took little more than half an hour to come to their conclusion. Based on his own confession, James Kerr, was guilty of assault. Turning to the second man in the dock, they found Robert Watt not guilty of assault but guilty of culpable homicide. Taking account of his previous good name, however, they recommended him to the mercy of the court. It now fell to the judge, the Lord Justice-Clerk, George Patton, to draw matters to a close by passing sentence.

Addressing his opening remarks to James Kerr, the judge announced that in redress for the part he had played in this appalling affair he would spend four months in jail. Then, turning to the second convicted man, he sentenced Robert Watt to eighteen months' imprisonment for being responsible for the loss of two lives. When Patton fell silent, his words were greeted by angry hisses from the public benches whose occupants deplored the leniency of the two men's sentences and wanted their views to be known. Their reaction was surely understandable, and it would be hard to argue that the punishments were an accurate reflection of the gravity of the two men's crimes.

So, the trial brought matters to a close - however unsatisfactorily - but it had gone no way toward solving the most pressing puzzle of all: why? What was Captain Watt's motive for abandoning six helpless boys to an unknown fate on the frozen ocean? And, in so doing, what could he possibly have hoped to achieve? The mate, James Kerr, is often depicted as the villain of the piece, the captain too weak to assert himself, but that reading of events seems not to take account of Watt's part in the flogging of James Bryson, or his violent role in ejecting the six stowaways. When all is said and done, the outcome of the trial left observers no closer as to the whys and wherefores of the case than they had been beforehand.

For what the future held for the story's main protagonists, we are indebted largely to the old Greenock historian, John Donald - apparently a would-be stowaway himself at the age of eleven. Both Watt and Kerr, he tells us, returned to the sea as captain and mate, but of different ships. Within a year or two of Watt's release, he died at Pensacola, Florida; but Kerr was more fortunate and lived on into his sixties. Ironically, the favoured stowaway, Peter Currie, died of tuberculosis while still in his early teens. Barney Reilly, as we know, travelled on to Halifax, Nova Scotia, where initially he found employment in the fishing fleet before moving on to work on the railways. The reviled James Bryson emigrated with his family to the United States where he worked as a New York streetcar conductor. John Paul became a foreman riveter in England, carrying out his trade at Caird's Yard, Wollaston Ironworks, in the Itchen district of Southampton where, due to his slight built, his workmates nicknamed him 'Sparrow'. He married a local girl and fathered no fewer than twelve children. Paul died, aged 56 in February 1913 and, sadly, he is buried in an unmarked grave at St Mary's Extra Cemetery. David Brand was the boy-stowaway who travelled farthest. Settling in Townsville, Australia, he founded a successful engineering company and lived out his remaining years far from the Canadian chill in the tropical warmth of northern Queensland. But for the two lost boys, Hugh McEwan and Hugh McGinnes, no such rosy future would unfold after their lives were needlessly squandered on the frozen seas off Newfoundland. As for the final character in the tragic tale, the *Arran* herself, she came to a sticky end when she was wrecked on Sand Island in the Gulf of Mexico during a voyage from Greenock to Mobile, Alabama, in 1886.

George Chalmers
Braco, Perthshire - December 1869

Shortly after six o'clock on the morning of Wednesday, 22 December 1869, Peter McLeish, a farm worker in Perthshire, was passing the Blackhill tollhouse, a mile or so from the village of Braco. He was surprised to see the house in darkness with no sign of the tollkeeper, John Miller, a bachelor in his mid-sixties who lived there alone. He reached out and knocked at the door, and when there was no reply he tried turning the handle but found it fastened from the inside. He was still pondering his next move when Archibald McLaren, the local miller, arrived at the toll and both men tried hammering on the door and calling out loudly, but still there was no response. Certain now that something must be wrong, McLeish set off for the blacksmith's forge just along the road, while McLaren left at a jog to alert the tollkeeper's sister who lived not far away at Garrick Cottage. When she heard the miller's story, Mary Bayne bustled back with him to the tollhouse where she tried a key in the lock which remained stubbornly secure. Eventually, as a last resort, McLaren took it upon himself to cut a pane of glass out of the window, broke open the shutters using a hatchet and clambered over the sill. He was not prepared for what he found inside.

Two days earlier - on Monday, 20 December - the tollkeeper had been visited by an enigmatic, late-going stranger. He had not yet gone to bed as a dance was being held at nearby Beannie farm and he expected that revellers would be late on the road. Presumably the stranger had spotted a light in the tollhouse window when he appeared on the doorstep at around eleven o'clock. In Miller's own words, his visitor was 'a big, stout, black-like man' whom he had seen earlier that day, loitering near the toll. Heedless of the hour, the stranger invited himself in, took a seat, lit his pipe and settled down for a blether, but the tollkeeper could not help noticing that he was careful not to give much away in terms of personal information. The only explanation he offered for his presence was a prior arrangement, so he said, to meet up with a certain unspecified someone returning from the dance. Once he had finished his smoke, he got to his feet, put on his coat and stepped out into the darkness, leaving Miller no wiser as to who he might have been. That said, there was nothing in the stranger's manner that had caused him to feel uneasy or in any sense under threat.

The following afternoon two of Miller's nephews happened to be working near the toll, and during the course of a conversation with their uncle, he brought up the subject of his mysterious guest who, he speculated, might be a newly-appointed gamekeeper on the Ardoch estate. Keepers had recently been active, he warned his nephews, and suggested that it would make sense for the time being to keep their dogs on a short leash. Later that evening he gave a similar account of the stranger's visit to an old friend, Walter McLaren, a shepherd at Inverardoch, by Muthill, who regularly dropped in at the tollhouse where the two men were in the habit of playing draughts together. Once again Miller voiced his theory that the stranger might be a new gamekeeper and, as he showed his guest to the door, he mentioned that he would leave it unlocked, just in case Archibald McLaren paid him a visit before bedtime. When Walter said goodbye at around eight o'clock, he turned out to be the last local man ever to see his friend alive.

After easing himself over the windowsill, what Archibald McLaren saw must have sickened him to the pit of his stomach. In the westernmost of the two small rooms, John Miller's body lay spreadeagled on the floor with his legs crumpled up beneath him. His head was badly cut, and blood had soaked his upper clothing before pooling on the floor where it had started to congeal. Bashed and bloodied, his hat lay beside him. It was clear to McLaren that Miller had been interrupted during his normal, everyday routine, since a plate of bread, ham and cheese was sitting undisturbed on a stool by the fireside. Placed alongside, a glass of the tollkeeper's favourite tipple, the dark sweet ale known as porter, had not been spilt. McLaren edged around the body, careful not to disturb the crime scene, then entered the narrow lobby leading to the front door which, as he had expected, was locked but with no key visible. In spite of the difficulty, he managed to raise the door from its hinges, letting it swing open and allowing Miller's relatives to come inside. As to the murder weapon, a hefty iron crowbar, streaked with blood and hair, had been abandoned behind the cottage. At around eight o'clock McLaren left to walk to Braco in order to telegraph news of the crime to police at Dunblane.

As Mary Bayne scanned the room where her brother's body lay, she noticed immediately that the silver pocket watch and chain that he wore every day were missing. All of the buttons had been torn from the front of his clothing. 'Being of a saving turn', John Miller had kept money hidden in a wooden chest which his sister now found locked and with no sign of the key. She swung open the lid of a second chest and saw straightaway that various articles of her brother's clothing had been removed: his grey tweed suit, made to measure by a tailor in Braco; his tartan shepherd's plaid; a red-and-black striped shirt; and a distinctive pair of fine blucher boots. Around midday Police Superintendent Peter Stewart and Constable John Ingram arrived from Dunblane, and immediately set about the task of examining the crime scene. From the pockets of a tattered waistcoat, presumably left behind by the killer, they extricated various odds and ends - a small comb, a pair of scissors, some needles and fishhooks, and a pawnbroker's receipt in the name of 'John Smith'. A well-worn pair of boots, distinctively lined with oat straw, had been tossed under the bed. When Superintendent Stewart forced open the locked chest, he found that it had been ransacked with one forlorn, solitary penny left behind. There appeared to be nothing to suggest that a forced entry had been made or, for that matter, that any kind of struggle had taken place. It looked very much as though the dead man had been taken by surprise. Outside the cottage, the two officers followed a series of footprints that led to a closet window looking directly into the west room where the tollkeeper would have been preparing his solitary, candlelit supper. It was easy to imagine that the killer had crept from the window to the front door and slipped stealthily inside before launching his attack. At the cost of a human life, his estimated total haul had amounted to a mere twenty shillings - roughly £100 today.

Later in the day Dr William Forrest of Stirling - a surname, as we know, familiar to the medical profession in that town - and two colleagues visited the tollhouse and carried out a post-mortem examination of Miller's body which revealed a total of three wounds on the head, inflicted, the doctors judged, between nine and ten o'clock the previous evening. The dead man's heart and blood vessels were entirely drained of blood, but the most disturbing conclusion they drew was that the tollkeeper had remained alive for some time after the attack. Once the post-mortem was completed and correct procedures followed, police authorised the release of Miller's body which was taken to his sister's home to await burial three days later in Braco kirkyard.

Suspicion fell immediately on any travelling folk who were known to have passed through the area in recent days. On the selfsame day that the murder was discovered, no fewer than three tramps were taken into custody - two at Crieff, five miles from the scene of the crime; and another a similar distance away at Comrie - only to be released a short time later for lack of evidence. A few days later a telegraph was received by the chief constable of Perth to the effect that on Christmas Day a labourer at Maryhill Spelter Works near Glasgow had come across two tattered cotton shirts and a 'semmit' - vest - lying in a ditch underneath two heavy stones. Apparently it was common for vagrants to sleep beside the furnaces and Maryhill police had suspected a possible connection with the Braco murder, but whether the Perthshire force pursued such a tenuous lead seems doubtful. One of the most curious aspects of the case was why it took local police a full week after the murder before they got round to searching the east-facing room of the cottage, by that time boarded up. Whatever the reason for the delay, during their belated search Superintendent Stewart and Constable William Morgan turned up more abandoned clothing, hidden beneath a pile of firewood. From the pocket of a loose-fitting 'sack coat' they retrieved a tobacco pipe and a shoemaker's tool known as an 'awl'. A pair of blood-spattered corduroy trousers and a man's cap were found nearby, which Mary Bayne assured them had not belonged to her late brother. It was a reasonable assumption that the clothing had been abandoned after the murderer got himself dressed in his victim's clothing. Its worn-out, tattered condition supported the theory that the 'big, stout, black-like man' police were seeking was likely to be a tramp.

Following what sounded like a promising tip-off, Superintendent Stewart travelled to Edinburgh in early January 1870 amid high hopes of an imminent arrest. A plasterer's labourer from Dundee, Owen McGachon, had been seen near Braco around Christmas-time and, after his description was circulated, he was traced to Edinburgh and eventually detained by West Lothian police at Addiewell, near Bathgate. Transferred to Dunblane, he was kept under lock and key for seven days, but at the end of the week it was concluded that the evidence against him was too flimsy to proceed with this particular line of inquiry. It took until the middle of the month before police were able to attach a name to the man they were looking for. Their breakthrough came about when the custodian of Alloa jail read press reports of the Blackhill murder and realised that he recognised the items of clothing that had been left behind, and some of the contents of the pockets. These, he believed, were the property of a prisoner he had locked up on Thursday, 9 December, following a conviction for disorderly conduct. At the end of a ten-day term the individual in question, one George Chalmers, was released on the day immediately prior to the murder. Curiously at odds with Miller's 'big, stout, black-like man', Chalmers was in his mid-forties, short in stature, with an estimated weight of little more than nine stones. His eyes were 'hazel or grey' in colour, and his hair and whiskers were reddish-brown. He had a long face with prominent cheekbones and a ruddy complexion, and a hollow to one side of his jaw suggested that he was missing a number of teeth. Believed to be a native of Aberdeenshire, he spoke with a stutter and walked with a slouch. With no positive sightings to go on, a £50 reward was put up the following month - February - but still Chalmers proved elusive. In late April a policeman stationed at Kenmore, Constable Kennedy, arrested a tramp who appeared to resemble Chalmers' description. The man was duly escorted to Aberfeldy, jailed overnight and transferred on to Perth the following day, but he too had to be released without charge. By this time news of the Blackhill murder had evidently spread far and wide, and improbable reports circulated during May that upwards of forty suspects had been arrested south of the border, every one of whom was subsequently freed. One unfortunate individual was brought all of 300 miles from Rotherham,

Yorkshire, to Perth, only to be promptly eliminated from inquiries.

Locating Chalmers' whereabouts presented more of a challenge than might have been expected, but at the end of the day a commendable piece of vigilance on the part of two Dundonian officers was what turned police fortunes around. In the early hours of Saturday, 14 May - nearly five months after John Miller's murder - Constable Edward Billington was on his regular nightshift duty in the Princes Street area when he spied a suspicious-looking character, dressed in worn and ragged clothing, who was walking the city streets. When questioned, the man stated that he had recently been made unemployed and was travelling via Arbroath to his home in Aberdeen. Following a short exchange, the two men parted company but Billington was left with a troublesome niggle that refused to let up. During a routine rendezvous with his superior officer, Sergeant Parr, he made a point of mentioning his encounter with the travelling man, and the description he gave was enough to jog the sergeant's memory. Some time earlier a document containing details of the Braco murderer had been circulated among Scottish police forces and, by sheer good fortune, the sergeant had a copy to hand. After poring over the paper for a few moments, the two officers decided that the likeness was close enough to merit further inquiry, and they set off along the Arbroath road without delay. After walking a few miles, however, they had seen neither hide nor hair of their suspect. Just beyond the Eastern Necropolis they intercepted a workman driving his horse and cart towards Dundee to ask whether he happened to have met anyone matching the wanted man's description, but it turned out that he had seen no-one at all in the last few miles. Reluctantly the policemen retraced their steps into the city, but when his shift ended at six o'clock, suspicion was still gnawing at Constable Billington who went straight home, changed into civilian clothes and left on a solo mission to locate the travelling man.

Billington took the Arbroath road once again, but this time round his quest was more successful. At around eight o'clock he caught up with his suspect near Claypotts farm where it transpired he had spent the night sleeping in a barn. When informed that he was being apprehended on suspicion of being the Braco murderer, the man vehemently denied the allegation, insisting that his name was not George Chalmers, but rather Andrew Brown, and that he was the innocent victim in a case of mistaken identity. Still unconvinced, Billington escorted him to Broughty Ferry police station where it was obvious to all that his appearance bore a strong resemblance to Chalmers' official description. He was taken on the eleven o'clock train to Dundee and interrogated at the city's main police station where he stated that he was a hawker to trade, occasionally turning a penny or two by singing in the streets, but he still flatly denied that he was the murderer: 'Na, na,' he told his interviewers, 'There's been a few ta'en up for that already. Ye'll need tae let me awa'.' Pressed further, however, his resistance gradually crumbled and he was left with no option but to submit to the inevitable. For the first time he admitted his true identity, and conceded at the same time that he had been released from Alloa jail on Monday, 20 December. He was charged accordingly with the murder of John Miller.

There followed an effusion of information - reliable or otherwise - and a number of minor confessions. By Chalmers' account, four or five years previously he had been obliged to flee his hometown of Fraserburgh and adopt the alias of James Wilson after purloining property belonging to one of his relatives. In the years that followed he had kept on the move, picking up work where he could find it, in positions varying from routine farm work on the one hand to crewing a whaling vessel on the other. During hard times, he repeated, he had been forced to resort to busking and begging in the street. He admitted to having served a term of imprisonment in Aberdeenshire after being convicted - somewhat bizarrely - of cutting a piece out of the hip of a sheep. Crucially, however, he insisted to officers that he had had no involvement in the murder of John Miller, nor indeed had he so much as visited the village of Braco.

He explained that, after being released at Alloa, he had made his way first to Stirling where he spent several hours viewing Wombwell's Show - a travelling menagerie, popular at the time, containing foreign and exotic beasts. He had then walked a few miles farther south and slept at a colliery near Bannockburn. The second night - Tuesday, 21 December - he spent in a haystack near the Carron Ironworks before moving on the following morning and reaching Edinburgh later in the day, where, signing in as Andrew Brown, he had found lodgings at a hostel for the homeless - the Night Asylum in the Canongate. (The use of an alias was a commonplace practice here since an individual's overnight stays were limited to three in any given month.) During the five months since then, he had worked his way south to Newcastle and found employment in herding cattle throughout Northumberland. When work dried up, he had returned to Scotland, drifting from Glasgow to Stirling and on to Perth. He had continued via Sheriffmuir - thus avoiding Dunblane - and arrived in Dundee on Friday, 13 May, where he had spent the evening drinking in the city's public houses. At eight o'clock the next morning - Saturday, 14 May - he had been placed under arrest by Constable Billington. Despite being manacled and kept under constant watch, Chalmers appeared relaxed and nonchalant, joking with his jailers that he would very soon be free. The following day he was taken by train to Dunblane, where it was now Superintendent Stewart's task to come up with evidence strong enough to link him with the murder. To that end, Dunblane officers escorted him back to Dundee where they paraded him through the city streets and public houses in the hope that someone might recall having seen him spending freely during the evening of Wednesday, 22 December - the day Miller's body was found. No witnesses, however, came forward. Inquiries in the towns of Linlithgow, Falkirk and Stirling similarly drew a blank. His photograph was distributed widely, but still no joy.

Back at Dunblane, a fortnight after giving his original statement, Chalmers indicated that he wished to make a correction. He had been guilty of an error, he explained, when he had previously stated that he spent the night of Tuesday, 21 December, sleeping in a haystack near the Carron Ironworks. There were witnesses, he claimed, who could confirm that on the night in question he had sought and been given leave to sleep in the corn-house at Easter Manuel farm, just west of Linlithgow, where he had been locked up between six o'clock in the evening and eight o'clock the next morning. But when officers followed up his claim, they found that none of the workers at Easter Manuel was able to corroborate his story due to uncertainty over the precise date of when he had stayed there. So, dismissing his attempted alibi as unverifiable, they returned to the thorny task of sourcing hard and fast evidence. Had Chalmers been in possession of some of Miller's clothing or other belongings at the time of his arrest, then their job would have been a good deal more straightforward - but he wasn't, plain and simple. As things stood, they knew that their best chance of convincing a jury depended upon two things: first, to place their man at Braco on the day of the murder; and secondly, to establish beyond doubt that the various items abandoned in the tollhouse belonged to him.

At one point the case took an unexpected detour when five-year-old Margaret Burns was found grievously injured at the foot of a dimly-lit stairwell in Glasgow. The doctors who treated her put the child's injuries down to the result of a brutal attempted rape, and ultimately it proved impossible to save her life. Local police put out a description of a man they were seeking to assist with their inquiries: roughly five feet seven inches in height, he had red or fair hair and whiskers, and 'a very dirty appearance'. The resemblance to Chalmers was unmistakeable, on top of which he was known to have been living rough in Glasgow shortly before the atrocity, sleeping at the foot of stairwells and in outhouses. Two children who had caught a glimpse of the murderer were brought to Dunblane where they concluded that Chalmers looked more like Margaret's killer than any other suspect they had been shown. At the end of the day, however, there was insufficient evidence to justify laying charges and, despite arrests stretching from Rothesay to Lockerbie - plus an unfounded confession from a mentally ill man in Haddington - Margaret Burns's murderer was never traced.

Back at Dunblane, efforts to pin down Chalmers' movements were starting to bear fruit. The warder at Alloa prison, William Wallace, reported that prior to his release Chalmers had told him that he planned to go first to Stirling where he would cross the River Forth before striking south-east towards Falkirk and Edinburgh. William Muirhead, an engineman at Low Plean colliery, south of Stirling, told investigating officers that Chalmers had spent the night of Monday, 20 December, bedded down beside the pit furnace - a place where travelling folk regularly gathered for warmth - and had departed the following morning. But not, as it turned out, towards Edinburgh. Contrary to his earlier statement, police discovered that Chalmers had turned instead in a northerly direction, joining forces somewhere along the way with an unknown companion. Partway between Dunblane and Braco a housemaid at Upper Whitestone farm, Isabella Robertson, reported having seen two men begging: the tall one wearing a blue overcoat; and the second whom she described as shorter in height, and who spoke with a stutter and moved with a shambling gait. Steadily, police were able to build up a picture of Chalmers' movements throughout the rest of the day. Robert Whyte, an innkeeper at Braco, had been making his way home from Greenloaning by moonlight when he met him walking in the opposite direction towards Blackhill. A shoemaker, John Dewar, crossed his path a short time later. He aroused the suspicions of three men - James Urquhart, John Finlayson and Robert Howden - when he stepped out of the darkness to ask if they were gamekeepers and to cadge a few matches. To a man, they found his manner a bit strange and disconcerting. And at around twenty minutes past eight a labourer, John McOwen, met him less than a mile from Blackhill.

When it came to identifying the items found in the tollhouse, Chalmers' shenanigans in early December rebounded on him with a vengeance. According to the Alloa policemen involved in his arrest - Constable Robertson and Sergeants Ferguson and Carmichael - the articles of clothing bore a striking resemblance to what he had been wearing at the time. The three officers were also able to identify some of the items retrieved from the pockets. The proprietor of the *Alloa Journal*, John Haldon, had sat through his trial and had no doubt that the cap, tattered coat and corduroy trousers belonged to Chalmers. Back at the prison, William Wallace recognised the distinctively straw-lined boots and, since part of his job involved emptying a prisoner's pockets, he was certain that the various small items - the comb, tobacco pipe, cobbler's awl, needles, scissors and pawnbroker's ticket - belonged to Chalmers. According to Sergeant Carmichael, finding fishhooks in a prisoner's pockets was an unusual enough occurrence to be fairly memorable.

While police inquiries were ongoing, details emerged concerning Chalmers' background and character. In early July the Procurator Fiscal for Aberdeenshire, William Boyd, visited the accused's hometown of Fraserburgh where he spoke to a number of individuals who had known Chalmers since childhood. The doctor who had attended him as a boy stated his opinion that his brain showed signs of being defective from a very early age. His maternal aunt cited various instances of petty mischief for which he had been responsible. A gardener and his wife were questioned who had been his neighbours for a number of years, as was James Burnett, farmer at Kirkton, who had been his employer. A postman, James Gray, told the Fiscal that Chalmers had on one occasion threatened him with violence. All those interviewed concurred that he was a fairly spineless individual, of notably low intelligence, but there was general consensus that he made for an unlikely murderer. All in all, Boyd's investigations were a low-key affair whose findings were relatively restrained. Others opted for a different approach. An altogether more colourful depiction of Chalmers' character appeared in press reports and focused squarely on his 'vicious and unrestrainable temper' and tendency to 'bodily violence'. From early childhood, it alleged, he suffered from a form of 'semi-madness' and was subject to 'fits of rage', growing in time to become 'the terror of the neighbourhood'. Such was his reputation among the douce townsfolk of Fraserburgh, it said, that 'to hear him a suspected murderer does not seem to have very much surprised them'. Almost certainly such lurid reporting was aimed at satisfying the public's appetite for sensationalism, and it is perhaps significant that none of the opinions expressed was attributed to any named source.

When George Chalmers appeared in court at Perth on Tuesday, 6 September 1870, without hesitation he pled not guilty. His strategy, it quickly became clear, was to deny everything. No, he'd had nothing to do with John Miller's murder, and he repeated his earlier assertion that he had never set foot near Braco. Shown the clothing recovered from the tollhouse, he stated that, no, these were not the clothes he had worn during his prison term at Alloa; and, no again, he recognised none of the contents of the pockets - at no time, specifically, had he ever carried fishhooks. Weighted against his blanket denial was the testimony of multiple witnesses - a total of 46 for the prosecution - which placed him in the vicinity of Blackhill Toll on Tuesday, 21 December; which showed his attempted alibi to be false; and which identified the clothing and other odds and ends found at the tollhouse as his belongings. Granted, the absence of definitive evidence might have worked in his favour, coupled with the authorities' failure to recover any of John Miller's stolen clothing, but at the end of the day the weight of circumstantial evidence proved persuasive and, following an absence of less than an hour, the jury returned to the courtroom. 'Gentlemen,' said the Clerk of Court, 'have you agreed upon your verdict?' 'We have,' replied the foreman of the jury. 'What is it?' asked the Clerk. A profound hush descended as the foreman gave his reply: 'The jury, by a majority, find the prisoner, George Chalmers, guilty as libelled.'

The revulsion that the Lord Justice Clerk, James Moncrieff, felt for Chalmers' crime was reflected in his words when he turned to sentence him: 'I shall not aggravate the position in which you stand,' he said, 'by saying anything in regard to the nature of the crime of which you have been found guilty.' He went on to advise Chalmers to devote what time he had left - 'short as it is [but] much longer than that which your victim was allowed' - to preparing himself for his inescapable fate. Then, placing the black cap upon his head, the judge pronounced that a month hence, on Tuesday, 4 October, Chalmers would be executed within the precincts of Perth County Prison, and he concluded with the formulaic phrase - 'May God Almighty have mercy upon your soul.' Throughout his trial Chalmers had given an impression of being unable to concentrate, or fully grasp his position. It was said that he had entered the dock with a smile on his face, and even during the airing of the most gruesome details of his crime remained apparently unmoved. Only now, as proceedings drew to a close, did he display any emotion, breaking down in tears and sobbing pitifully as he was led from the court.

For the most part, he was a good deal more composed while awaiting execution in Perth prison, reportedly eating and sleeping well on his straw mattress, despite being handcuffed at night and kept under constant watch. In daytime he was allowed a fellow prisoner for company. Various clergymen visited him regularly for whom he recounted his recent history. Until seven or eight years ago, he told them, he had lived with his mother and father on a 'pendicle' - a smallholding on a large estate near Fraserburgh. His parents, he said, were decent and respectable folk, and it was only after they died that his life went into a downward spiral. Evicted from the family home, he had no option but to take up a wandering life, carrying out spells of casual work and begging in the streets when there was no alternative. Through a growing dependency on alcohol, he acquired a reputation for disorderly behaviour which inevitably led to his name being linked with any instances of wrongdoing in the locality. He freely admitted to having been a thief, but was insistent that he had not at any time been guilty of robbery or burglary. The murder of John Miller he consistently denied, claiming that those who testified against him had perjured themselves. In spite of his shady past, a widely supported petition was raised in Fraserburgh by a local minister, Rev. McLaren, and was one of two such submissions to the Home Secretary, Henry Bruce, attempting to stave off the execution, mainly on the grounds that Chalmers' conviction was entirely circumstantial and therefore unsafe. In a further example of pastoral concern, Rev. McLaren made the journey to Perth where he visited him in the condemned cell on two occasions. But in the end the petitions changed nothing, and on the day prior to his execution the director of the prison, Sheriff Barclay, read him a communication received from the Home Secretary intimating that after careful consideration he had decreed that the law must take its course. Despite listening closely, it was obvious that Chalmers had been unable to grasp the substance of the letter, and, following Barclay's departure, it fell to the prison chaplain, Rev. St Clair, to break to him the news that his last chance of a reprieve had failed. Although he had been given no inkling through official channels of efforts made on his behalf, it seems likely that he had received a sideways hint from one of his fellow inmates. It was a painful occasion for all concerned when Chalmers received a final visit from his two brothers - James Chalmers, an Arbroath shoemaker; and William, a labourer back home in Fraserburgh. The two men were accompanied by their brother-in-law, William Macdonald, a slater at nearby Peterhead. Such was the weight of emotion, so it was said, that for a time none of the men was able to utter a word for fear of breaking down, and only through the compassionate intervention of a prison official was the silence finally broken. When the time came to say a last farewell, all four shed tears at their final parting.

On the last night before his execution Chalmers retired at ten o'clock. Rev. St Clair and one of the warders stayed with him and reported in the morning that, though he lay still through the night, he managed to snatch no more than a few minutes' sleep during the early hours. When breakfast was brought to him at six o'clock, he drank tea but showed no appetite for bread. At around half-past seven Rev. Fleming of St Paul's Church joined the prison chaplain. The two ministers were saddened to find Chalmers largely unresponsive to their 'devotional exercises' and equally unaffected by two edifying tracts - *Baxter's Call to the Unconverted* and Bunyan's *Jerusalem Sinner Saved* - they had provided him with. Meanwhile, Lord Provost John Pullar, town magistrates, dignitaries and a number of local pressmen had assembled in the Town Hall and, preceded by scarlet-robed officers, walked in procession to the prison where Chalmers' death warrant was handed over to the Provost to be read aloud. On entering the building, they were led along narrow corridors, flanked on both sides by the inmates' quarters, until they reached the cell of the condemned man. Opposite his open door, a table had been put in place, and chairs set out. Bibles were distributed, then Rev. Fleming began proceedings with various readings from the scriptures. A paraphrase was sung, following which Rev. St Clair took over and read aloud the aptly-chosen 51st Psalm - 'Have mercy on me, O God [and] blot out my transgressions.' Leaning listlessly against the door jamb, Chalmers showed little interest but, as the last 'amen' died away, he was inevitably drawn into the day's events. Provost Pullar stepped forward to address him, and the short exchange that followed was widely reported -

Provost: *I have been asked by my brother magistrates if you have anything to convey to your friends, or any communication to make?*

Chalmers: *I have nothing to say, but I would like the letter that he* - there indicating Rev. St Clair - *wrote to be sent to my sister.*

Provost: *That is the only communication you have to make to your friends?*

Chalmers: *Yes.*

Provost: *You have nothing else to say?*

Chalmers: *No, sir.*

Provost: *I will give you another opportunity of saying whether you have any other communication to make. You have nothing more to say, except that you wish this letter to be forwarded to your sister?*

Chalmers: *No.*

Despite Pullar's promptings, Chalmers refused to take the bait. Responsibility for cranking up the pressure now passed to Rev. Fleming. 'I have just one word to say to you,' he began, but immediately went on to say a good many more. 'Sin unconfessed is sin unpardoned and sin unforgiven,' he lectured Chalmers, 'and those who are guilty expose themselves to an everlasting doom. If you go into the great eternity with a lie upon your lips, we have reason to fear that you are ... upon the very verge of a bottomless pit.' He continued in much the same vein for a time and concluded by inviting the prisoner to clear his conscience. Chalmers, however, would not budge. 'I am innocent, sir,' he insisted. 'That is all I can say to you.' The clergymen's efforts had hit a brick wall, so they had no option but to step aside and give way to the veteran hangman, William Calcraft, brought from England for the occasion and notorious for his bungling. With him Calcraft carried the ropes and straps of his profession which he used to pinion the condemned man's arms to his sides, assisted by Chalmers himself in tightening an obstinate knot. Finally, when all the straps had been secured, he led him to the prison's internal courtyard where the provost and magistrates were gathered in the shadow of the scaffold. Following the passage of the Capital Punishment Amendment Act of 1868, Chalmers' execution was the first in Scotland to be conducted behind closed doors. Blank walls overlooked the yard, and the drop was partially screened by a curtain of black material.

As church bells tolled solemnly in the background, Chalmers walked to the scaffold calmly and unassisted, and quickly mounted the staircase, easily outpacing Calcraft and Rev. Fleming. Observing the hangman's final preparations with interest, he gave an enigmatic smile, and just as the noose was being looped around his neck, he spoke out clearly: 'I know nothing of this affair,' he proclaimed. 'I will die like a man for it; yes, I will. I was not there at all. I am innocent.' After Rev. Fleming's final prayer, Calcraft placed the white hood on the prisoner's head and drew it down over his eyes. Yet again Rev. St Clair offered him an opportunity to admit his guilt, but Chalmers' reply was unhesitating: 'May the Lord have mercy on me. Goodbye to you all. Farewell for evermore. Thank God, I am innocent.' At that, Calcraft gripped his hand in a final handshake, drew back the bolt and Chalmers plunged from sight. His struggles were mercifully short-lived and, once the requisite length of time had elapsed, his body was cut down and a black flag hoisted above the prison walls as confirmation that the death sentence had been carried out. In marked contrast to the droves of spectators who had attended public executions in the past, no more than a handful had turned up outside the prison who, on seeing the black flag, dispersed quietly. With the exception of Provost Pullar and his circle, there was no-one to witness Chalmers' refusal to crumble under pressure and his bravado in the face of death. Even Calcraft, with his years of experience, was struck by his defiance.

The letter that Chalmers had asked to be sent to his sister, written on his behalf by Rev. St Clair, was published throughout the length and breadth of Scotland:

'Perth Prison, 3d October, 1870

My dear sister - I received both your letters, the first was read to me by the Governor of the Prison; and the last one by Sheriff Barclay, and oh! I felt very sad when listening to your kind and faithful words, while tears ran down my cheeks, as I know they are the last letters I will get from you. I confess with sorrow that I have been a most wicked man for the last twelve years. I disobeyed all the good counsels of our dear father and mother.

I left my home and took to a wandering life, which led me into every kind of evil company, and which I do now most bitterly regret.

O, my dear sister, strong drink has been my ruin; it has been the cause of all my troubles. O, that I had taken your many advices, and kept from that accursed drink; it has brought thousands of men and women to shame and misery, and so it has brought me. I now see the folly of all my sinful ways, and what my reckless life has brought me to. I feel thankful to the Rev. Mr Fleming, the Rev. Dr Manson, Sheriff Barclay, and also the Chaplain of the Prison for all their Christian labours on my behalf.

I have also to thank the Governor of the Prison, as well as all the other prison officers for their uniform kindness to me while here.

My dear sister, I wish you would allow this letter to be made public after my death for the benefit of my fellow creatures, that they may take warning from my sinful and profligate life, and its melancholy end.

So farewell, my dear sister, while I remain your loving but unfortunate brother,

(Signed) George Chalmers.

Joseph Sime, witness.

Andrew Syme [sic], witness.

P.S. - I must add my thanks to my counsel and the agents who did all they could for me.'

In the circumstances Chalmers' letter was a little strange and much of its content was surely not his own work. The wording, we might suspect, was down to Rev. St Clair, and the confessional tone hard to square with the prisoner's consistent denial of guilt. Notably, there was no direct reference to his conviction for murder. When the letter was published, it only added weight to the suspicions of those - two jury members among them - who still held to the belief that, through no fault of his own, Chalmers was an innocent party who became tangled in a web of circumstances beyond his control. But as soon as Calcraft drew back the bolt, their point became an academic one.

In early November Constable Edward Billington received his £50 reward - roughly £5,000 today - for his vital role in the apprehension of George Chalmers. And, aside from the reservations of a few, the entire affair of the Braco murder was finally done and dusted. Or was it? An abiding mystery of the case is the 'big, stout, black-like man' who materialised at John Miller's home on Monday, 20 December, just as George Chalmers was bedding down for the night twenty-odd miles farther south. Who was this night-walking stranger who entered the tollhouse, lit up his pipe and settled down for a smoke? Seemingly forgotten in the clamour surrounding Chalmers and his trial, his part in the story has never been explained. But whoever he was and whatever his motives, one thing we may be sure of is that now, a century and a half on, the stranger's identity is never likely to be known.

VILLAINS AND VICTIMS

Thomas Scobbie
Monifieth, Angus - September 1872

It was only a pair of old flannel shirts, washed and worn many times over, but for folk of modest means they were a loss nonetheless. Somewhere between ten and eleven o'clock on the morning of Tuesday, 24 September 1872, Jean Spalding had hung them out to dry, not far from the cottage at Kingennie, Angus, she shared with other family members, but when she returned in the early afternoon she found them gone. Thinking back, it struck her that she had seen a tramp passing by and, when she told her brother, George, about this he hurried out with his retriever bitch, Juno, in hopes of overtaking the likely thief. Just newly returned from herding livestock, Jean's eleven-year-old son - also named George - followed on behind but reported back a short time later to say his uncle had apprehended the stranger not far away and was questioning him about the stolen clothes.

The man's appearance was highly distinctive - his complexion deeply ravaged by the scars of smallpox. When Spalding ordered him to 'deliver up the shirts', the tramp admitted knowing their whereabouts but maintained that it was not he who had stolen them but rather an acquaintance whom he did not name. Nevertheless, he led the gamekeeper to where they had been hidden beneath a hedge, saying, 'There's them.' Despite the man's repeated protestations of innocence, Spalding remained unconvinced and made his mind up to hand him over to police at Monifieth, a 45-minute walk away. Some six hours later at around 10 p.m. Juno returned to Kingennie alone. Jean sat up for a time, thinking her brother would follow soon after, but when he failed to turn up, she was not unduly concerned. She knew that his job as a gamekeeper meant he was in the habit of keeping irregular hours.

When there was still no sign of him the following morning, she started to feel a niggle of worry. Her sister, Susan, and young George left home to search, half-expecting to meet him striding home, but as Juno led the way along a narrow footpath between high hedges, they could not help noticing that the dog seemed uneasy, frequently looking back over her shoulder as though to check that they were still following. At a certain point she froze, began to growl and finally let out what young George later described as 'a great yowl'. When he turned to investigate, he discovered that what was troubling Juno was the sight of her master lying motionless in a ditch, his cap askew and his body part-covered over by a tangle of long grass and bramble twigs. Vicious wounds could be seen on his head and livid bruising around his neck as though he had been strangled. When Susan reached out and clasped his cold hand, she was left in no doubt that all traces of life had departed. An area of trampled grass nearby indicated where a struggle appeared to have taken place and the missing shirts lay abandoned with a length of unfamiliar black ribbon lying beside them. Shocked at their discovery, young George and Susan hurried from the scene to Ethiebeaton farm where they blurted out their story to two workers, Robert Alexander and George Nicoll, who straightaway fitted out a horse and cart which they brought alongside the bramble thicket where Spalding's body lay. Here they waited for Police Constable Marnoch to be called from Monifieth and give the go-ahead for the dead man to be removed to his home.

Based on information supplied by a number of local people, police were able to track the stranger's movements the previous afternoon. Shortly after 1 p.m. Alexander Scott had been working in the stackyard of his smallholding when an unfamiliar tramp stopped off to pass the time of day. After chatting for a few minutes, the man left, heading in the direction of the Spaldings' cottage a few hundred yards to the north. He reappeared within the hour, Scott told investigating officers, walking alone and carrying a small package which he was taking great care to conceal beneath his jacket. He kept his head down and no conversation took place. A couple of hours later, two farm workers at Ethiebeaton, James Haxton and Robert Alexander, saw this same man in the company of George Spalding who closely watched his every move as they walked south towards Monifieth. At one point a scuffle broke out when the tramp tried to make a run for it, but Juno, it seems, saved the day when she pursued the fleeing figure, seized his coat with her teeth and refused to let go. Furious at his failure to escape, the man raged at Spalding, threatening that he 'wad do for [him]', but his angry words came across as empty bluster. Two slaters currently employed nearby, David Molison and Melville Suttie, also witnessed the tussle but they had no doubt that Spalding had the situation well under control by the time they left him frogmarching his captive down the road to Monifieth. 'The damned rascal has been stealing,' the burly gamekeeper told them.

Late in the afternoon an elderly woman, Ann Henderson, was making her way home through the gathering gloom when she was startled by the dishevelled figure of a man who materialised out of the darkness ahead of her. When he spoke to ask her the time, she was so taken aback by his sudden appearance that it took her a moment or two to recover before she could reply. In spite of her shock, she was sufficiently alert nonetheless to spot a tear in the material of his blue Balmoral bonnet and noticed that one of its two black ribbons was missing. The man was alone; of George Spalding there was nary a sign. After taking statements from all witnesses involved, police reeled in a string of tramps for questioning whose alibis, one after another, were tested and found to be watertight. As the list of suspects was steadily whittled down, it struck on one Constable McIntosh, so it is said, that there was one man he'd had dealings with in the past who matched the witnesses' descriptions and had still to be interviewed. He was a wanderer who went by the name of Thomas Scobbie.

Scobbie had been born around 1840 near Dunfermline, Fife, the son of a cobbler. During his youth he undertook a variety of jobs - farm worker, weaver, rope-maker and general labourer. It appears he lapsed into criminal activity in his early teens, receiving a conviction for theft by housebreaking for which he served a prison term. But he seemed to turn his life around a few years later when he enlisted in the 92nd Gordon Highlanders and travelled overseas. During the Indian uprising of the 1850s he was praised for his good conduct and admirable personal qualities, and he chose to stay on in the country even after the rebellion was crushed, transferring to the 79th Cameronian Regiment. After suffering heart problems, he was invalided home in 1865 and, following several months' treatment at Portsmouth Hospital, was transferred north to Aberdeen where he met and married a mill worker, Ann Rough, before being moved on once again to Fort George, Inverness-shire. It was after his discharge in 1866 that things began to spiral downwards. Finding a return to civilian life intolerable, he took to a life on the road as a 'gaun' body', seldom staying in one place for any length of time and returning home to his wife only intermittently. Reverting to old habits, it wasn't unusual to find him on the wrong side of the law. In March 1869 he went on trial on a charge of purloining various items from washing lines in Dunfermline and district: shirts (four); linen sheets (three); two linen collars; two petticoats; a window blind; and a pair of heavy-duty woollen drawers. It emerged in court that he had a similar previous conviction, and he was sentenced to six months behind bars. In 1871 Ann gave birth to a daughter, Elizabeth, but he appears to have been no more than a passing presence in his child's life with varying degrees of involvement, financial or otherwise, in her upbringing. He carried on with his roving life and in areas where he became known he was given the cruel nickname of 'Bonnie Scobbie', the result of his heavily pockmarked complexion.

Seeking him in connection with the death of George Spalding, police inquiries led them to the Victoria Model Lodging House in the Overgate, Dundee, where the superintendent, James Oudney, confirmed that Scobbie had stayed at the hostel from time to time over recent weeks. The officers were disappointed, however, to learn that he was currently absent and had not spent a night there since Monday 23 September - the night immediately prior to Spalding's disappearance. He had returned to pay a brief visit to his room two days later, Oudney continued, but had left again before nightfall. When they opened up a small wooden chest in his room the officers found inside two pawnbrokers' receipts, one issued by Edward Rowan whose premises were located a short distance from the model. When they visited Rowan, he could tell them that the nine-shilling ticket had been issued against a jacket and pair of trousers which had been pawned by a customer giving his name as John Young. When examined, these garments were found to be torn in places (courtesy of canine teeth?) with grass seeds and thorny burrs adhering. The second receipt had been issued by Margaret Bryan, an employee of Peter Millan's business in the Overgate, and related to several shirts pawned by a man calling himself James Smith. It turned out that both tickets had been issued on the Tuesday evening within the space of an hour. It all made sense: it isn't hard to see why a man who feared being accused of the most grievous crime imaginable would make a change of clothing an early priority.

It took till Thursday the 26th for police officers' patience to be rewarded. When Scobbie reappeared at the model lodging house he was immediately arrested by Constable McIntosh and taken into custody. While being admitted to jail at Dundee Police Station, a clasp-knife (a knife whose blade folds into the handle) was removed from his pocket by the turnkey, William Fraser, the butt end of whose handle was undoubtedly capable of inflicting wounds such as those to be seen on the dead man's head. The effect of the victim's being stunned, it was suggested, would have made death by strangulation a good deal easier to accomplish though it would still have taken a determined effort lasting a minute, maybe two. Interviewed by Inspector Adams, Scobbie attempted to account for deep scratches to be seen on his face by insisting they had been inflicted during an altercation some days earlier in which he was struck by an umbrella. Adams was sceptical. It looked to him as though fingernails had been applied, then raked down across his cheeks with some force. On top of that, Scobbie's claim that he had spent all day Tuesday at the home of a blind fiddler, Peter Kelly, in Spence's Close, Dundee, was easily dismissed. And if all this wasn't enough, it was not easy to explain away the Balmoral bonnet with one black ribbon missing that Scobbie was wearing at the time of his arrest.

No-one who had seen the suspected murderer on the day of Spalding's death had the smallest doubt that he was one and the same as the prisoner under lock and key in Dundee. The day after his arrest, police took Scobbie back to Kingennie where Jean Spalding recognised him instantly as the man she had suspected of stealing shirts from her line. Some say that her brother's dog snarled at him and had to be restrained. The crofter, Alexander Scott, recognised him, not only him by his appearance, but also his voice. 'I'm not the man,' came Scobbie's instant retort. When James Haxton, one of farm workers at Ethiebeaton, visited Dundee Prison some weeks later he had no difficulty in picking him out from an identity parade of four men. His pockmarked complexion, of course, was hard to mistake.

A curious tale is recounted by Alexander Hastie Millar, Dundee's City Librarian, in his book, *Haunted Dundee*, published some half a century after the murder of George Spalding. According to Millar, the same day that Scobbie was returned to Kingennie to be identified he was subjected to a variant of the ancient bier-right, in this case by unscrewing the dead man's coffin-lid and exposing his face to his alleged murderer. Asked whether he had ever set eyes on George Spalding before this moment, Scobbie had no hesitation in denying it. 'No, no,' he said - 'I'm bad and bad eneuch, as the polis ken, but I'm no' a murderer.' At the time of Spalding's death Alexander Millar was a grown man of 25 and, while it is not impossible that he was privy to some source of confidential information, it has to be conceded that supporting evidence for his disturbing anecdote is not easy to come by.

It was another six months before Scobbie appeared at Dundee Circuit Court before Lords Deas and Jerviswood. It had been put about that the trial had been delayed after the prisoner allegedly tried to poison himself by swallowing limewash, scraped from the walls of his cell. This was officially denied. Asked by Lord Deas how he pleaded, Scobbie replied firmly, 'I am not guilty.' During the ensuing trial, there were witnesses aplenty whose testimonies suggested otherwise and, piled one on top of another, they amounted to a persuasive case for the prosecution. The defence, by contrast, called no-one. As far as the fifteen-man jury was concerned, it was an open-and-shut case and its members took a mere ten or fifteen minutes to reach the unanimous verdict that Scobbie was guilty of murder. There was, however, a proviso attached. By a margin of fourteen to one they had appended an appeal for clemency, largely in response to the circumstantial nature of the evidence presented plus the degree of provocation to which they believed the prisoner had been subjected. In spite of their recommendation, Lord Deas advised Scobbie not to invest too much faith in a possible reprieve, then, placing the ritual black cap on his head, he announced that he would be returned to Bell Street Prison until Tuesday, 29 April - three weeks hence - when he would be escorted from his cell between the hours of 8 and 10 a.m. to be 'hanged by the neck upon a gibbet... until he be dead'. Despite hearing his fate spelt out in those starkest of terms, Scobbie remained utterly expressionless and showed no emotion as he was led from the dock.

The aftermath of the trial saw public opinion divided. There were those who held that Spalding's actions in carrying out a citizen's arrest had been right and just, while others viewed those same actions as somewhat high-handed, even a touch arrogant, and well-nigh assured to provoke a hostile reaction. They pointed out that no evidence of premeditation had been presented in court and, other than those who saw Scobbie's attempt 'to break free and run away from his captor', there was a complete absence of eyewitnesses who could categorically nail down the facts. Whatever the truth of the matter, fourteen of the jurymen took it upon themselves to initiate a petition seeking clemency which was placed in the Free Library, the Royal Exchange and other buildings to which the public had access. Within a matter of days, it attracted well over 4,000 signatures which, if reports are to be believed, formed a paper ribbon stretching some sixty feet in length. This serpentine document was forwarded by Sir John Ogilvy, MP for Dundee, to the Home Secretary in Westminster, Henry Austin Bruce, to be delivered in due course to Buckingham Palace for Queen Victoria's consideration. The Society of Friends - that is, the Quaker church - followed up by submitting its own petition. In order to avoid buoying up Scobbie's hopes prematurely, he was deliberately kept in the dark about efforts being made on his behalf.

It didn't take long for his sang froid to desert him once his cell door clanked shut and the key turned firmly in the lock. Visitors found Scobbie restless and unsettled, tearful and distraught, and such was his level of distress that the prison authorities deemed it advisable to keep him under constant supervision with a light to be burned in his cell throughout the night. When he was afflicted by a troublesome boil on his neck, he refused medical treatment on the grounds that because he had such a short time left to live there was no point. However errant a husband and father he had been, his deepest concerns were directed towards his wife and daughter during whose visit to the prison he was unable to remain composed and contain his emotion. Throughout this time, he was provided with support by the prison chaplain, Rev. Reid, and, Episcopalian by upbringing, he was visited daily by Rev. Nicholson, the Bishop of Brechin, who felt sufficiently strongly about his case to back up the public appeal for royal clemency with a personal plea of his own. By whatever channel, it seems that Scobbie picked up on the activity taking place on his behalf, and the spark of hope it ignited allowed him to rest easier and sleep a little more soundly.

Following receipt of her Dundonian subjects' petition, no-one could have accused Victoria of responding with undue haste. While Her Majesty was busy making arrangements for her imminent spring visit to Balmoral Castle, a new scaffold was being constructed in Dundee Prison. While Scobbie endured a torturous waiting game, he was seldom out of the public eye and his plight featured regularly in the local and national press. A letter in the *Dundee Courier*, penned by a certain William Robertson of Broughty Ferry, bluntly described him as 'of a very low type' and went on to highlight his 'low standard of intellect' but, strange though it must seem, in reality Robertson was sympathetic to Scobbie's cause and he concluded his letter by highlighting the disparity between justice for the rich and privileged as against what was meted out to those on the lowest rungs of society. Meanwhile in Dundee Music Hall large audiences attended a series of lectures in which two preachers - a London evangelist, Charles Inglis, and his co-speaker, James Watson, a Glaswegian chimney sweep who had evidently seen the light - alluded to Scobbie's misconduct as a poignant reminder of man's sinful nature. Similarly righteous in tone, John Bowes delivered a lecture in Meadow Street Hall entitled 'Scobbie's History: important facts from which lessons may be learned'.

While moralists such as these made hay, there were grumblings among the wider public concerning whether the jurymen at Scobbie's trial had been adequately informed that a verdict of culpable homicide was available to them as an alternative to a cut-and-dried murder conviction. In a second letter to the press the same William Robertson of Broughty Ferry pointed out that if it were indeed the case that Scobbie had taken George Spalding's life by mistake - say, in self-defence - then it was a clear case of culpable homicide and the jury had been mistaken in finding him guilty of murder, a more serious crime by far. Meanwhile the clock continued to tick and in the small hours of Saturday, 26 April, the dapper form of the elderly hangman, William Calcraft, and his assistant, a whiskery red-faced Welshman, were seen disembarking from a first-class carriage at Dundee railway station. Calcraft was a devotee of the 'short drop' method of hanging which brought about a prolonged and painful death by strangulation, and the small trunk he carried excited a high degree of interest, rumoured as it was to contain the tools of his grisly trade. His assistant and he were transferred by horse-drawn cab to Bell

Street Prison where they were to be accommodated. Though under the same roof as the condemned man, their status was rather different. Their meals, it was noted, were prepared and delivered by the Royal Hotel.

Scobbie had languished in a state of uncertainty for nearly three weeks, hopeful and fatalistic by turns, until the morning of Saturday, 26 April, when (a matter of hours after Calcraft's night-time arrival) an official communication was received from the Home Secretary in Whitehall for the attention of Provost Cox of Dundee. After taking in the contents of the letter, Cox was accompanied by two town bailies as Prison Governor McQueen conducted him to the condemned cell. As Scobbie listened atremble, Cox broke the long-awaited news that 'the Queen commands that the execution of the sentence of death passed upon Thomas Scobbie, now in Dundee Prison, be respited'. Instead, he would be sent to Parkhurst Prison on the Isle of Wight where he would serve a life-term. Learning that he had been spared the noose, Scobbie broke down, repeatedly expressing his gratitude toward those who had helped to bring about the happy outcome. When news of his reprieve spread through the city it was met with widespread approval but when word reached Kingennie the reaction of George Spalding's family is not on record.

Of course, there was another gentleman still to be informed of the upturn in Scobbie's fortunes. When he learned that the condemned man had been reprieved, William Calcraft expressed deep satisfaction with the outcome and went on to state that the exercise of his professional duties grieved him almost as much as it did his victims. Sincere in his comments or otherwise, he certainly had no reason for complaint: he had been canny enough to settle in advance that his fee of twenty guineas (plus expenses) was payable whether or not his services were required. Before leaving, he was invited to inspect and pass his opinion on the prison's newly-constructed scaffold, but he chose not to do so. Then, after a flying visit of less than 24 hours, he was brought by coach back to the railway station where he was met by a throng of excited Dundonians who had assembled to see him depart. Strangely, some members of the crowd saluted him in a friendly manner while one individual, particularly enthusiastic, thrust his way to the forefront and shook the elderly hangman by the hand. As his train pulled out of the station, Calcraft leaned out of the carriage window and waved goodbye to the gathering of onlookers. There would be no further call for his professional skills in Dundee and this was the last time he would visit the city.

Strangely enough, Calcraft's trip north was a wasted journey on two counts. After attending to the case of Thomas Scobbie his intention was to travel on from Dundee to Ayr where he had been led to believe that his services were needed to dispatch a convicted murderer, Henry Reid. It was a case which bore some startling similarities to Scobbie's. Reid too was a travelling man, a gypsy bagpiper, and a crucial factor in his conviction was a rosette recovered from the crime scene which was found to be missing from his Balmoral bonnet. Like Scobbie, ultimately his death sentence was commuted to a lifetime of hard labour and Calcraft's expertise was not required.

Back at Dundee, the gallows prepared for Thomas Scobbie's final moments was dismantled and placed in a vault beneath the floorboards of the Sheriff Courthouse where it remained mothballed for the following sixteen years. Not until 1889 was it brought back into service for the execution of William Henry Bury, a convicted wife-killer whom some believed to be the Whitechapel murderer, Jack the Ripper, and whose hanging turned out to be the last ever to be conducted in the city.

So, Scobbie's fate had been settled beyond doubt but discussions continued throughout the city concerning the judge's specific wording when passing the original death sentence. Following the guilty verdict, Lord Deas had announced to the court that Scobbie would be executed on 'Tuesday the 29th April next to come' when he would be hanged until dead. This created a problem. Scobbie's trial concluded on 8 April 1873, therefore 'April next to come' must refer to the following year, i.e. 1874. And if that wasn't problematic enough, it led in turn to a further complication. In 1874 the 29th of April would fall, not on a Tuesday, but on a Wednesday, and not until 1879 would the 29th be a Tuesday. Clearly it was hardly reasonable to expect a man to spend six years on death row and, according to one school of thought, this was the true reason why Scobbie's death sentence was commuted - less, it was suggested, an indicator of Her Most Gracious Majesty's great compassion, and more a means of sparing His Lordship's blushes.

Whatever the truth of the matter, even before Scobbie left Dundee he had grown noticeably frail and, in the light of his fragile health, it is a wonder that he survived the following 22 years at all. Finally freed on licence in September 1895, he made his way home to Fife and during the rail journey north he reportedly engaged in conversation with a fellow passenger who happened to be a native of Dundee. Even after all this time he continued to assert his innocence, claiming he had been a victim of mistaken identity, followed by a gross miscarriage of justice. On the face of it, what had he to gain by lying? And yet the facts seemed indisputable. His facial appearance, after all, was not easily mistaken - and who could explain away the question of that crucial black ribbon? Back in Fife, he settled at Lower Oakfield, Kelty, and found work in the pits at Glencraig but the years of hard labour had taken their toll. Still in his fifties, his death was reported early in the new year of 1898, little more than two years after his release from jail. At the end of the day, as we look back over Scobbie's life and death, is it wrong to feel a grain of sympathy? He had been a sound and solid soldier - invalided out, unable to settle to civilian life and guilty of a moment's loss of control. And yet, his actions left a family bereft and with a void that was unable to be filled. Perhaps, as so often, Scobbie's case shows that there are few blacks and whites, mostly shades of grey.

Somewhere between Monifieth and Kingennie there was until recent times a circular copse of trees which over the years had acquired for itself the name of Scobbie's Roundie and a reputation for being haunted. Today the scrap of woodland is no more, its trees fallen victim to road development and unstoppable urban creep. Of the hundreds who now pass by daily, how many, I wonder, are aware of the fatal clash that took place just a stone's throw away? Few, I suspect, if any. A century and a half on, the story of a life that was lost and a second irreparably broken has largely been erased from local memory.

Unidentified Assailant
Moscow, Ayrshire - March 1884

In August 1933, the Vice-Principal of Glenfield Ramblers, Walter Emery, guided a party of walkers on a weekend jaunt in countryside near Kilmarnock. Conditions were less than ideal - one account refers to a 'torrential downpour' - but Emery put a brave face on it and did his best to distract his companions from their soggy socks and dripping collars. No-one doubted that he'd done his homework. Arriving at the tiny settlement of Moscow, he gave an account of research he had carried out into a cluster of unusual place names in the locality: the Volga Burn, flowing down from high ground to the east; the farms of High and Low Rushaw - pronounced locally 'Russia' - a stone's throw across the fields; and, of course, the name of the hamlet itself. In search of an explanation, Emery described how he had approached the Ordnance Survey service, one of whose officials had indicated that the place names went back as far as the Napoleonic Wars when Moscow, Russia, was burned to the ground in 1812 - 'the first house having been erected [in Moscow, Ayrshire] about that period'. A representative of Ayr County Council had provided an alternative explanation, suggesting instead that the names dated back to the 1850s when prisoners and other refugees from the Crimean War were relocated to the area. But once Emery had exhausted the possibilities of a Russian connection, he could hardly have avoided touching on a shocking event which brought tragedy to the sleepy hamlet in the late nineteenth century.

In March 1884, Robert Rankin, a bachelor in his mid-fifties, had been living at Moscow for five years. In keeping with the Russian theme, his house went under the name of Volga Bank and was somewhat at odds with those around it. A handful of modest cottages formed the main - and only - street in the village, and Rankin's home projected its gable-end toward the topmost of these. His front windows had an open outlook over a small grassy meadow bordered on one side by his neighbours' cottages and by a strip of woodland on the other. At the far end of the field, maybe one hundred yards away, stood a coaching inn, the only other building of note in the village. Substantial and commodious, Rankin's home had a large outhouse to the rear, used for storage by the previous owner, Robert Muir, a cheese and grain merchant. The closest neighbouring cottage was unoccupied.

In contrast to his rustic neighbours, Rankin had a very well-to-do background. His father, also Robert, had been proprietor of a long-established bakery business in Duke Street, Kilmarnock, and the owner of some of the town's grandest buildings. For a time, young Robert operated his own successful grocery store but, following his father's death, he took on the running of the family business. Then, in his early fifties, something changed. Rejecting town life, he bought a house in one of the loneliest corners of the local backcountry, far from any main roads, where he settled down to a solitary existence, withdrawing to a large extent from the company of others and living off the rental income he received from his properties in town. For the most part self-sufficient, he did his own cooking, carried out his own domestic chores, and was polite but distant toward his neighbours. Callers were few, and those he invited into his home even fewer, and he was particularly reserved when dealing with strangers. That said, he showed no hostility to those around him and, quite the reverse, he was known to have been responsible for various acts of kindness in the village. And so Rankin lived quietly and unobtrusively, apparently content with his own company and a source of trouble to no-one.

So when he knocked on the door of the village inn during the late evening of Tuesday, 11 March, his action was totally out of character. The landlord and his wife were already in bed, and the door was opened by a servant girl who was presumably taken by surprise when Rankin explained that he had a young male visitor who he 'thocht would be better for a hauf-yin'. The girl invited him into the kitchen but he chose to wait outside, handing over an empty bottle to be filled with whisky and remarking only that it was a cold night. When the full bottle was returned to him, he turned immediately and left. A neighbour who paid him a quick call half an hour later - and was kept standing on the doorstep - was the last local to see him that night. The first sign of anything amiss the following morning was when the window blinds at Volga Bank remained drawn for longer than usual, and the fact that no movement was to be seen caused a degree of concern among his neighbours. Their anxiety was compounded by the fact that a few months earlier, at New Year time, Rankin had been away from home for a short spell and on his return had lain unwell in bed for several days without anyone knowing it. As the day wore on and he still failed to appear various neighbours knocked on his door and windows but they could elicit no response. Finally in the early afternoon the local shoemaker, Hugh Fulton, tried the handle of the back door and, finding it unlocked, stepped into the kitchen where he was met with a horrifying sight.

What Fulton saw was the body of Robert Rankin, lying motionless in a pool of blood. A report of his shocking discovery was immediately sent to police, and Inspector Innes of Galston - the station closest at hand - hurried immediately to Moscow, while Superintendent Menzies of the county force despatched one of his constables from Kilmarnock. Not until these officers were present was a detailed examination of the crime scene carried out. Robert Rankin was lying face-up with one eye closed and his mouth sagging open. A severe wound had been inflicted high on his forehead, and a deep gash could be seen beside his left eye. His right hand appeared to be holding a hammer but any thought of suicide was quickly ruled out when it was noticed that the shaft was held loosely, not gripped, suggesting that it had been deliberately placed there after his death. The hammer was stained with blood, and it seemed likely that this was the weapon which had been responsible for his head wound. Dark bruising and finger marks could be seen around his throat.

It looked as though the murderer's motive had been robbery, pure and simple. The dead man's gold pocket watch - number 34611 - was missing, plus its associated 'Albert' - the chain that was normally threaded through a buttonhole on the wearer's waistcoat. Only a small piece of the guard chain had been left around Rankin's neck. An unsuccessful attempt had been made to break into a bedroom wardrobe before the murderer had given up and turned his attention instead to an adjoining table whose drawer was forced open and the letters and photographs within, many of them spattered with blood, strewn about the room. The cash that Rankin was known to keep in the desk drawer had been removed with the sole exception of a small silver sixpence which appeared to have been overlooked. The dead man's pockets had been turned inside-out, but in his hurry to depart the robber had failed to spot a gold ring and threepence in coppers. Various clues scattered across the ransacked rooms helped police reconstruct the previous evening's events. On a table at the side of the kitchen were two cups containing the dregs of cold tea. A pot of boiled potatoes suggested earlier preparations for a supper that never took place. Two glass tumblers and a paraffin lamp lay shattered on the floor, and on top of a second table a stable-lamp appeared to have been left burning but whose oil had eventually run dry. Beside the back door a candlestick had been abandoned, presumably after being used to light the robber's getaway. The back court of the cottage was paved, so there was no possibility of finding footprints, and the fact that fifteen hours had elapsed before his crime was discovered had given the murderer a significant head-start on the pursuing authorities.

Later in the day the Procurator Fiscal for Ayrshire, James Pollock Stevenson, arrived at Moscow, followed the next morning by Captain Hardy McHardy, Chief of the County Constabulary, whose job it was to superintend the large body of police officers involved in the case. That same day a post-mortem examination of Rankin's body was carried out by Drs McFarlane and Munro who deduced that the murderer had caught his victim off-guard, seizing him by the throat with his left hand while using his right to administer hammer blows to the head. Death, the doctors concluded, had been the result of strangulation, as the blows to the head were not severe enough to prove fatal on their own. When Rankin's murder became known, it created a sensation throughout the surrounding area. The local press reported that the Kilmarnock area was 'perhaps the most free of serious crime of any town and district of similar size... in the kingdom'. Perhaps it was not surprising, then, when hordes of ghoulish sightseers descended on Moscow - 'attracted thither by morbid curiosity and the fineness of the weather'. Such was the demand that on Sunday, 16 March, the village inn was obliged to admit customers in relays until its stock eventually ran out.

How, we might ask, had the killer gained the trust of a man, solitary by nature and reclusive by habit? What means might he have used to insinuate himself into Rankin's confidence and breach the walls he'd built around him? We can only speculate. That the two were already on familiar terms seems highly likely, though almost certainly Rankin had no advance notice of his late-night guest's arrival or he would surely have had refreshments on hand. Strangely, in their quest to identify the murderer, police appear to have given little consideration to the possibility that Rankin and his attacker were already acquainted, and although their inquiries turned up a number of leads, ultimately none stood up to scrutiny. An early suspect was a young man who had been absent from his lodgings in Fore Street, Kilmarnock, during the late evening of Tuesday, 11 March, and had not returned until the early hours, but in the end it was established beyond doubt that he had been nowhere near Moscow. A second line of inquiry looked more promising. Thomas Borland was a native of Newmilns who had been working as a miner at Quarter, near Hamilton, for the last year or so. A known reprobate with a previous conviction for theft, he had enlisted in the Lanarkshire Militia at the beginning of February but promptly deserted a month later. A few hours before Rankin's death, Borland was spotted on the banks of the Polbaith Burn near Moscow, and he was known to have arrived at his father's house in Newmilns some time later. When he heard he was the subject of police inquiries, he vanished from the area but within 24 hours he was traced to Quarter, arrested and brought back to Galston. On Monday, 17 March, he was escorted to Kilmarnock and examined before the sheriff. It emerged that in autumn 1882 he had been employed as a harvest labourer at Hemphill farm, a few minutes' walk from Moscow, but a rumour to the effect that he had recently carried out gardening work at Volga Bank was dismissed as unreliable. Since no concrete evidence to implicate him in the murder was forthcoming and his alibi for the night in question was judged to be sound, police eliminated him from their inquiries and he was sent on to Ayr to be locked up as a deserter. And thereafter, nothing. Despite nationwide publicity in *The Police Gazette* and an offer to the general public of a £100 reward, Rankin's murderer was never brought to book.

Inevitably the unsolved murder spawned various theories but, perhaps surprisingly, the possibility of an unscheduled sexual encounter appears not to have been considered - at least not officially. One of the most colourful explanations was picked up a few years later by John Aitken, an itinerant merchant who tramped the roads around Kilmarnock, hawking books out of a barrow. One Christmas night, Aitken tells us, a policeman by the name of McNabb recounted for a group of listeners a bizarre series of events he had been involved in while employed as an officer of the Royal Irish Constabulary in a small town in Fermanagh. By McNabb's account, Barney Scollan was a local tailor who was a firm believer in the existence of the fairy folk, and who claimed to have good reason. Any work he left unfinished in the evening, the tailor insisted, would invariably be completed by 'the wee folk' overnight and not only that, he added, but 'in the most artistic and latest style'. Sceptical to say the least, McNabb concealed himself in Scollan's shop one evening to verify - or debunk - the tailor's claims once and for all. He was just beginning to doze around midnight when he was startled into wakefulness by the sound of movement. Peering through the darkness, what he saw was the sleepwalking tailor, threading his needle and settling down to work by candlelight. And with that, the mystery of the fairy folk had been solved. Similar to the Irish situation, McNabb stated his belief that the Moscow killer had been a near neighbour of Robert Rankin's who had acted whilst sleepwalking, and ever since that night had remained entirely unaware of his - or her - gory involvement. The policeman finished up by confiding that, at the time of the murder, he had kept his speculations to himself for fear of 'being laughed out of the force'. That, it seems fair to say, was an odds-on certainty.

A good deal more fanciful than it was enlightening, McNabb's theory left no-one any the wiser as to the murderer's identity. For many people's money, the army deserter, Thomas Borland, remained the prime suspect, and there were those who questioned whether police had perhaps acted a little hastily in dismissing him from the investigation. Based on the time he spent at Hemphill farm, there could be little doubt that he had sufficient local knowledge to allow him to slip in and away, unnoticed under cover of darkness. His sighting near the village earlier that day looks highly suspicious and, even though it was officially discounted, it is hard not to wonder about his gardening work at Volga Bank. One thing looks certain. The shadow of Thomas Borland never falls far from the hub of the action, and he may well be the undetected villain of the piece.

Hector Mackenzie
Ardersier, Inverness-shire - December 1888

On a vantage-point overlooking the Moray Firth, Bombardier Robert Brobson was on sentry duty on the ramparts of Fort George in the forenoon of Saturday, 15 December 1888, when his eye was caught by an object floating on the surface of the water. When he looked more closely, he realised with a start that he was looking at a human body, bobbing back and forth on the ebbing tide. He immediately sent word of what he had seen to his superior officer, but by the time Lieutenant Lang arrived the body had already been recovered from the water and found to be that of a tall, stout female. The cause of death seemed obvious: the top of the woman's head was brutally stoved in and her throat had been cut. After arranging for a guard to be placed over the body, Lang left the scene to send off a telegram to the chief constable of Inverness-shire. Meantime three Seaforth Highlanders - Privates Archibald Allan, Murdoch Macaulay and Donald Smith - kept guard over the body to ensure that nothing was tampered with until a police officer, Constable Hird, could be called to the scene. Initially Hird was unable to identify the bloodied corpse, but after it was removed to the mortuary some hours later, he recognised it as the body of Isabella Lamont, a widow in her fifties who had lived at nearby Campbelltown, Ardersier, for the past seven or eight years. The local postmaster, John Leitch, confirmed his identification.

Some time around eight o'clock the previous evening, a knock had come to the door of John McQueen, a farm worker at Viewhill, a short distance inland from Campbelltown. It had already been dark for easily four hours and he was not expecting visitors. When he opened the door, he found a stranger there who asked him whether he knew anything of a woman called May Gordon. The name rang no bells with McQueen but, thinking she might be a resident of a nearby lodging-house, he stepped outside to show the stranger the way. After a short walk the two men arrived at the lodging-house where McQueen left the man in conversation with the landlady, a Mrs Dey. Part-way home he was intercepted, this time by a woman he did not recognise, who also asked for directions to Mrs Dey's establishment. Mere coincidence? Or possibly something more? McQueen didn't stop to think about it. He simply pointed her in the right direction, then turned on his heel to go home.

The woman in question was Isabella Lamont and the fact that she needed directions seems a little odd, given that she lived locally, was already known to Mrs Dey, and it was not the first time she had visited the lodging-house. In those days before widespread electric lighting, we can maybe put her being lost down to nothing more than the deep midwinter darkness - or perhaps there was another reason. By the landlady's (later) recollection, Isabella and the strange man arrived at the lodging-house together, though in reality they must have been a few moments apart. Once inside, the man spoke first to ask the landlady about this same May Gordon. She was able to tell him in reply that, while she had been acquainted with May in the past, she had seen nothing of her since she left the lodging-house three years earlier. At that May Gordon dropped out of the conversation. Switching to Gaelic, the stranger changed the subject and asked whether the landlady was acquainted with Mrs Mackenzie of Flowerburn House, a gracious mansion on the far side of the firth. Mrs Dey replied in Gaelic. 'Oh yes,' she said, 'I know her.' Believing he had established his grand credentials, the stranger then proceeded to introduce himself as Hector Mackenzie - a man of some substance, as he would have it, and owner of Flowerburn farm, complete with its sixteen dairy cows, a short ferry ride away. He turned to Isabella Lamont and, as the conversation alternated rapidly between Gaelic and English, the landlady found herself struggling to keep up. She did, however, catch the gist.

With Mrs Dey listening in the background, Mackenzie returned to the subject of his farm and asked Isabella if she might be interested in working for him. Yes, she told him, she would. Had she any previous experience of working with milk kye? She replied that she had, though admittedly never as many as sixteen. Her wages, Mackenzie told her, would be £6 plus two bolls of oatmeal (approximately twenty stones) payable at 'the term' - that is, when her contract expired at the end of May. He went on to say that he lived with his sister, his brother and their widowed mother, and added that if she were 'kind' to the old lady she could expect an extra ten shillings on top of her regular wages. When Isabella agreed to his terms, Mackenzie immediately started drawing up a contract but before he was satisfied, he crushed up and discarded several sheets of paper, giving the impression perhaps that he was unaccustomed to writing. Dey could not help noticing that, alongside his pen, he was carrying a small pocketknife, a few inches long, with several blades folded neatly into the handle.

Now that agreement had been reached, Mackenzie told Isabella that they would cross the firth that same night and that his brother would bring a dogcart - a lightweight horse-drawn vehicle - to meet them at Chanonry Point and carry her goods to the farm. At this point Dey intervened to point out that it was far too late to catch the ferry, but, not put out in the least, Mackenzie had a ready answer. By paying double-fare, he told her, he was in the habit of crossing the firth at any time he chose. As Isabella prepared to leave in order to pack clothing and other belongings, Dey warned her that going with an unfamiliar man at such a late hour and in darkness might be viewed as improper, but she was not to be dissuaded. In an apparent - fairly feeble - nod to propriety, Mackenzie insisted that when the time came for them to leave, she must wear her bonnet, and to this Isabella raised no objection. During her absence, Mackenzie continued to chat with the landlady, telling her that he was in the habit of attending markets and had recently sold prize cattle for the sum of £150 - something that surprised Dey in light of his well-worn clothing and general personal appearance. He had 'a good gift of the gab', she could tell, and there was certainly no chance of the conversation flagging before Isabella reappeared with her belongings. When they left the lodging-house at 9.45 p.m., Dey had no fears for Isabella's safety since she and her new employer appeared to be on perfectly cordial terms.

Ten minutes after leaving Dey's establishment, Mackenzie appeared at the bar of the Ship Inn where he ordered two glasses of whisky: one for himself, he explained to the proprietor, George Cowan, and one for a woman outside. Looking out, the landlord immediately recognised Isabella as one of his customers - not someone he would have described as a heavy drinker but who could 'take her dram' nonetheless - an observation that would later be brought into question. Leaving her bundle of possessions at the door, she came inside where she heard Mackenzie tell Cowan that they were planning to take the ferry that night. Their visit to the Ship Inn was necessarily a short one, and at closing-time - ten o'clock - she suggested that Mackenzie have 'one for the road'. He declined on the grounds that there would be plenty to drink on the other side of the water at Grant's Royal Hotel.

Private James Hastie of the Seaforth Highlanders was on sentry duty that night. It was not especially dark, though from time to time clouds passed across the face of the moon. At around eleven o'clock - an hour after Isabella and Mackenzie left the Ship Inn - he heard voices coming from below the ramparts and, when he looked down, he saw an unfamiliar man and woman walking in the direction of the pier. The two were huddled close together, and the man's arm was draped around the woman. Hastie noticed that she was wearing a bonnet. A few minutes later the mood had apparently changed when he heard raised voices, the woman's most distinct, and from what he could tell, she was indignant at her male companion. Private Hastie continued to watch as they stopped and turned back until they reached a place where steps descended to the breakwater. Although he was no longer able to make out what was being said, he heard the murmur of conversation passing between them for the next half hour. By the time that Hastie was relieved at midnight all had gone quiet, and the sentry who followed him, Private Arthur Jones, heard nothing and saw no-one during the next two hours.

And things at Fort George remained quiet until word got out of Bombardier Brobson's grim discovery. Although the cause of Isabella's death was obvious, still there were forms to be adhered to. The hospital sergeant, Charles Philips, arranged for her body to be brought back from the beach and he had begun preparing for the post-mortem when his work was interrupted by the arrival of a telegram from police at Inverness asking him to leave everything exactly as it had been found. Accordingly, he secured the remains under lock and key in the mortuary until Sunday, 14 December, when the examination was carried out by Drs Alexander of Fort George and Chapman of Inverness. In their findings, the doctors wrote that there was no doubt in their minds that Isabella's death had resulted from the wounds she had sustained and the consequent loss of blood. They were careful to rule out any possibility of death by drowning. Her wounds had been inflicted, they believed, while she was still alive, with the single exception of one on her head. A loose flap of skin, roughly two and a half inches across, had been torn in an upward direction from the lower part of the chin - an unusual wound, they said. And finally, Isabella's throat had been slit by a 'cutting instrument [such as] a pocketknife'. No other weapon, the doctors stated, would have been required. They added in conclusion that (contrary to the impression of the landlord of the Ship Inn) the dead woman had been 'addicted to alcoholic liquor'. Drunkenness would certainly provide an explanation for her becoming disorientated on her way to Mrs Dey's lodging-house.

Meanwhile investigations on the ground proceeded apace. During their examination of the beach, Sergeant Alexander Chisholm of the Inverness-shire Constabulary and Constable Hird found what looked like traces of a struggle and followed a bloody trail that led from there approximately thirty yards to where it had been washed away at high tide. There were three conspicuous places where blood had pooled and clotted, and the officers judged that the track was likely to have been made by an inert body being dragged along by the feet. A 'guano bag' (one made from rough, loosely-woven material) had been abandoned near the breakwater which the policemen found to contain articles of women's clothing. A stain on the neck of the bag looked as though it had been grasped by a bloody hand. At Fort George, they were given an assurance that the entire garrison had been inside the walls by ten o'clock on Saturday evening, the sole exception being the Sergeant-Major who was absent at Inverness. Any object entering the water, they were told, would be prevented from being washed away by an eddy that customarily formed near the breakwater.

It did not take long after the discovery of Isabella Lamont's body for the crime-scene to become an attraction for morbid sightseers. On Monday, 16 December, workmen were sent out to obliterate all traces of blood and, during the course of digging up an area of the beach, one of them came across a detached button - a find that would later prove highly significant. By this stage Hector Mackenzie was the wanted man, and an unsuspecting tramp who apparently answered his description found himself taken into custody. The unfortunate soul was released soon after. Eventually Sergeants Chisholm and Philips traced Mackenzie to the farm of Mains of Bunachton, twenty miles south of Campbelltown, where they found him working in the stackyard. When cautioned and charged, he denied any involvement in the crime and, before his clothing was even mentioned, volunteered the fact that he was not the only man in the habit of dressing in grey. He was taken by dogcart to Inverness where he was challenged by Isabella's cousin and friend, George Mackintosh, regarding his whereabouts 'that night'. In reply Mackenzie insisted that he had spent the Saturday evening visiting an uncle at Urray, a village fifteen miles north-west of Inverness. Once he had been placed behind bars, his clothing was removed and examined by Dr Chapman who found what looked like stains and smears of blood on his waistcoat, under his collar and on the lapels. The front of his shirt was stained as though 'by a spray of blood from a small artery which had been cut while the person wearing the shirt was in close proximity'. Attempts had been made to wash the garments, apparently in salt-water. Turning to Mackenzie's boots, the doctor saw immediately that one was missing a toecap which had caused nails, two on either side, to become exposed. A quick check was all it took to confirm that these four nails corresponded exactly with the wound on the dead woman's chin where she had been on the receiving end of a vicious kick. Not until the final day of the year was the jigsaw completed when Mackenzie's overcoat turned up, found by Constable William Macdonald at Inverfarigaig on the eastern shore of Loch Ness. The sleeves, the policeman noted, were stained red and - most notably - one of the buttons was missing.

Given the weight of evidence stacked up against him, it must surely have come as a surprise when Mackenzie chose to plead not guilty at his murder trial in Inverness Castle on Tuesday, 5 February 1889. Things went increasingly badly for him as a string of witnesses placed him in Isabella Lamont's company late on Saturday, 14 December: the garrulous 71-year-old landlady, whose rambling testimony provoked frustration from the bench and hilarity in the public gallery; George Cowan, the landlord of the Ship, who served up their final drams; and Private Hastie, the last witness to have seen Isabella alive. Much of the defence case looked weak: Helen Macdonald was called to the stand to testify that Mackenzie had been employed in the slaughter of sheep - rather different, it must be said, from his imagined dairy farm - and she claimed that she recognised his bloodstained shirt as one he had worn while at work. (Had modern-day forensic methods been available, of course, human and animal blood could have been distinguished in an instant.) The representative of an Inverness clothing manufacturer, Macdougal & Co., stated that the buttons used as evidence were produced in large quantities and widely worn on everyday garments. And finally, the curious case of a witness named Jean Gillies who understood only Gaelic and refused to give evidence, standing her ground despite offers of a translator and even the threat of imprisonment. The impasse was broken only when her testimony - whatever it might have been - was deemed unessential to the case, and she was excused court duty.

Following his attempt to cast doubt on Mackenzie's involvement in Isabella's death, his lawyer opted for a different approach when he called into question the state of his client's mental health. Against a background of unkind laughter, one of Mackenzie's boyhood associates in Applecross, Wester Ross, recalled how, as a seven-year-old, he would stand on a chair and ramble incoherently. His sister, Catherine, voiced similar reservations regarding his mental state. Two farmers he had worked for were equally dubious. Charles McPhail of Mid Lairgs, Daviot, told the court that he would never have trusted Mackenzie with horses, and could not rely upon him to complete a task unsupervised. The second farmer, James George of Muirton of Drumbuie, near Daviot, stated that he believed he was 'of weak mind'. In his final summing up, Mackenzie's lawyer made a last-ditch effort to sow uncertainty in the minds of the jury and, as his fallback position, argued that a mentally-impaired individual could be found guilty not of murder, but culpable homicide. Speaking last, the judge, Lord Kingsburgh, was forthright in his disagreement. While acknowledging that Mackenzie was undoubtedly 'an eccentric and curious' individual, he told the jury that he was not convinced that his actions were beyond his control.

Shortly after the jury withdrew to consider their verdict, a curious little scenario played out in the courtroom. Following an absence of fifteen minutes, a messenger arrived from the jurors, indicating that they needed advice on a specific point of law. Lord Kingsburgh sent back instructions that the entire jury should return to the courtroom but a few moments later the same messenger reappeared, this time to inform the judge that his assistance was no longer required. A further thirty minutes later the members of the jury emerged from their deliberations and their representative, Colonel Johnston, spoke on their behalf. They found the prisoner guilty of murder, he announced, but added that they recommended him to the leniency of the court. This put the judge in an awkward position. The penalty for murder - death - was set by statute and so outwith his jurisdiction. In such circumstances leniency was not an option. 'Your best course,' he advised the jurors, 'would be to recommend him to mercy generally.' A few moments later their revised verdict was put on record as 'guilty as libelled, but recommended... to mercy.' Once the matter had been settled, Lord Kingsburgh turned to the man in the dock. 'Hector Mackenzie, the jury have been unable in this case to come to any other conclusion than that you have been guilty of this very terrible crime of murder,' he intoned, and went on to warn that, despite the plea for mercy they had made, he should 'place no reliance upon that recommendation receiving any effect.' He urged him to devote what time he had left to spiritual matters, and finally brought proceedings to a close when he placed the black cap upon his head and spoke the words that condemned him to death. His execution, he stated, would take place in Inverness a month hence, on Monday, 4 March.

But before Lord Kingsburgh's words could be put into effect there was still a major stumbling-block to be overcome. In assessing the jury's appeal for mercy the question of Mackenzie's mental health took centre stage, and on Wednesday, 22 February, Sir Arthur Mitchell, the bluntly titled Chief Commissioner for Lunacy, arrived in Inverness. During the course of his investigations, he learned that Mackenzie had always been viewed by those who knew him as being a little simple - a trait that apparently ran in his family since his father and two uncles were similarly 'of low intellect'. As a result of 'bad habits and idiotic manners', it emerged that Mackenzie had twice been discharged from the army - first from the Ross-shire Militia, and second from the regulars. Once Mitchell's inquiries were complete, it was believed that the evidence he had garnered was sufficient for him to recommend that Mackenzie be reprieved and, sure enough, on Wednesday, 27 February, a telegram was received from

Robert Cochran-Patrick, Under-Secretary for Scotland, stating that the death sentence was to be commuted to penal servitude for life. A letter to this effect had been sent to Henry Macandrew, Provost of Inverness, so that plans for the forthcoming execution could be abandoned.

And so, Hector Mackenzie's life was spared, but his motive for murder was no clearer. That he was a liar is certain, but he was surely also a fantasist whose claims of wealth and hinted connections with the gentry were all concocted for effect. Perhaps he too was drawn in by the fictions he wove - for a time at least - but when reality kicked in again, he knew his deceptions would be seen for what they were. There would be no waiting dogcart on the far side of the Moray Firth, no sixteen cows and no Flowerburn farm, so he resolved to settle his problem in the most brutal way imaginable.

Loreto Palombo
Possil, City of Glasgow - December 1890

Occupying the darker recesses of Italian tradition, the term 'vendetta' refers to a savage feud, often sparked by insult or trivial grievance, whose actions steadily escalate in a spiralling cycle of violence. A thousand miles distant from its place of origin, might such a word lend itself to the series of events that rocked Glasgow's Italian community in November of 1890? Some might say that to a certain extent, yes, there could be more than a grain of truth in this.

Throughout much of the year strains had been evident among the city's Italian population and, when not in the thick of it, twenty-one-year-old Loreto Palombo was more than likely to be there or thereabouts. Employed in the ice-cream trade, relations with his peer-group were from time to time a little problematic. Volatile by nature, in the spring of the year he had been seen brandishing a razor and uttering threats, but mercifully the fracas had been averted before any serious damage could be done. Around the same time, he had quarrelled with his countryman, Michael Gizzi, but cordial relations were apparently restored and since then the two men had been seen in one another's company, sometimes playing cards with a third ice-cream seller, Andrea Luciano. Palombo displayed similar flashes of temper when relations soured with his lady-friend, Fanny Hamill. In the light of his fiery temperament, therefore, there was some uncertainty as to whether he should be extended an invitation to wedding celebrations due to take place on Monday, 3 November, in the Possil district of the city but eventually after discussion it was decided to invite him.

Of course, the plan was for a joyful occasion. In a downstairs tenement flat at 19 Rodney Street, festivities had been organised to mark the marriage of Margaret, daughter of the householder, James Powell, to a young ice-cream dealer, Lorenzo Lanni. Both native Scots and members of the Italian community featured on the guest list. Well acquainted with Palombo's quick temper, the groom attempted to nip potential trouble in the bud by taking him aside beforehand and warning him against stirring up trouble. For a time at least, Lanni's words seemed to penetrate and things got off to a positive start. Before the celebrations proper got underway Palombo treated two of the other guests, Andrea Luciano and his brother, Giuseppe, in a nearby public house, and when the three arrived at Rodney Street a little later he was still in party mood to the extent that he stood up to perform a song for the pleasure and entertainment of the company. But as the evening wore on, his mood steadily darkened. He could hardly have avoided being conscious that he was persona non grata with certain of his fellow guests and when he started to react and make a nuisance of himself Andrea Luciano politely asked him to leave. 'If you please,' he told him, 'Walk out.' Palombo immediately exploded. 'We [sic] will go,' he snapped, 'but we will do you tonight.'

His first stop was Saverio di Marco's shop on Garscube Road, just south of the River Clyde, where he gave vent to his outrage at having been ejected from the wedding reception, vowing grimly not to let the matter rest. True to his word, he reappeared at Rodney Street an hour or so later with his brother-in-law, Lorenzo Marcantonio (whose name was absent from the guest list) in tow. As the bridegroom, Lorenzo Lanni, was making his way back to the party after slipping out briefly to buy tobacco, he found the two men loitering at the close-mouth: Marcantonio with his cap drawn ominously low over his brows; and Palombo still patently seething with resentment. Lanni suggested that it would be best for all concerned if they let the matter drop and at first his overtures seemed to have their desired effect. But only for a time. When they turned up yet again a short time later, he was forced to opt for a different tack and invited both men into the kitchen where in an effort to defuse the tension his new wife, Margaret, presented each of them with a glass of wine. But to no avail. Dismissing her peace offering, Palombo refused to be appeased.

The main focus of his bitterness was Margaret's bridesmaid, his former paramour whose crime - in his eyes - was the simple act of socialising with the other wedding guests in the adjoining living-room. Employed as a dressmaker, Fanny was the daughter of the late John Hamill - an ironworker who had died suddenly when she was only months old - and his wife, Jane. By coincidence the day of Lorenzo and Margaret's wedding happened to be her eighteenth birthday. Special day or not, Palombo's anger spilled over into outright aggression when he started making threats of violence: 'Send out Fanny,' he demanded, before adding unambiguously - 'I want to kill her.' The young woman's understandable failure to appear infuriated him even further. 'If you don't put Fanny Hamill out,' he raged, 'I'll murder the first one that comes. Send Luciano out. I'll kill him too.' When Fanny stayed put, on the surface at least he appeared to concede defeat. 'Jesus Christ,' he muttered to Marcantonio, 'come out of this.' At that, the two men made for the door but unfortunately that wasn't the end of the matter and there was more trouble to come. Palombo left the house with his dander up, still smarting with indignation.

In the flurry of events that followed it is hardly surprising that the recollections of those involved - James Powell's neighbours in Rodney Street and the wedding guests themselves - did not correspond entirely. A top-floor resident, Jane Reid, was preparing for bed when she heard a loud banging in the close below. Leaving her sister Mary upstairs, she crept down in the half-dark and saw two men violently kicking against James Powell's door. Her first thought was that they had been drinking. Amidst a cacophony of voices shouting in Italian she picked out a single sentence spoken in English - 'By Christ, the first one that comes out, I'll do for them.' By then she had seen enough and hurried back upstairs to her flat. From the front window, her sister and she looked down to where a three-way conflict broke out and spilled on to the street. Angry words were exchanged then, in a flash, either Palombo or Marcantonio - the watching sisters were unsure which - struck Andrea Luciano a mighty clout that sent him reeling. Marcantonio and Palombo immediately took flight but a few seconds later the latter apparently had second thoughts and returned to deliver a second blow. Andrea Luciano let out a scream, uttered the words, 'Jesu Maria!' and staggered a few paces before falling to the ground where he lay motionless. At this point his friend, Michael Gizzi, emerged from the close and set out in pursuit of Palombo, who had retreated into a dimly-lit back lane nearby. Jane heard Gizzi emit what she later described as 'an unearthly yell' and, as she continued to watch, his assailant fled in the direction of Possil Road.

Others had their own distinct memories of the night's events and the part they had played in them. Questioned later, the bride's sister, Susan Powell, recalled that the first she knew of anything wrong was when she heard a loud banging on the door and, too terrified to leave through the close, she had slipped outside via the front window. Out on the street she saw 'a clear thing like the blade of a knife' as it arced down through the lamplight towards Andrea's chest. When she came closer, Susan realised straight away that the wound he had sustained was life-threatening and she did her best to hold him upright but, unable to support his weight indefinitely, she lowered him to the ground as gently as she could. Meanwhile, her sister, Margaret, heard Susan cry out 'Andrea is murdered!' and rushed out on to the street where she found the injured man unconscious. Michael Gizzi was standing not far away with blood running from a gash on his leg. 'Loreto [Palombo] has done it,' he told her. Arriving on the scene, Giuseppe Luciano knelt by his brother's side and for a short while he could see that Andrea was still breathing but a few moments later his life ebbed away. It was surely a vision Giuseppe would find hard to erase from his memory throughout the rest of his life.

By a stroke of good luck Constable Kenneth Mackay of Glasgow Northern Division happened at that time to be patrolling the Rodney Street area and when he heard Susan Powell's cry for help he instantly came running. The first thing he saw was Andrea Luciano's body lying sprawled on the ground and when he shone his lamp down it illuminated a gaping wound in his chest. A second or two later Mackay heard a voice calling out, 'There's one of them!' He spun around and spotted Lorenzo Marcantonio trying to sidle off unnoticed and immediately secured him and placed him under arrest.

At first light his colleague, Sergeant Donald McLachlan, was combing an area of waste ground directly opposite James Powell's flat when amongst the scrubby vegetation he came across an abandoned knife. Its position and angle led him to suspect that it was likely to have been thrown from the far side of the road, a distance of perhaps forty yards. A neat piece of detective work linked his find with Arthur Wallace's hardware store in Herbertson Street where the proprietor confirmed that the previous forenoon 'a foreigner' had visited his shop and examined the various items he had for sale. According to Wallace, the stranger's eye had been caught by an expensive three-bladed knife displayed inside a glass case, but he had finally opted for something more modest for which he paid one shilling. The ironmonger could confirm that the knife found by Sergeant McLachlan was the same one he had sold to the customer whose description matched that of Loreto Palombo. Following a useful tip-off, it did not take long to track Palombo down to an ice-cream shop in Dumbarton, fifteen miles away, where he was arrested by an officer of the local force. Initially he gave a false name and claimed he lived in Port Glasgow but, pressed further, he caved in, admitted his true identity and was promptly returned to Glasgow. Regarding the part played by alcohol in the whole fatal affray, we know for sure that it was present at Margaret and Lorenzo's festivities but how much bearing it had on Palombo's actions is impossible to quantify. That said, his erratic behaviour and eruptions of rage look very much like signs of overindulgence.

In the last week of the year, Lorenzo Marcantonio and Loreto Palombo appeared side by side in the dock at the High Court in Glasgow, each of them facing charges of assault and murder. Their trial was presided over by Lord Stormonth Darling. As proceedings got underway, the various witnesses were called to the stand, one after another, to give their own particular version of events and despite the minor (and not-so-minor) discrepancies in their accounts, the jury took only twenty-five minutes to conclude that Marcantonio had been responsible for nothing more grievous than loitering with - or without - intent and consequently he was cleared of both charges. In relation to Palombo, on the other hand, their verdict was of guilty, but with a recommendation to mercy attached. Hearing their decision, the judge turned to address him. 'I will not aggravate your position,' he told him, 'by alluding to the heinousness of the crime by which you launched your countryman into eternity amidst a scene of rejoicing and without a moment's warning.' Of course, in so saying he had done just exactly that. Then, placing the black cap upon his head, His Lordship announced that Palombo would be executed in the prison of Glasgow in three weeks' time on Monday, 19 January 1891. Hearing his fate spelt out, the condemned man remained impassive but as he was being led from the dock his emotion spilled over and he threw his arms around the neck of his co-accused and kissed him with what looked like great affection. He left the courtroom in tears, waving his hand to his friends in the public gallery as he did so. His father made a desperate effort to reach out to him but was prevented from doing so. A few moments later the court proceedings concluded when Marcantonio was set at liberty.

Even with his trial at an end and a conviction secured, Palombo's case showed no sign of fading from the public eye. Petitions demanding clemency were placed in public buildings throughout the city and soon amassed a great many signatures. Various individuals were prompted to air their views in print. In a letter to *The Glasgow Herald* of Thursday, 8 January 1891, a correspondent signing herself simply M.N.M. argued the case for mercy, voicing her concern that 'as a foreigner [Palombo's] case may not excite the pity usually extended to our own countrymen and women in like dire extremity'. Highlighting the fact that the jury had agreed its verdict by the narrowest of majorities, she went on to present what she saw as possible mitigating factors: namely, that his crime had been committed 'in hot blood' while he was, she believed, under the influence of alcohol and that at its root was the legacy of a failed love affair. She drew attention to the fact that at the time of his conviction in Scotland, the death penalty had already been abolished in Palombo's native land. While this was certainly the case, depending on the point of view of *The Herald's* readers it might or might not have been seen as relevant.

And at this point the letter took a more personal turn, offering an unexpected insight into a side of Loreto Palombo's character hitherto hidden from view. M.N.M. revealed that for the previous four years or so he had acted as a model for several highly-esteemed painters in Glasgow's art schools where, in her words, he had 'conducted himself with the greatest propriety, giving entire satisfaction'. Such esteem was he held in, she continued, that he had been engaged as a member of staff during one such artist's family summer vacation in the country where once again he 'behaved in a most exemplary manner, giving ... the impression of being a most gentle, unassuming and obliging youth'. (The possibility that Palombo's form might yet grace a canvas, buried deep in the vaults of a city gallery or even on public display, is a tantalising thought. Nor, for that matter, is it completely out of the question that his likeness might be an object of admiration on the walls of a private residence.) In any case, the sensitive soul evoked by M.N.M., currently languishing behind bars, comes across as utterly at odds with Luciano's hot-headed murderer. So - an unbiased appeal for forgiveness for a man's drunken errors? Or might there be something more to it? The final paragraph of her letter drilled down to the nub of the matter. 'It is now almost the universal opinion in this country,' she asserted, 'that capital punishment should be abolished', and went on to suggest that, by supporting this specific petition, signatories were giving voice to their objection to the death penalty in principle. Granted, her earlier remarks leave no doubt that she was familiar with Loreto Palombo's specific circumstances, but her broader agenda is also crystal clear.

Printed in the same issue of *The Herald* is a second letter, this one a good deal shorter and of a different cast entirely. Reproduced, we might suppose, in its original, unedited form, it had been submitted by 'Un Italiano' living in the Yoker district of the city. Through the newspaper's columns the writer begged the 'Italian Counsel Representative of the noble Italian nation' to orchestrate a petition on Palombo's behalf which 'implore from the Most Graciouse and Good Mother the Queen, the Commutation from the Pain of Death to Penal Servitude for Life, if nothing else but for the Old poor Father sake.' The writer closed on a more upbeat note. 'Italy being so friendly with this Great noble and Christian nation,' he concluded, 'I am almost certain of the magnanimity of the So biloved Queen's Pardon.' However awkward its phrasing, the letter comes across as a sincere and heartfelt plea on behalf of a fellow countryman. A good deal blunter in his approach, however, was a correspondent calling himself 'Justice' who stated in *The Glasgow Evening News* that 'if [Hangman] Berry does his work in this case, Italy will be dismayed and Scotland disgraced'.

Meanwhile, locked up in Duke Street Prison Palombo was kept under constant watch for his own safety but gradually he became resigned to his situation, grew calmer and reportedly devoted much of his time to drawing and sketching. At first he spurned any offer of spiritual support but in time came to accept daily visits from Father Paul Jones, a fluent speaker of Italian, with whom he came to form a close bond. He declared that he was willing to forgive his enemies - though the question of whether his victim's friends would be prepared to reciprocate did not appear to enter his head, nor indeed the couple whose wedding day was tainted for ever. In a scene of heightened emotion he was visited in jail by his brother-in-law, Marcantonio, and his elderly father for whom he had a particular fondness. When the time came for their visit to end all three were weeping and in considerable distress. In a poignant moment Palombo asked his father to bless him in the traditional Italian manner by placing both hands upon his head. Despite his precarious situation, what sustained him throughout this time was his confidence in the likelihood of a reprieve. A good deal less certain, Prison Governor Alston opted for what seems at best a questionable strategy. Ostensibly to prepare him in advance should his hopes be ultimately dashed, Alston advised him that in his personal opinion efforts being made on his behalf offered little if any chance of a favourable outcome. The success of the governor's tactic could be judged when Palombo had to be restrained from crashing his head against the walls of his cell in despair.

Following her former lover's conviction for murder, Fanny Hamill, it would seem, experienced a radical charge of heart. Despite not meeting face to face, the two exchanged letters during his time in prison in which she vowed to remain true to him regardless of his fate. In the event of his death, she undertook to remain forever celibate and her letter concluded by expressing a hope that at the end of life's journey they would rejoin one another in the great hereafter. (Clearly she took it for granted that they would both be granted admission.) Such was her apparent commitment that she travelled to the Secretary of State for Scotland's offices at Dalkeith in the hope of gaining an audience with Lord Lothian himself in order to make a plea for her lover's reprieve. Strangely enough, His Lordship was unavailable that particular day though he deigned to receive her letter. That Fanny's actions read like a work of romantic fiction did not go unnoticed at the time, prompting some commentators to make comparisons with Jeanie Deans, Sir Walter Scott's noble heroine in one of his best-loved novels, *The Heart of Midlothian*. Any suggestion that Fanny might have enjoyed basking in her moment in the limelight would not, I hope, come across as overly cynical.

There remained the question of the petition in support of Palombo which, by the time it reached Lord Lothian on Monday, 12 January, had been successful in attracting more than 5,000 signatures. On Friday the sixteenth - a mere three days before the date appointed for the execution - the Lord Provost of Glasgow, John Muir, received a letter from the Scottish Secretary which read as follows:

> My LORD PROVOST, - I am to signify to you the Queen's commands that the execution of the sentence of death passed on Loretto [sic] Palombo, presently in Her Majesty's Prison at Glasgow, be respited until further signification of Her Majesty's pleasure.
>
> I am, My Lord Provost,
> Your obedient servant,
> LOTHIAN.

Arriving at Duke Street to break the news, Provost Muir was shown to Palombo's cell where he is said to have found him on his knees at prayer. The prisoner rose to his feet but, hearing of his dramatic change of fortune, such was the effect that his legs folded beneath him. Once he had recovered himself sufficiently, he spoke out to express his appreciation to the Lord Provost and to the people of Scotland and to give thanks for God's goodness. Now his life had been spared, he swore that he would ever after be 'God's man' - possibly easier to say than to stick to. Before leaving the condemned cell, Lord Provost Muir offered his congratulations and shook him by the hand. In light of Palombo's changed circumstances the governor decided that keeping a watch over him was no longer necessary.

Needless to say, not everyone approved. A crusty contributor to *The Glasgow Evening News* kicked off with the blanket assertion that 'every reasonable, right-minded man and especially those who are admirers of justice' must necessarily have opposed Palombo's escape from the gallows. Even if his sentence was to be commuted to a life-term of penal servitude, 'Medicus' went on to predict that 'he [would] regain his freedom in some sixteen or eighteen years' and be at liberty to pick out his next victim. Unimpressed by the fact that the death penalty had already been abolished in Italy, Medicus continued: 'I [cannot] see why he should be allowed to settle in this country and enjoy the privileges and protections of its law and then, on violating them so seriously, to be judged in the eyes of the Italian law.' Clearly, unlike M.N.M. in *The Herald*, Medicus took the view that when in Rome... and possibly he had a point.

In his eyes it was not Lord Lothian who was at fault but rather all of those 5,000-plus signatories to the petition which the Scottish Secretary had been obliged to reflect on - 'Many of whom,' Medicus asserted, 'are personally against capital punishment' but, no less than M.N.M., he too had his personal axe to grind. The majority of Scotland's population supported the death penalty, he claimed, but they didn't go signing petitions to say so. 'It would be a pity for our noble nation,' he bemoaned, 'if capital punishment ceased to exist.'

But too late; the matter was already done and dusted and, just as Medicus had anticipated, Palombo's death sentence was commuted to a lifetime of hard labour. After a spell of oakum picking at Duke Street - a common activity for prisoners at the time which involved teasing slender fibres from old ropes which, impregnated with tar, could be used to 'caulk', or seal, gaps in the wooden hulls of ships - a task undeniably sore on the fingers. During this time, it is on record that he received a final visit from Fanny. He was then transferred to Perth where he spent several months before being forwarded 120 miles farther north to his ultimate destination, Peterhead Prison, where he was put to work, most likely either quarrying granite or alternatively engaged in the back-breaking labour of constructing a new harbour breakwater. A drear prospect indeed and what a price to be paid for his uncontrolled anger at Rodney Street.

In the fullness of time it transpired that Medicus' prediction very nearly came to pass. In November 1900 - almost exactly ten years after his conviction - Palombo was discharged from Peterhead Prison on compassionate grounds after his health broke down as a result of a stomach complaint. He was little more than 30 at the time. As a condition of his release, he agreed to leave the country, cross the North

Sea to Rotterdam by ferry and travel on to Italy, but a few weeks later he appeared at the Central Police Court in Glasgow, charged with having breached the terms of his release. The Magistrate accepted his defence that he had misunderstood what was required of him and he was dismissed from the bar, though his plea that he had no means of support in the city of Rotterdam went disregarded. Despite this minor brush with the law, he was still in Glasgow a few months later, living with his younger sister, Maria; her husband - that same Lorenzo Marcantonio with whom we are already well acquainted; and their five young daughters. And then the trail goes cold when Loreto Palombo effectively disappears off the radar. Whether he ever made it back to Italy is impossible to say.

The contentious issues raised by his case continue to rumble on in our own time: the place and status of immigrant communities and their acceptance (or otherwise) by their host populations; the misuse of alcohol and its repercussions, both social and personal; and, of course, the thorny question of capital punishment, as certain to divide opinion today as it was at the latter end of the nineteenth century.

But in conclusion, what became of Fanny Hamill and the undertaking she gave to Loreto Palombo in 1891? Well, it turns out that by the time of his release from Peterhead Prison she had already been married, widowed and was subsequently remarried. In March 1903 she gave birth to her first child, Josephine, but by six years later, though still only in her mid-twenties, she had lost her second husband. In 1909 she made the decision to emigrate with her young daughter to Canada where, employed as a waitress in Montréal, she learned to speak French and married for a third time to American-born John Williams. In 1914 she had a second child, a son named John, and some ten years later she and her family moved south to settle in the USA. Young John, of course, was still a schoolboy at the time of the move and Josephine, now 21, had taken up her mother's former trade of dressmaking. Seemingly Fanny's story came to an end in 1934 when she died in her early sixties in New York City. However sincerely meant, the youthful promise she gave Loreto Palombo forty-odd years earlier was but one small incident during the course of a full and eventful life.

Afterword

'I would rather know the histories of these humble, unremembered lives than [those] of the great ones.'
(William Henry Hudson, A Shepherd's Life.)

While I was researching the cases featured in this book there was a question that refused to be ignored. If the hands of time were reversed and I found myself in the shoes of the individuals involved, what would I have done? Sometimes I had no difficulty answering. No decent person wants to believe he would deprive an innocent eleven-year-old of life for no other reason than an uncontrolled surge of ill-temper - as a Lanarkshire schoolmaster did in the spring of 1838. Or that he would abandon his fellow-mortals, emaciated and abused, to whatever cruel fate might await them off the icy Newfoundland coastline as happened thirty years later. And these are by no means the only actions contained within the preceding pages that would be hard to justify, prompted by impulses such as greed, callousness or self-interest.

I'm fairly confident too that I know what I'd have done if my family was struggling to keep body and soul together and my neighbour was a duke or an earl whose woods were stocked with pheasants aplenty. Balanced against the prospect of bedding down on an empty belly, a plump gamebird or two gone missing would surely seem neither here nor there. Tragically, men like Richard Jones - the gamekeeper shot and killed while protecting the Marquis of Ailsa's birds in 1859 - were collateral damage, victims of a system skewed to protect the interests of the rich and privileged.

As I made my way through page after page of archived newspapers, the fact was inescapable how poverty and hardship gave rise to crime and frequently erupted into violence. In the case of the former soldier, Thomas Scobbie, trouble flared over what looked on the face of it like a petty theft but, even so, the matter quickly escalated and culminated in the loss of a man's life. In an age without safety nets, all that was needed to slip through the cracks was a spell of ill-health, a job loss or the death of a family's breadwinner. Unemployed, homeless and well-nigh destitute, John and Catherine Stuart were forced to take desperate measures in 1828 and although it would be hard to deny that the plan they came up with was deeply irresponsible, still the argument might be made that the couple were themselves casualties of a system that offered those on the margins of society few prospects or positive destinations to be aimed for. Villains? By their deadly actions, undoubtedly yes. Or victims? Well, readers will have to decide that for themselves. The distinction is not always an easy one to make, and if placed in the Stuarts' position who among us can say for sure what we ourselves might have been capable of?

The fact is that times may change and circumstances with them, but human nature remains remarkably constant. Need, greed, anger, despair, wickedness, temptation, a disordered mind or injured pride... All of these can lead people down dangerous paths, often carrying others in their wake.

Index

Aberdeen 59, 64, 111, 214, 230
Adam, John 103-123
Airdrie, King's Arms Inn 98
Alloa 31
Alness 168
American War of Independence 12
Anatomy Act of 1832 50
Applecross 251
Ardrossan 205
Arran, Isle of 82, 197
Arran, sailing ship 197-207
Arthur, Alexander 97-102
Ayr 157, 160-162, 179, 182, 236

Balerno 45
Banns, calling of 110
Bastard verdict, the 152
Bathgate 98, 213
Bayble, Isle of Lewis 125-130
Beaton, Catherine 171-176
Beauly Firth 111, 112
Begbie, William 19-27
Belfast 82
Berry, James (hangman) 261
Bier-right 116-117, 232
Biggar 92
Billington, Constable Edward 214-216, 225
Black Isle 112
Boer War 56
Borland, Thomas 243-244
Bowers, Peter 41-47
Boxing 98-100

Boyd, Matthew 29-37
Braco 209-225
Braemar 107
Brash, Thomas 136
Brechin, Jane 104-123
Brechin, Royal Burgh 104
Broadsheets 9
Broadsides 9
Bruce, King Robert 11
Buccleuch Estate 157
Burke & Hare 81, 149
Bury, William Henry 236

Cairngorm Mountains 107
Calcraft, William (hangman) 234-236
Calcutta, India 38, 74, 78
Campbellton, Ardersier 245
Campbeltown, Argyll 82
Canonbie, Dumfriesshire 159-160
Cape Town 56, 194
Cardenbarns 74
Carlisle 75, 137
Carsphairn 158
Chalmers, George 213-225
Citizen's arrest 233
Claddach Kyles, North Uist 167-176
Clyde, River 14
Cockburn, Lord Henry 14, 26, 77, 131-132
Coldstream 177
Colquhoun, Ludovic 11-17
Counterfeit coins 91, 101

Craigshiel, New Cumnock 154-163
Crimean War 56, 239
Culpable homicide 133, 136, 182, 204, 234
Cumnock 156-157

Dalkeith 102, 262
Deans, Jeanie 262
Dee, River 63, 107
Derby, Red Lion Inn 106
Dingwall 107-119
Dolphinton 133-135
Dowd, Theodore 153-165
Drumlanrig Castle 158
Dumbarton 14, 259
Dumfries 91, 93, 160
Dunblane 211-216
Dundee 161, 214-216, 230-236
Dunlop, Ayrshire 137-152
Dunlop Kirk 139, 148
Dunfermline 229, 230
Dunning Fair 29
Dunoon 85

Edinburgh 19-27, 31, 67, 70, 105, 160, 215
Edinburgh, High Court 32, 43, 46, 52, 59, 81, 88, 98, 102, 133, 151, 162, 190, 204
Edinburgh, Hogmanay of 1811 34
Edinburgh, Traditions of, Chambers 21
Elliott, Dorothy 106-123
Eskgrove, Lord 14-16

Falkirk 50
Fenwick 137
Forfar 63, 103, 106
Forres 114
Forrest, James 133-136

Forrest, John 49-57
Fort George 230, 245-249
Forth, River 31
Frankenstein, Mary Shelley 88
Fraserburgh 215, 218-220
Furie, Darby 153-165

Gaelic 13, 14, 89, 120, 126, 130, 174, 246, 251
Galston 241
Gifford 41
Gilmour, Christina 137-152
Gilmour, John 137-152
Girvan 178-179
Glasgow 14, 26, 34, 56, 75, 97-98, 105, 138-139, 212, 217, 255-265
Glenluce 90
Gourock 85, 202
Grampian Mountains 107
Grave-robbery 49-55, 148
Gray, Peter 11-17
Greenock 197, 202-204
Greenock, Seaman's Friend Society of 205
Gretna 92

Haddington 41, 217
Hamesucken 14-16, 46
Hamill, Fanny 255-265
Handbill 115, 117
Haunted Dundee, Millar 232
Hawick 159
Hervie, Alexander & Christian 61-64

Inchinnan 137-151
Indian Rebellion 229
Inverness 107-123, 131-132, 174, 248-253
Istanbul 56

k the Ripper 236
nstone 14
es, Richard 181-183, 267
nping the gun 67
iper Green 185-191

nnay 61-64
r, James 197-206
swick 75
marnock 157, 240-243
tyre 82
kcaldy 67
kintilloch 105
koswald 180-183
hapur, India 56
es of Bute 83

e District 76
nont, Isabella 246-253
nont, Robert 81-96
ark 45
dale, David 67-79
bert 51
danum 87-89
rencekirk 110, 111
vis, Isle of 125-132
lithgow 50, 52
erpool 137, 151
chgilphead 82
ch Lomond 11
chmaddy 167, 170-175
ckerbie 217
d Lothian 262-263
ciano, Andrea 256-260
ss 11
ll, Adam 29-33
ll, John 29-39

ckenzie, Hector 245-253
ckoull, James 23-26

Maclean, Margaret 167-176
Macleod, Henrietta 125-130
Macleod, Malcolm 125-132
Malta 56
Marcantonio, Lorenzo 256-265
Martin, Alexander 59-65
Maybole 34, 37, 178-182
McCallum, Colin 11-17
McKay, Superintendent George 137-150
McNab, James 49-55
McNaught, John 155-162
McNaught, Robert 154-162
Menstrie 30
Millbuie, Black Isle 112-123
Mitchell, Daniel 49-55
Moniaive 158
Monifieth 227-237
Montréal 265
Montrose 108-110, 117
Moray Firth 111, 122, 245
Morgan, George 68-79
Moscow, Ayrshire 239-244
Moscow, Russia 239
Muirkirk 46, 157

Napoleonic Wars 68, 69, 79, 239
Newcastle, New South Wales 38
Newcastle-upon-Tyne 22, 82, 215
New Cumnock 153-163
Newfoundland 198-204
Newmilns 243
New York, USA 137, 149-150, 265
Nightingale, Florence 56
Nith, River 158

Paisley 14, 138-151
Palombo, Loreto 255-265
Patterson, David 133-136
Peel, Robert (Home Secretary) 100

Perpetual motion 128
Perth, Scotland 76, 219, 264
Perth, Western Australia 164, 194
Peterhead Prison 264
Poe, Edgar Allan 9
Poison 87-89, 140-149, 151-152

Quaker Church 233
Quebec City 197, 202
Queen Victoria 56, 57, 192, 233-235, 261, 263

Rankin, Robert 240-244
Rape 59
Reform Act of 1832 78
Renfrew 142-151
Renfrew Ferry 85
Ross, Thomas 177-183
Rothesay 217

Salt, Edwin 185-196
Salt, Mary Anne 185-193
Saltcoats 197
Sanquhar 158, 162
Scobbie, George 227-237, 267
Scott, Sir Walter 15, 26, 262
Scottish verdict, the 152
Shakespeare, William 22
Sheriffmuir 29, 32, 216
Smallpox 14, 109, 116, 227
Society for the Abolition of Capital

Punishment 132
Society of Friends 233
Spaewife 169
Spalding, George 227-237
Spring-guns 177
Sri Lanka 38
Stevenson, Thomas 50-52
Stirling 30, 32, 49-56
Stornoway 126, 129, 130
Stouthrief 64
Stowaways 197-207
Strang, William 97-102
Stranraer 90
Stuart, John & Catherine 81-95, 26

Tarbert 82
Tasmania 102
Thames, River 37, 102
The Heart of Midlothian, Scott 262
Tomintoul 107

Ulva, Isle of 81

Vendetta 255

Watt, Robert 197-206
Whiteford, James 41-47
Williams, Thomas 95
Wombwell's Show 215

Xhosa Wars 56